PART-TIME GLAMOUR PHOTOGRAPHY FULL-TIME INCOME

Part-time Glamour Photography Full-time Income

Joe Farace

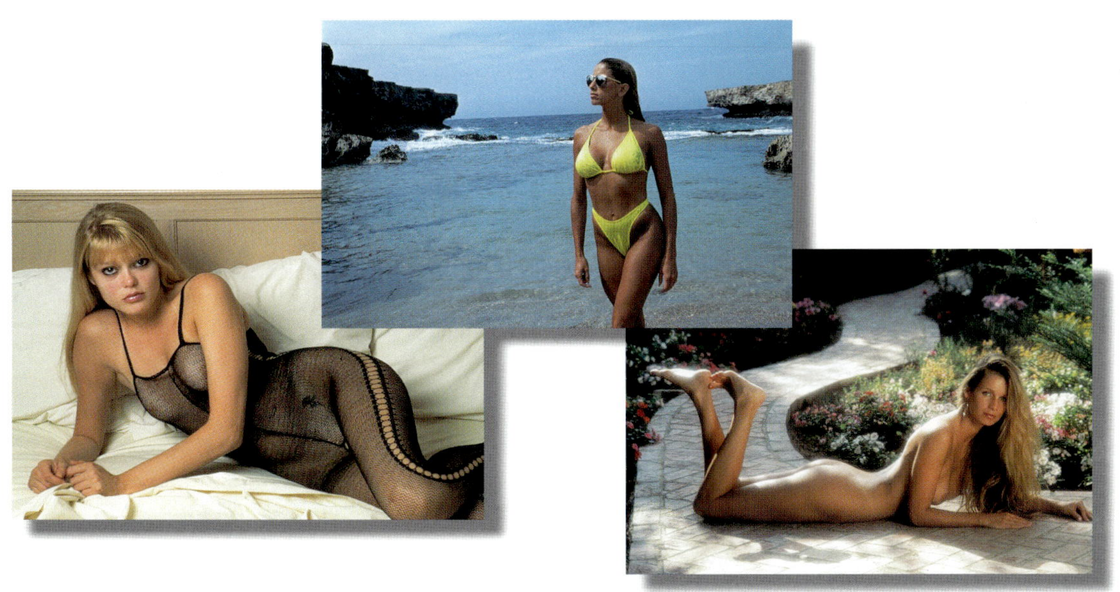

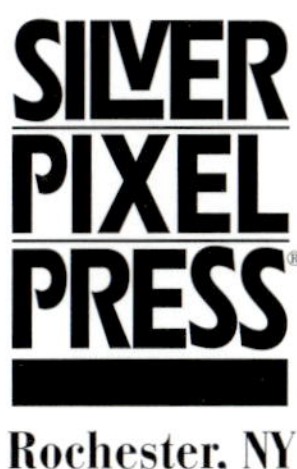

Rochester, NY

Part-time Glamour Photography—Full-time Income
Written by Joe Farace

Cover images ©Glamour Portfolios

Published in the United States of America by
Silver Pixel Press®
A Tiffen® Company
21 Jet View Drive
Rochester, NY 14624
Fax: (716) 328-5078
www.saundersphoto.com

ISBN 1-883403-49-9

Printed in Belgium by Die Keure n.v.

Library of Congress Cataloging-in-Publication Data

Farace, Joe.
Part-time glamour photography : full-time income / Joe Farace.
p. cm.
ISBN 1-883403-49-9 (pbk.)
1. Glamour photography--Handbooks, manuals, etc. 2. Photography--Business methods--Handbooks, manuals, etc. I. Title.
TR678.F37 1999
778.9'24'068--dc21 99-18349
CIP

About the Author

Joe Farace is the author of twenty books, including *The Photographer's Digital Studio*, *Stock Photo Smart*, *Plug-in Smart*, and, with co-author Barry Staver, *Better Available Light Photography*. He has written over 800 magazine articles about graphics, photography, and digital imaging. He is editor-at-large to *The Press* and a regular contributor to *Shutterbug* magazine, with a monthly column, "Digital Innovations." His column "Graphics," aimed at digital designers and artists, appears monthly in *ComputerUser* magazine. He also writes a monthly column, "Pixography," for *Professional Photographer Storytellers* magazine. Joe lives in northeastern Colorado with his wife, Mary. His World Wide Web address is http://www.hyperzine.com/writers/joef.html.

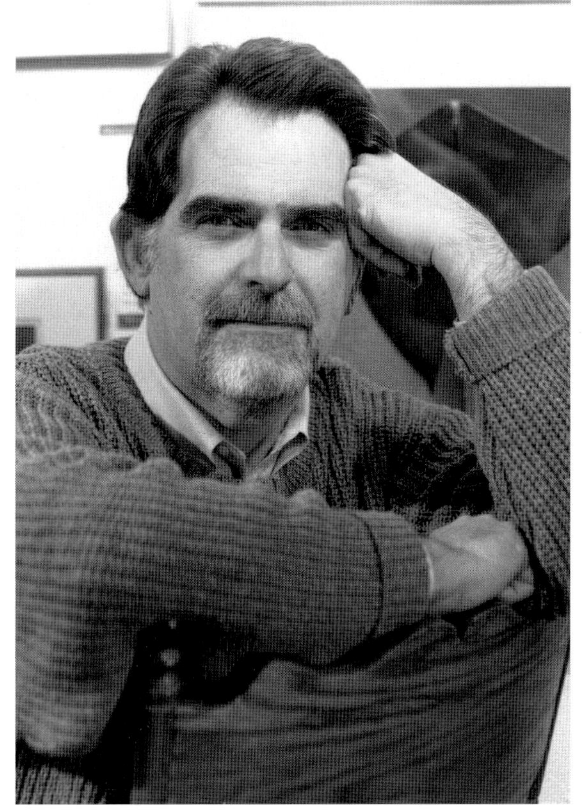

Acknowledgments

I would especially like to thank Len Kaltman for his creative input and all of his great photographs that appear within these pages. Without his talent and photographic skills, there would be no pictures in this book; in fact, there would be no book at all. I would be remiss if I did not acknowledge the contributions of all the models who appear in this book. What makes them so special is that they are the type of "girl-next-door" models I expect that many of you will be photographing after reading this book. That's just part of what makes their contributions so important.

This book would have never been published without the help and encouragement of Silver Pixel Press' Marti Saltzman. For some time, she kept pressing me to submit book ideas to her, and when the *Part-time Glamour Photography* concept was introduced to me by Glamour Portfolios' Len Kaltman, I immediately thought of her. Thanks, Marti, for giving me the chance to write this book.

Books like this are never written in a vacuum, and I would also like to thank my own support team who alternately inspire me and bail me out of technical and creative problems. This includes *Denver Post* photographer Barry Staver for his continuing friendship and inspiration. A special thank you goes out to legendary camera technician Vern Prime. He has been a constant source of information and a helping hand whenever I needed one. The same is true for Kevin Elliott, general manager of Cies-Sexton Visual. Kevin combines a photographer's skills with those of someone who can fix anything—including my computer that crashed and burned just as I was completing this book. Thanks, Kevin, I couldn't have finished this without your assistance. Lastly, I would have never been able to complete this book—or my first one—without the love and support of my dear wife, Mary. She is my biggest fan and, for that, I will always be grateful.

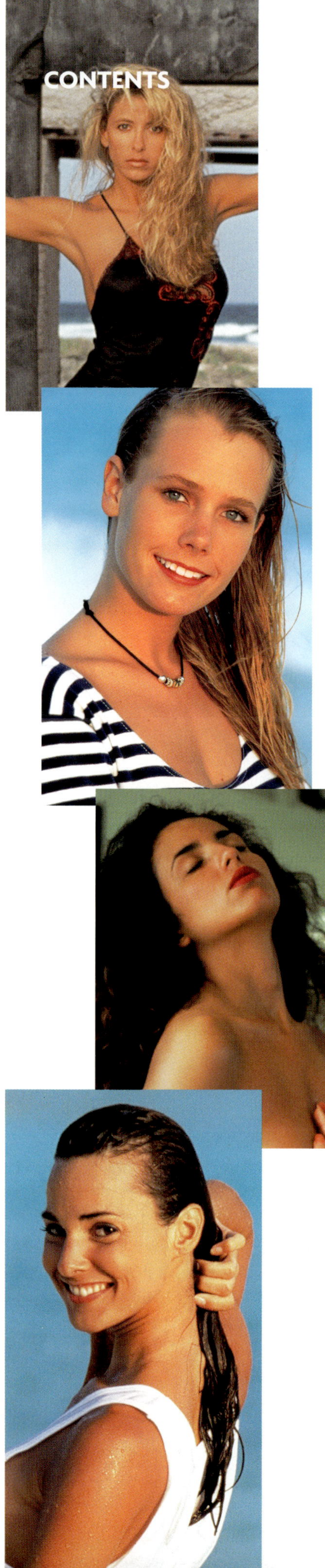
CONTENTS

CONTENTS

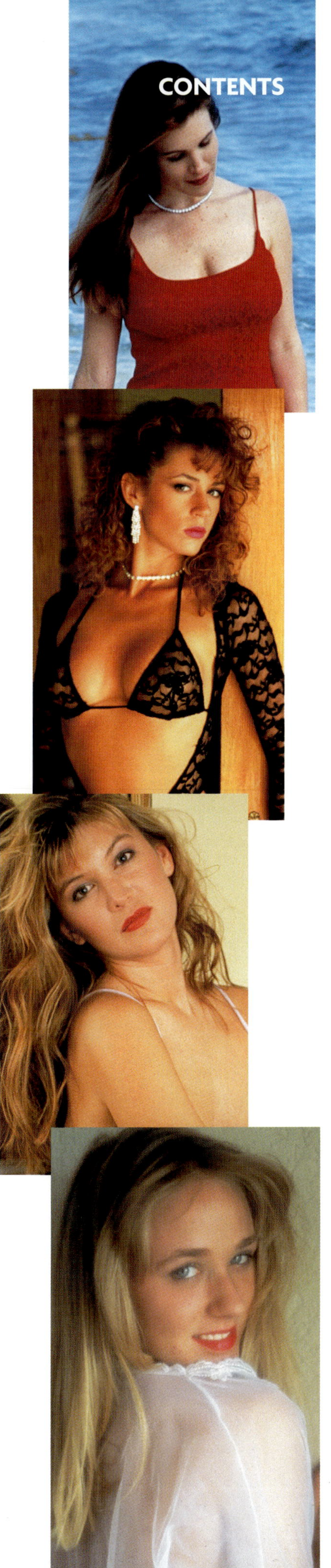

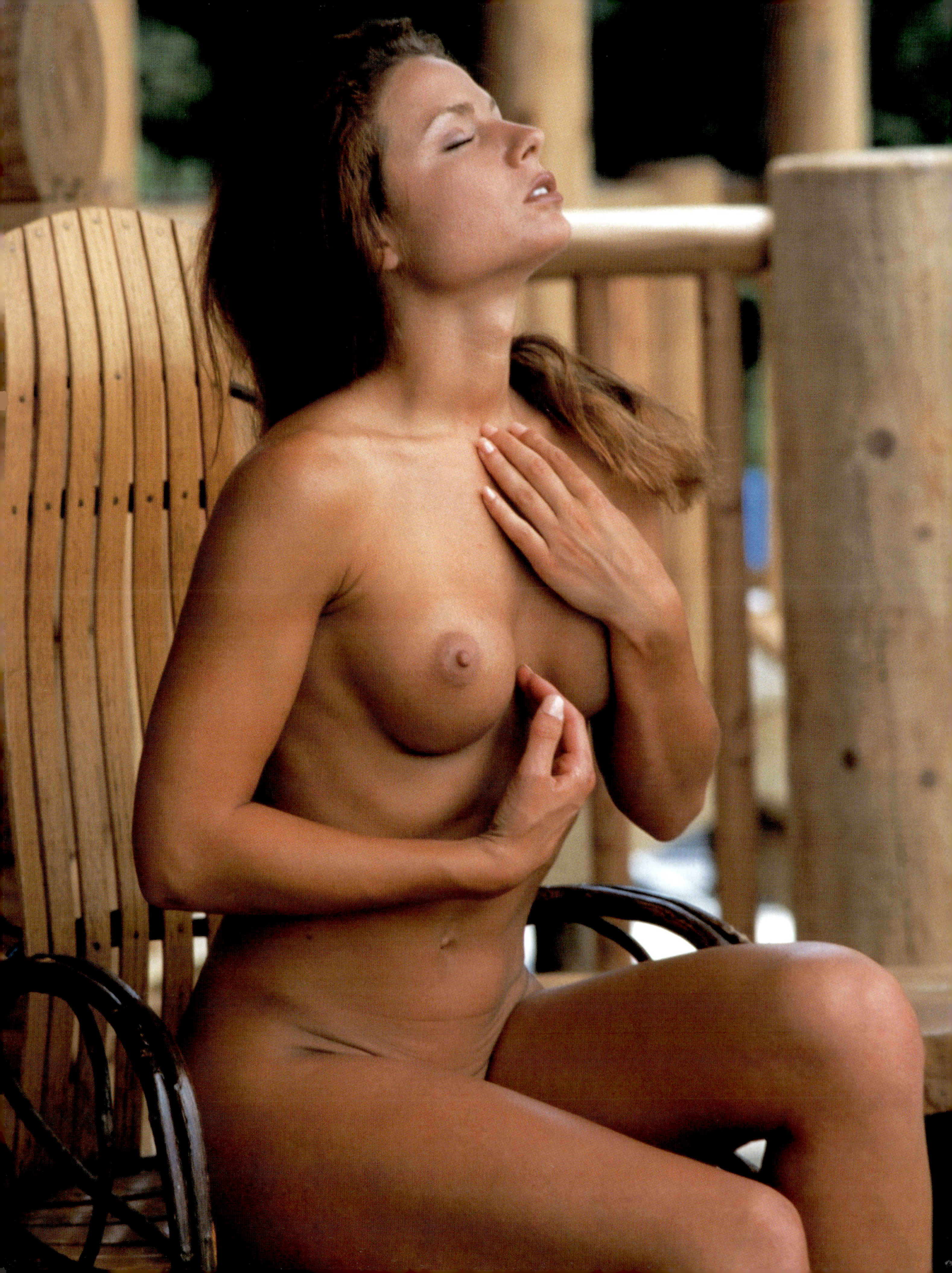

Introduction

The nude has long been a subject for artists—no matter what form of media they prefer to work in. Photographers in particular have been creating images of beautiful women ever since the invention of the photographic process over 150 years ago. Yet there is a difference between the art of the nude and glamour photography. Glamour photography combines the art of photography with the economic realities of the marketplace. It is not enough that a glamour photograph be artful, to be truly successful it must also be commercially viable.

If you are like most photographers, you may have dabbled in some form of glamour photography. Many wedding and portrait photographers create boudoir portraits for clients, or produce portfolio images for models and aspiring models. You may have even submitted photographs of a particular model to a men's magazine such as *Playboy*. Although glamour photography can be enjoyable, creative, and profitable, chances are you may never have considered expanding your marketing efforts into this lucrative field. This may be especially true for the part-time or aspiring professional photographer who has an interest in glamour photography but thought because of location and equipment limitations that this goal was unattainable. You will be glad to learn that nothing could be further from the truth.
One of this book's goals is to change the way you think about the creation and marketing of glamour and centerfold photographs.

Part-time Glamour Photography—Full-time Income is designed to take you beyond the creation of traditional boudoir portraits and help you discover the large market for high-quality centerfold photography. If you follow the steps outlined in this book and heed the advice from the glamour photographers who created the images on these pages, you will be able to create exciting images and earn a good income at the same time.

Glamour photography is not limited to full-time professional studio owners. Opportunities exist for part-time or aspiring professionals to make a good income creating photographs of beautiful women and marketing those images. Photographers just getting started should keep in mind that it will take time to develop creative, technical, and marketing skills. Whatever your level of experience, your ultimate success is limited only by your talent and how much energy you are willing to expend to improve your technical and marketing skills.

FANTASY VS. REALITY

Many male photographers fantasize about being a staff photographer for *Playboy*, but that's not the path you will find here. *Part-time Glamour Photography—Full-time Income* is not about shooting images while on assignment for a men's magazine. Instead, you will find information on how to directly market your photographs worldwide, working part-time for a full-time income.

To create this image, the photographer rented a house for the shoot, then took advantage of the natural light he found on the porch. Heather is a popular model on the Internet and regularly meets professional photographers on-line. ©Glamour Portfolios

Take the case history of Len Kaltman, founder of Glamour Portfolios and whose photographs appear in this book. Originally a major part of his business was commercial and fashion photography. Over the years, Kaltman gradually stopped doing these kinds of assignments and now specializes in shooting centerfold images that he markets himself. By using several innovative methods to sell his glamour photographs, he has made more money from centerfold photography than he ever did from commercial and fashion assignments. Instead of working 9 to 5 each day, he now only shoots once or twice a month. The rest of the time, Kaltman spends with his family or working on his hobbies.

WHAT'S IN THE BOOK

Here is just some of the useful and practical information that you will find inside this book:

- How to find beautiful and talented models in your area—even if you live in a small city or rural town

- How to communicate honestly and effectively with models so they will pose for you with confidence

- How to use model releases and deal with the basic business and legal issues of glamour photography—you will find sample model release and casting forms

- How to shoot just once or twice a month and earn a full-time income from glamour and centerfold photography shoots

- How to pose your models in tasteful but sexy ways, including frank advice on how to create poses that minimize a model's imperfections and create great glamour photographs

- How to use natural light and a minimum of equipment to create attractive and marketable photographs—you don't have to own expensive equipment to create successful glamour images

- How to travel to exotic locations with beautiful models at little or no cost—you'll find sample marketing letters and contracts used to establish barter relationships for photo shoots at exciting locations

- How to take advantage of computer technology to sell your photographs, including how to market your glamour images on CD-ROM discs and on the greatest moneymaker of all—the Internet

ARE YOU TALKING TO ME?

Yes. This book has been written for the professional, part-time, or aspiring photographer who enjoys photographing beautiful women and would like to make money doing it. *Part-time Glamour Photography—Full-time Income* contains start-to-finish, proven strategies on how to find glamour models, photograph them, and then market those images—all of the tips, tools, and techniques you need to be successful. All you need to add is your own hard work and creativity.

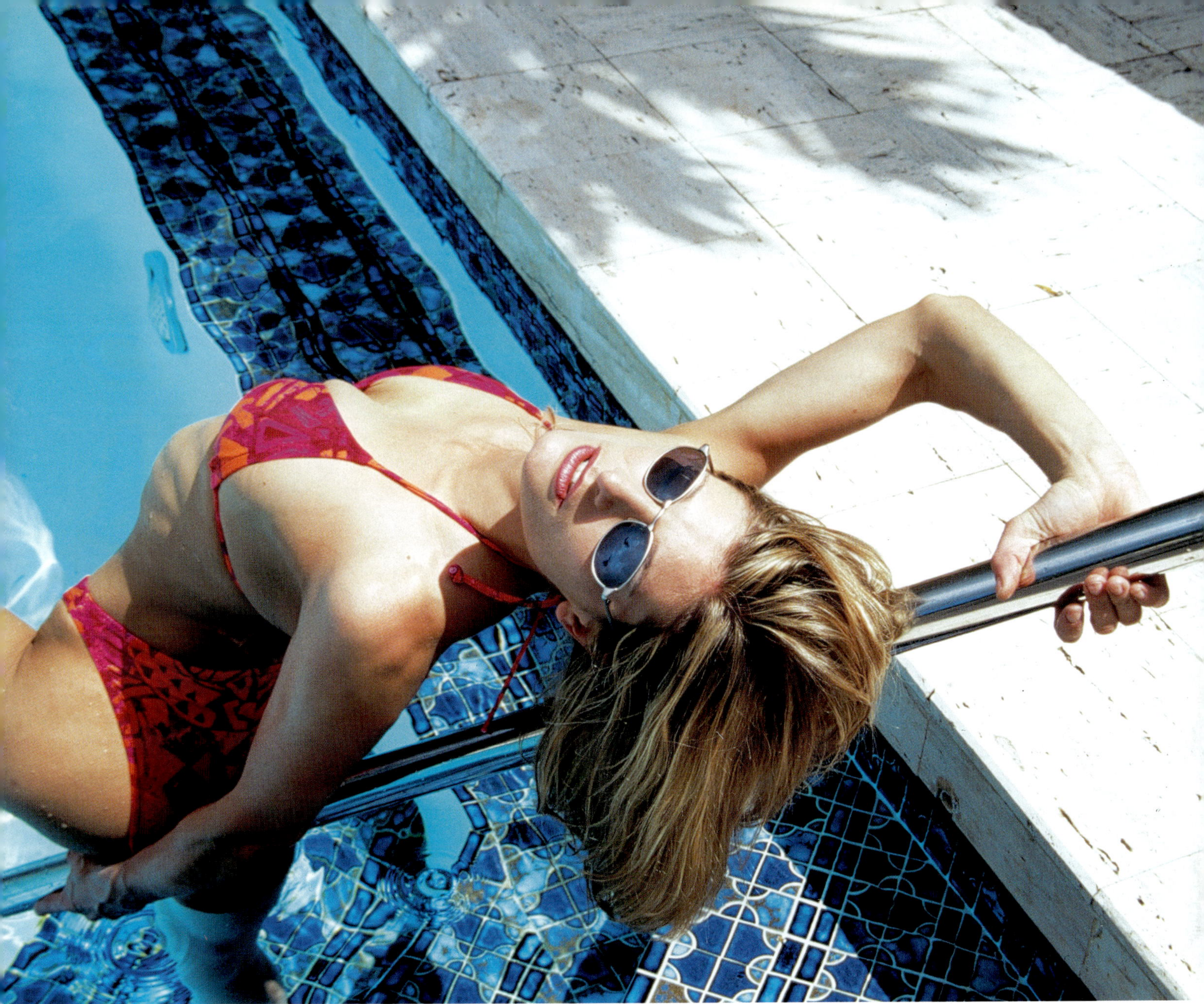

©Bob Shell

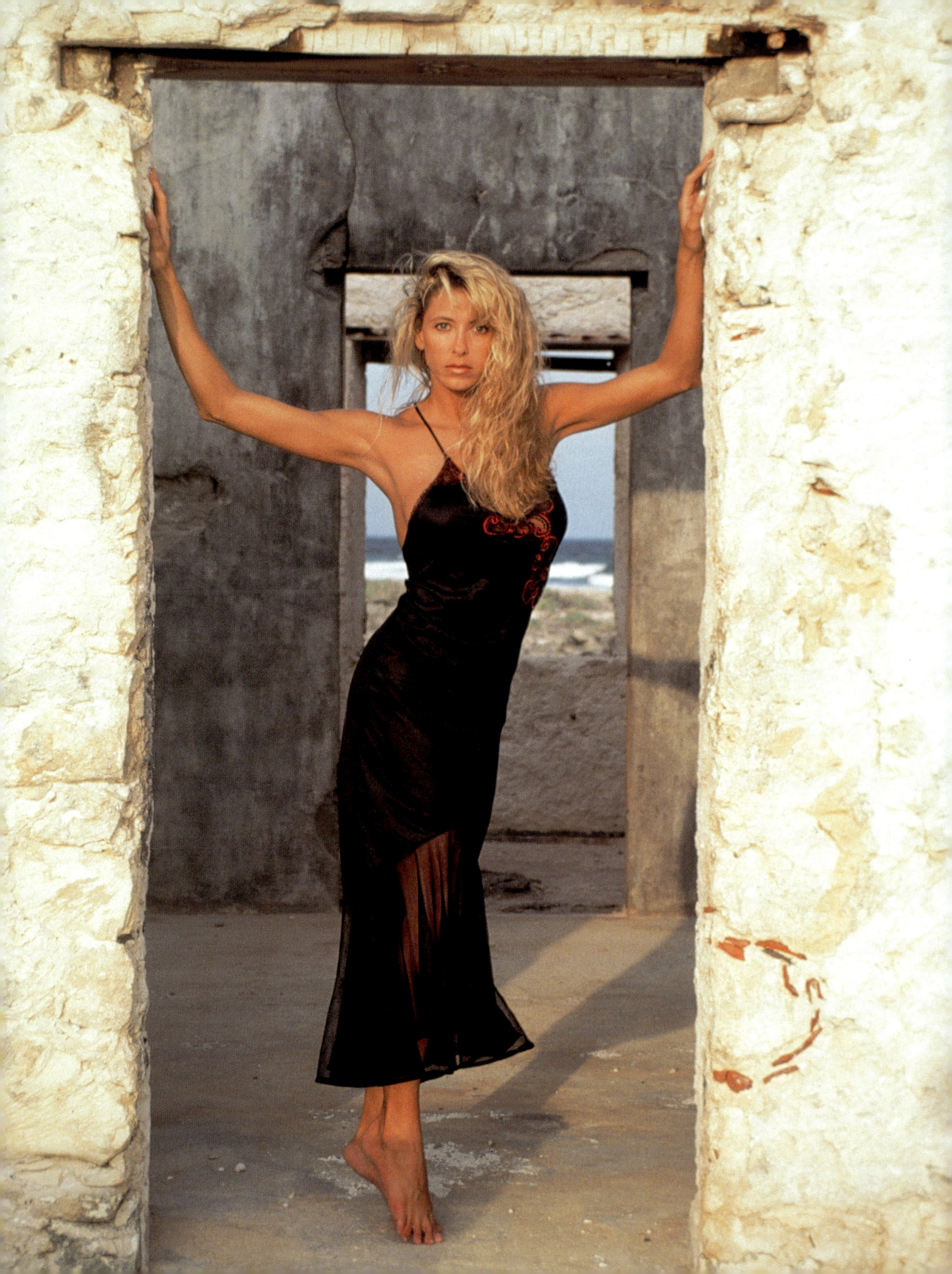

1

Shooting Part-time

...and making a full-time income

Sooner or later it happens to almost everyone who enjoys taking photographs: You get a set of prints back from the photo lab, and while flipping through them, you say to yourself, "Hey, these pictures are good enough to appear in a magazine." Maybe you're showing your vacation photographs to your wife, and while holding up a beautiful sunset photo, she remarks, "That looks like a travel poster. Maybe you should try to sell it." Then it dawns on you. Maybe you *can* take photographs and make money doing it! I know about these little incidents, because that's what happened to me.

If you hear a little voice in your head saying you can do more than just fill your family's scrapbook with snapshots or hang a few framed photographs on your wall, now is the time to start thinking about becoming a "pro." Why not take your photography beyond the snapshot phase and produce images you can sell? If you have enough skill to take sharp, properly exposed photographs and are willing to learn, chances are with a little effort you can enjoy photography as a hobby while turning it into a part-time profession.

One of the advantages of being a part-time pro is that you won't have many of the headaches and pressures that full-time professionals have to deal with on a daily basis. The typical professional photographer produces images on an assignment basis—the photographer is hired by a client who has very specific ideas and requirements about how the final photographs will look and how they will be used. In addition, there are deadlines that must be met, layouts that must be followed, budgets that must be kept, and models, hair and make-up artists, and stylists to hire and manage. As a part-time glamour photographer, most of the time you will be working in a less complex manner, shooting what, when, and where you want. You will have the enjoyment of shooting the kind of photographs you're interested in, with few of the headaches associated with typical assignment photography.

MAKING THE JUMP

I can guess what you may be asking at this point: Can you make any money just shooting part-time? The short answer is yes. The reality of the photography business is that while many of the images that appear in magazines, posters, books, ads, and calendars are taken by full-time professional photographers, a number are also made by part-time pros and amateur photographers. Every day, thousands of part-time and aspiring professional photographers—people who have full-time jobs—are shooting images and selling them. Some of these shooters may make only a few sales each year, but others develop their photographic and marketing skills and will make more money shooting part-time than they do from their full-time jobs.

Be sure to take advantage of farms, parks, beaches, old buildings, and other locations near where you live. Shooting on location often provides a part-time photographer with interesting backgrounds that can't be duplicated in a studio setting. ©Glamour Portfolios

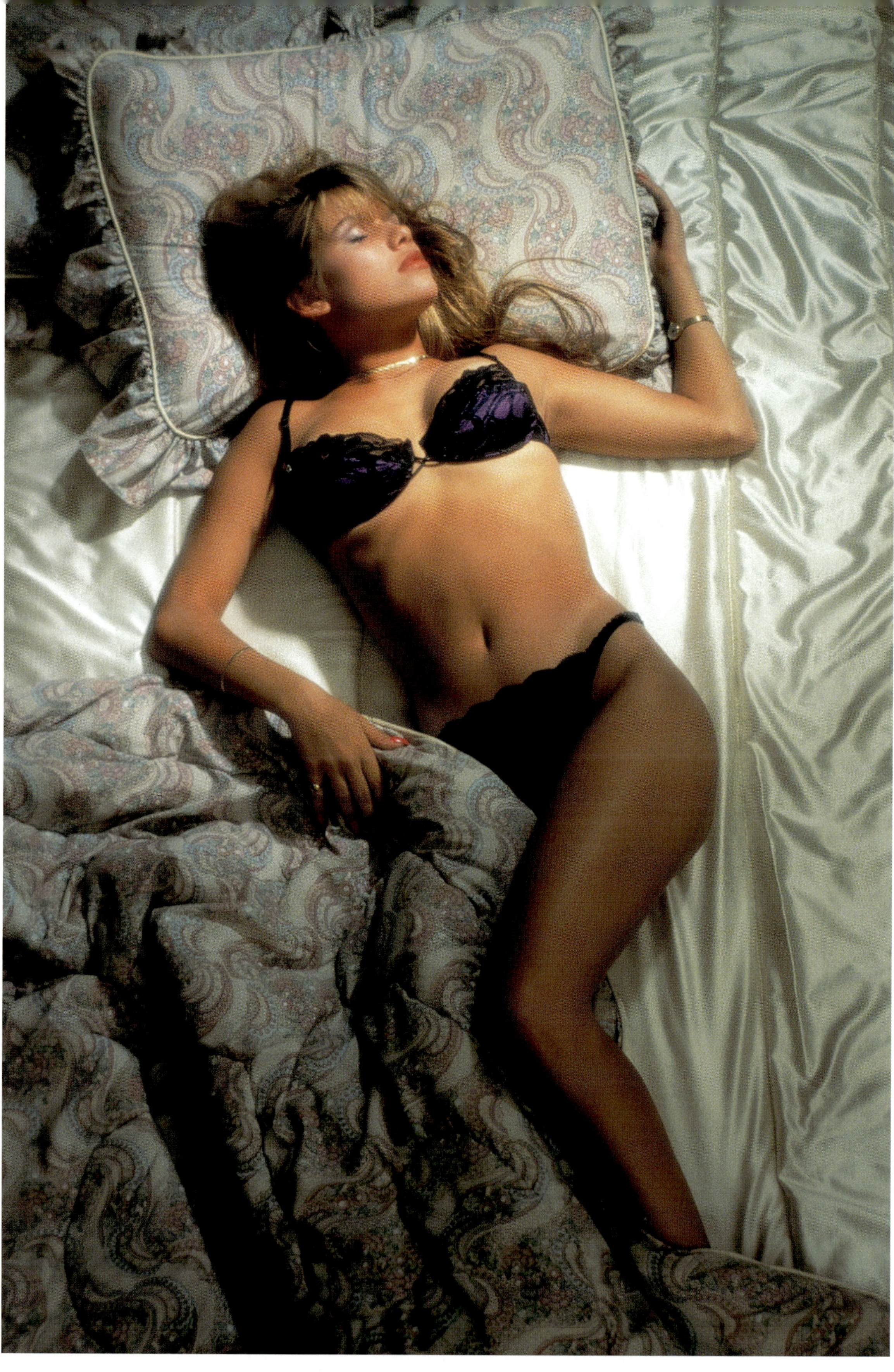

Studio setups in your home don't have to be complicated. This "bed" is really just a sheet and some pillows that were placed on the floor. Standing on a ladder and looking down gave the photographer an interesting perspective. The lighting is simple, too—just one monolight and an umbrella. ©Glamour Portfolios

If you happen to enjoy taking photographs of people, particularly beautiful women, chances are good that you've also thought about becoming a glamour photographer. While there is some potential for selling almost any type of photograph, such as a landscape, still life, or general images of people, photographs showing women in an attractive, healthy, and sexy manner are always in demand. If you've ever picked up a copy of *Playboy* or flipped through the pages of the *Sports Illustrated* swimsuit issue and thought, "That's the kind of photographs I'd like to make," you can consider yourself a potential glamour photographer. First, let's take a reality check: Can you develop the basic skills necessary to shoot professional-quality images? Can you find models and hire them to pose in swimwear, in lingerie, or even nude? More importantly, can you find ways to market your photographs and demand a respectable price for them?

You will be glad to learn that the answer to all of these questions is yes, you can, but (and you knew there had to be a "but" in there somewhere) to do so means you will need to look honestly and critically at your own photographic and marketing skills and make efforts to improve them. If you work hard on improving your photographic craft and learn how to sell the images you create, chances are good that you will be able to exceed your expectations and make a full-time income from your part-time glamour photography.

Backlighting is a technique that can often produce dramatic results without requiring complicated lighting setups. ©Glamour Portfolios

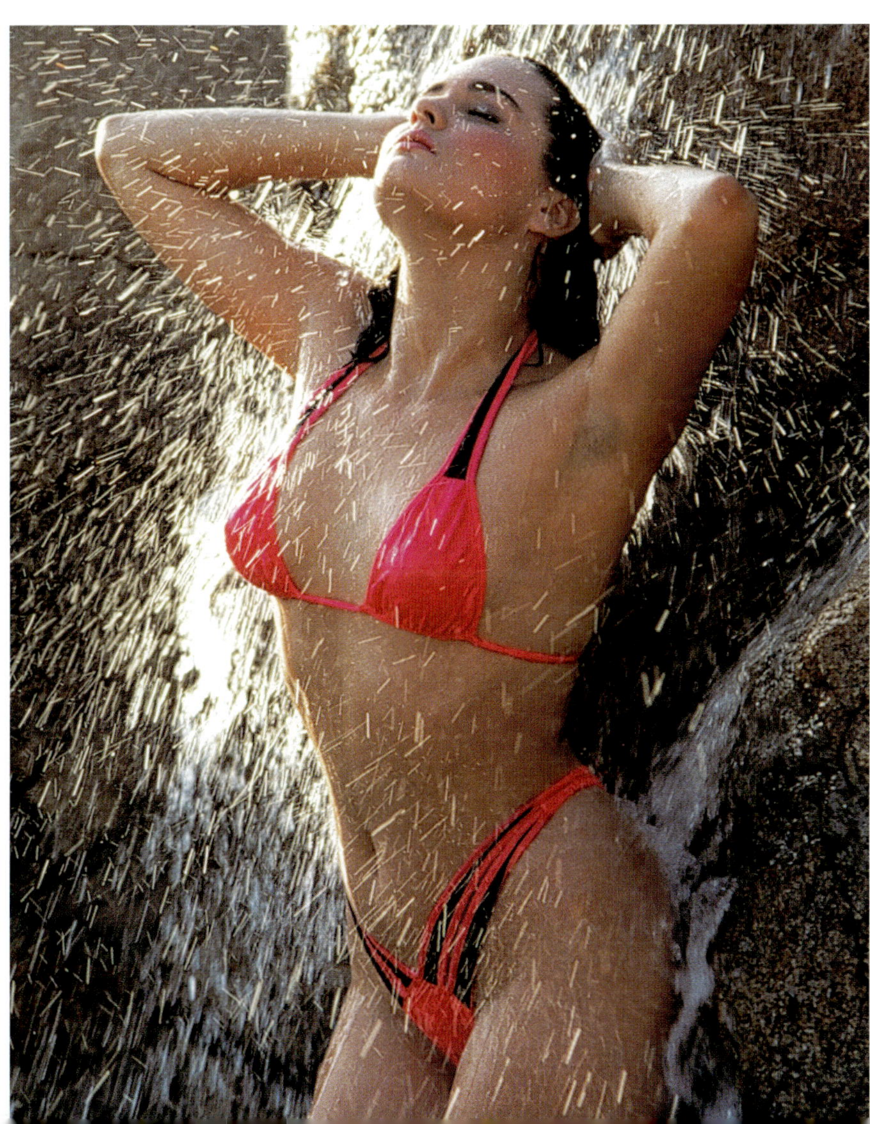

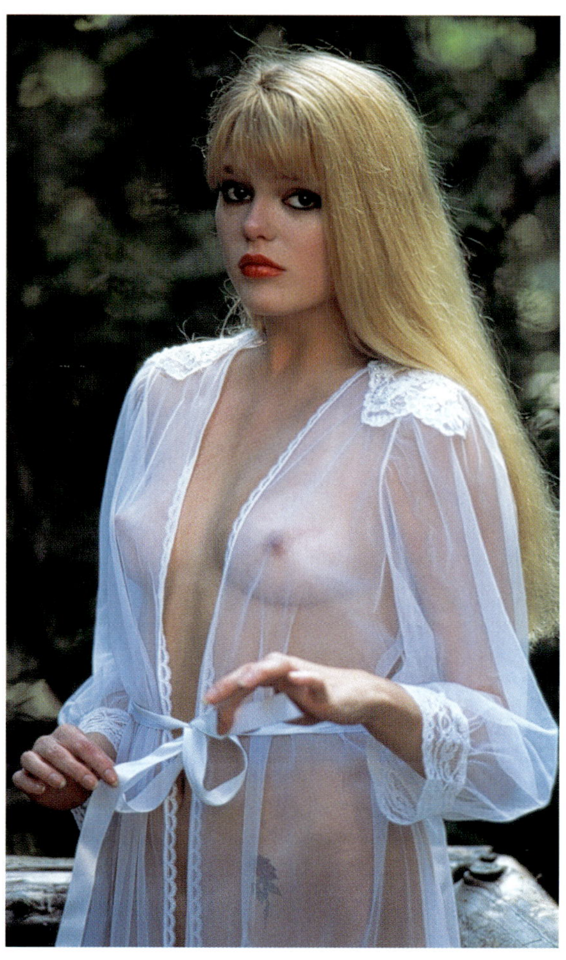

If your model is not comfortable posing nude, she may consider working in lingerie. Consider purchasing a variety of clothing that your models can wear during your shoots; don't rely on models to bring lingerie that will work for your photographs. ©Glamour Portfolios

Getting Started

The place to begin your quest is to make an honest assessment of your photographic skill. In order to create photographs that are good enough for a client to purchase, you need to attain a certain minimum level of technical and artistic skill. There is no shortage of amateur photographers who can point their automatic cameras at just about anything and get a sharp, well-exposed image, but you need to be able to produce images that are much more than that.

The best place to start improving the quality of your images is to study photographs you see published in magazines, calendars, posters, and books, and compare them to your own. Pay special attention to those technical and aesthetic qualities that these images have that are lacking in your own photographs. Is it lighting, posing, or composition? If you can learn to become your own harshest critic, you will have taken the first and most important step in turning your hobby into a part-time profession from which you can derive personal satisfaction and, possibly, a good income.

It may come as no surprise that in order to be a part-time professional, you will need more than a point-and-shoot camera, but as you pursue your career, don't give in to the myth that if you buy the best or most expensive equipment, your photography will automatically improve. The truth is that it won't. The most important equipment you have can be found inside your head, not a camera bag. If you put a low-cost SLR (single-lens-reflex) camera with the most basic controls and features in the hands of a good photographer, the results will be outstanding. On the other hand, if you give an expensive camera to an amateur who has no appreciation for lighting, composition, or exposure, the results are going to be mediocre at best.

Because your initial budget for purchasing photographic equipment will probably be limited, you need to carefully consider what type of camera, lenses, and lighting you'll need in order to get started. Later in the book, I'll introduce you to a basic camera and lighting kit for glamour photography, but for now here are a few basic points to keep in mind.

You don't have to spend thousands of dollars on equipment to make high-quality photographs. Although many professionals shoot with cameras made by companies such as Nikon, Canon, and Hasselblad, it's not necessary for you to. There are dozens of good cameras available from many different manufacturers that are reasonably priced, offer interchangeable lenses, and have adjustable shutter speeds and apertures. If you decide you want to own a Nikon, Canon, or Hasselblad, take the time to check out their lower- and mid-priced models instead of expensive top-of-the-line cameras. As a beginning glamour photographer, you will find it much more useful to have a $400 - $600 camera with a few lenses and a couple of electronic flash units instead of a $2000 camera with a single lens.

When starting out on their new career path, many aspiring professionals make the mistake of trying to duplicate a photo studio inside their homes. They hang up seamless paper on light stands and set up electronic flash units in their living rooms or basements, thinking that is how to create a professional look for their photographs. Even the most casual glance at any glamour or men's magazine will reveal how far this idea is from reality. It is better for you to save money by not buying seamless paper or muslin backgrounds and invest the time in locating attractive or dramatic backgrounds for your glamour images. These might include taking photographs in a friend's home, at a nearby park, beach, farm, or even in a nightclub. Chances are that the photographs you create using an interesting, real-life background will be more visually pleasing and more marketable.

Remember this photograph when you think you need a studio to produce great glamour images. Photographed in the Valley of Fire National Park, just north of Las Vegas, it is an excellent example of how you can take beautiful and highly marketable photographs with only an attractive model, a nice location, and a basic camera. ©Glamour Portfolios

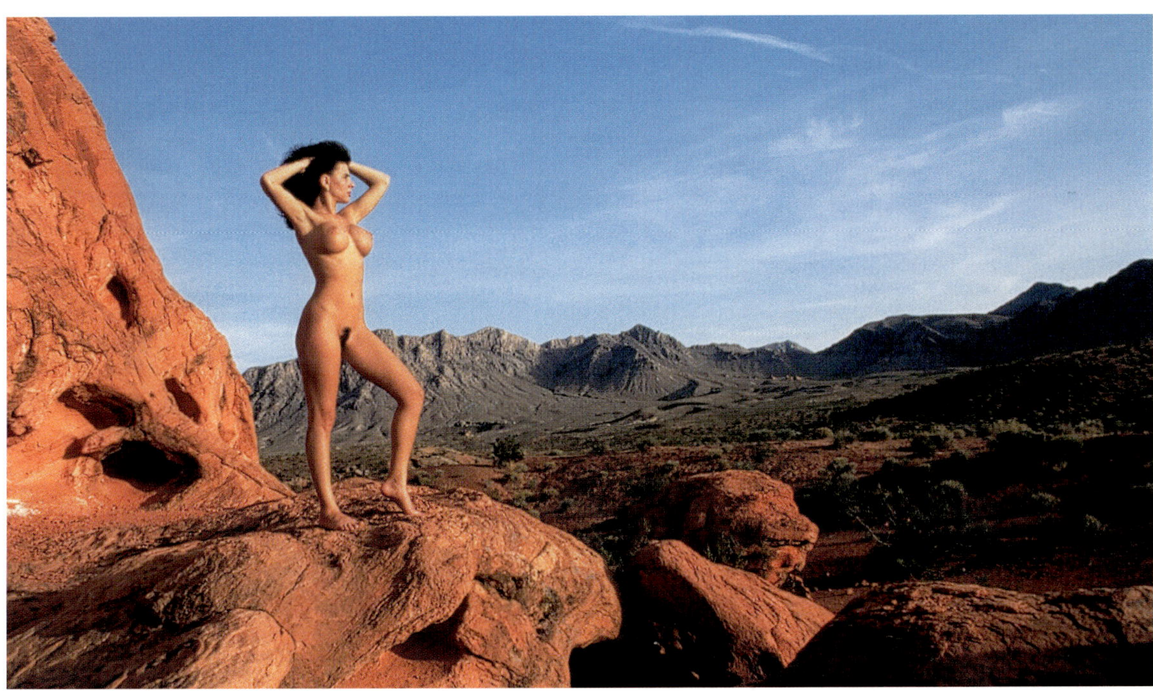

Just as it makes sense not to spend more money than necessary on cameras and lenses, the same is true for lighting equipment. You can easily get started in glamour photography with a pair of monolights that shouldn't cost more than $200 each, plus some reflectors and umbrellas. In fact, that's what I did. When I started my business, I purchased a pair of used Bogen 400 monolights for just a little over $400. The package also included a pair of light stands, two umbrellas, and a case. As you can see, it's not necessary to spend thousands of dollars on studio electronic flash units if you shop wisely and consider purchasing used equipment. Depending on the type of images you like to make, you may not need any lighting equipment at all! A few well-placed reflectors may be all you need.

One of the most important aspects of creating successful photographs is learning how to control light. Whether you enjoy working with natural light, electronic flash, or "hot lights," it's important that you feel confident in your ability to control the light and accurately measure it. The sooner you master the basics of lighting and exposure, the sooner you'll be on your way to creating marketable images.

Learning Your Craft

There are several ways to improve your skill level in lighting, exposure, and the other technical aspects of photography. You can take a course at a local community college, many of which offer evening courses in photography. Years ago, I taught classes in basic and intermediate photography at Howard Community College in Columbia, Maryland, and I have many fond memories of the experience and the students. Taking a night school class is a great way to learn hands-on photography from full-time pros who are eager to share their experience with others.

If you prefer, you can take one of the home-study courses offered by photo schools advertised in many photographic magazines. When looking for ways to improve your photography, don't forget the Internet. The Photoflex Institute of Photography (www.photoflex.com) and Robert Farber's 3D Virtual Internet Workshop (www.farber.com) are just two of the Web sites you can try in order to learn more about photography. The least expensive method for improving your technical skills is to read a few good books on the subject and do a lot of experimenting followed by a critical examination of the results.

Lighting Equipment

There are two popular types of electronic flash units. One uses a common power supply with separate heads (mounted on light stands) that are connected to the power source with cables. The other type, called monolights, combines a small flash head and power pack into a single unit. Both types of lighting gear will do the job equally well, and it's often a matter of personal style and preference as to which type of light is best for you. Another choice, the so-called "hot lights," use a light source, often quartz, to produce continuous light. Quartz lights are usually less expensive than electronic flash units, and since they provide a continuous source, you can actually see the effect of the lighting on your model. The disadvantage is that quartz lights are "hot" (which is how they got their name) and will make you and the model uncomfortable after working under them for even a short time.

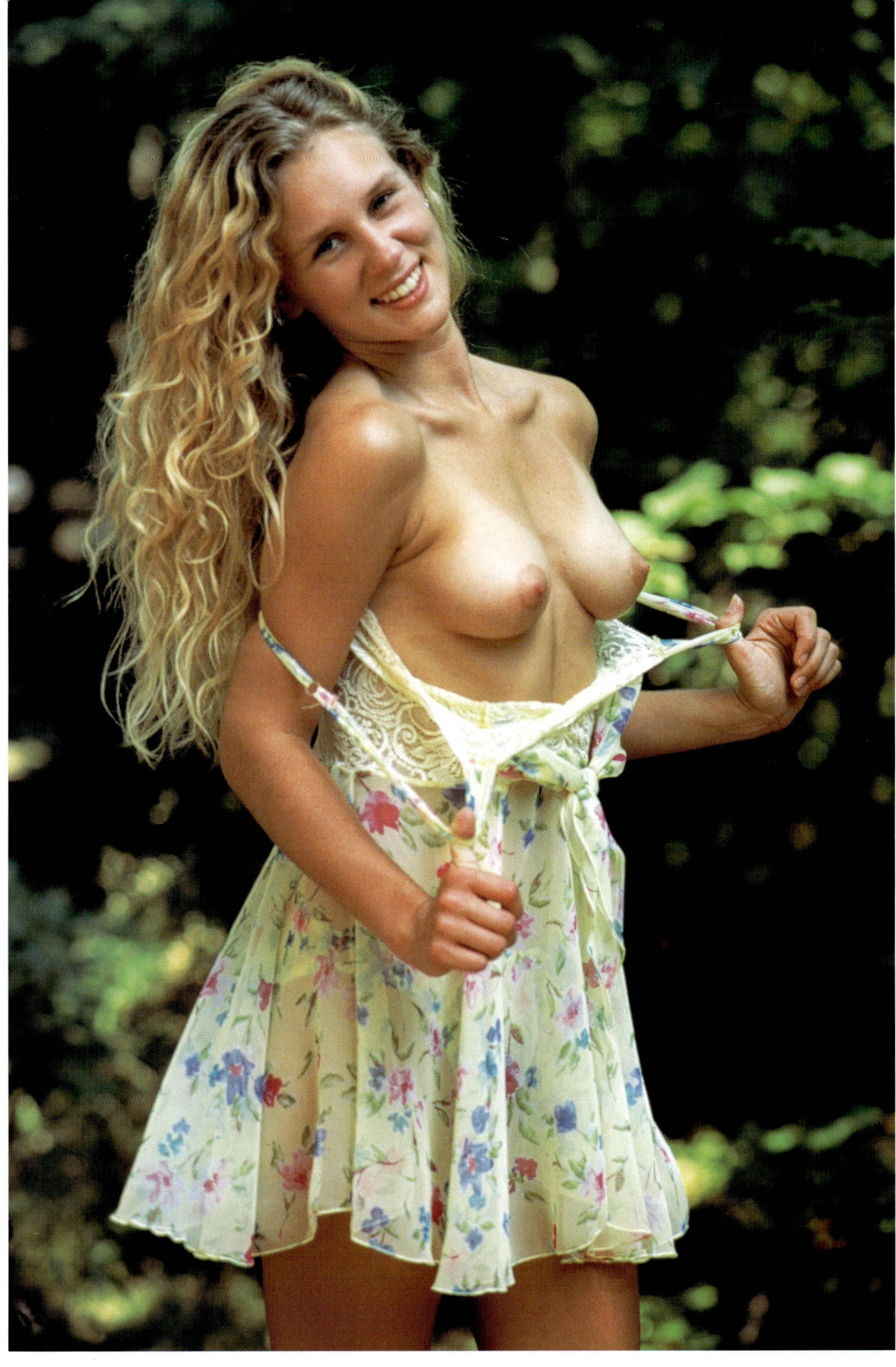

Your photos don't have to be "high concept" to be marketable. Here, Glamour Portfolios' model Jessie is simply lowering her lingerie, yet her beautiful smile and energy make this photo successful. ©Glamour Portfolios

Another important aspect you'll need to consider is your ability to work with people. As simple as this may sound, it's not uncommon for a photographer who may be technically proficient to have difficulty working with models. Some people are simply shy, while others are nervous around people they don't know. If you plan on photographing young women in sexy or erotic poses, it's important you develop the necessary "people skills" to effectively communicate with them. You want to feel secure and comfortable during a shoot, and you want your model to feel the same way. There's no easy way to learn this. It's usually a matter of practice, and after photographing several different models over a period of a few months, you'll begin to feel comfortable talking with and directing them.

Some of the most important skills you will need to develop deal with the business and marketing aspects of glamour photography. If your interest in photography ends when your photographs are returned from the lab or hung on a wall, then you will be missing out on the satisfaction of seeing your photos appear on calendars, posters, and magazines, as well as the financial reward. The skills you need to acquire include finding markets for your photographs, pricing your work, protecting your copyright, and keeping all of your images organized.

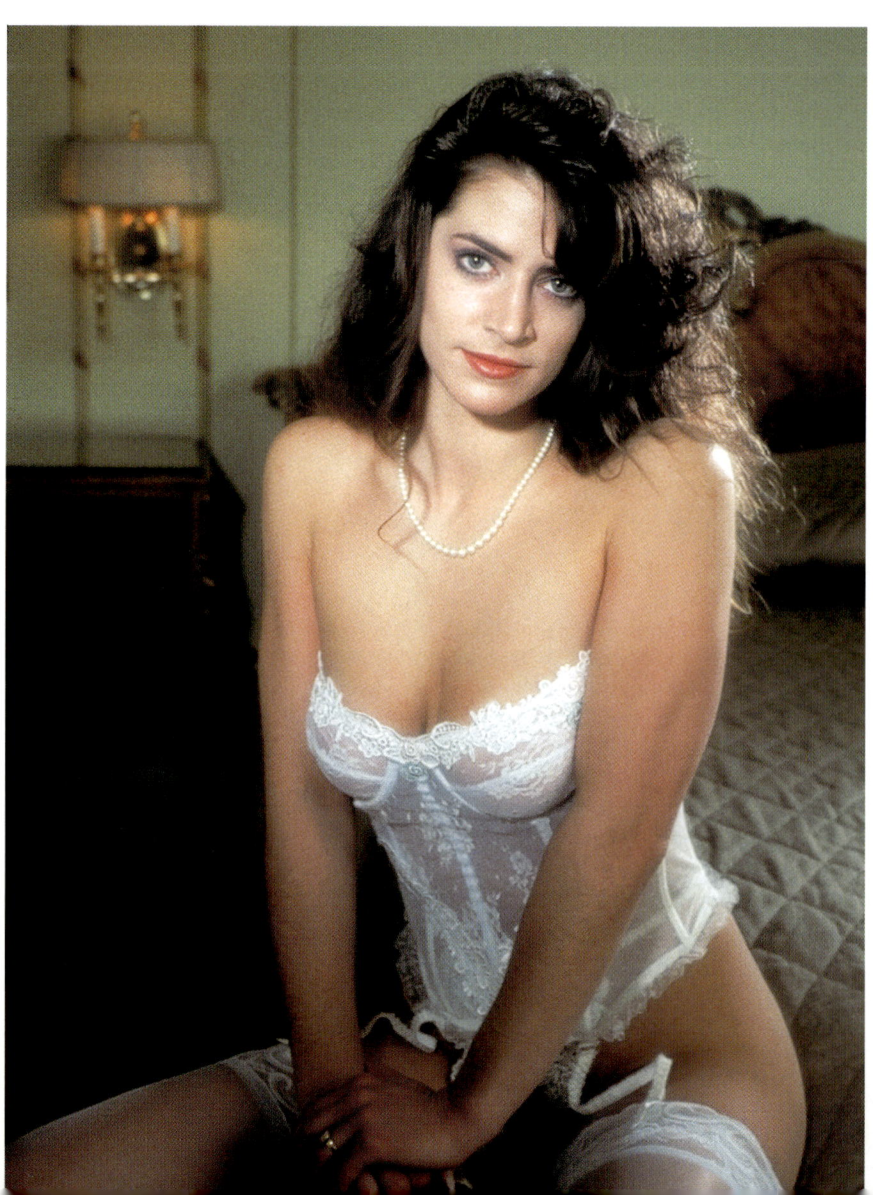

If you are looking for places to photograph models, look around for hotels that have nicely decorated rooms or "fantasy suites" that can provide interesting backgrounds. ©Glamour Portfolios

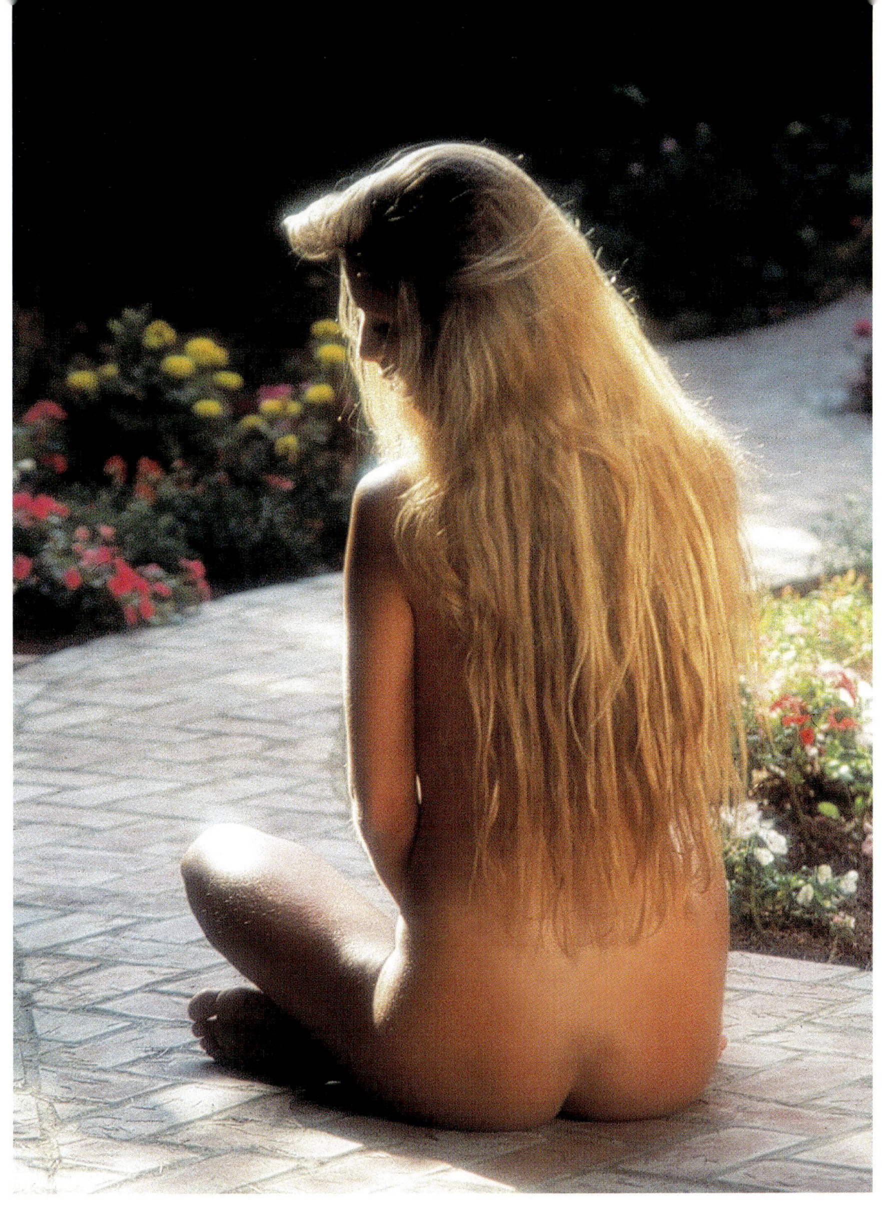

Controlling light is one of the most important skills to master. Here the photographer utilized a single reflector to create a simple yet dramatic image. ©Glamour Portfolios

Luckily, there are many excellent books covering all of these subjects. Any library or bookstore with even a modest section of photography books will have several titles relating to selling your photos.

Pricing is always a question for new photographers, and the best source I've found for pricing information is in a software package called FotoQuote, available from Cradoc Corporation. FotoQuote provides access to over 2000 prices in over 140 categories and is based on actual sales records from national stock agencies and photographers. All of the data, from a working price range for a specific sale to guidance on how to get your price, is available on one screen. FotoQuote is available in Windows and Macintosh versions and lets you print a quote on a fax cover sheet or on your own letterhead. FotoQuote includes 30 electronic categories, including Web banner ads, editorial and advertising photos on the Internet, CD-ROMs, electronic brochures and catalogs, in-store point-of-purchase kiosks, and on-line corporate annual reports. Other categories include stock photo sales to the music and sports industries, and still photos for documentary and feature films. A "sales coach" provides tailored advice to sellers, and the program displays prices in international currencies.

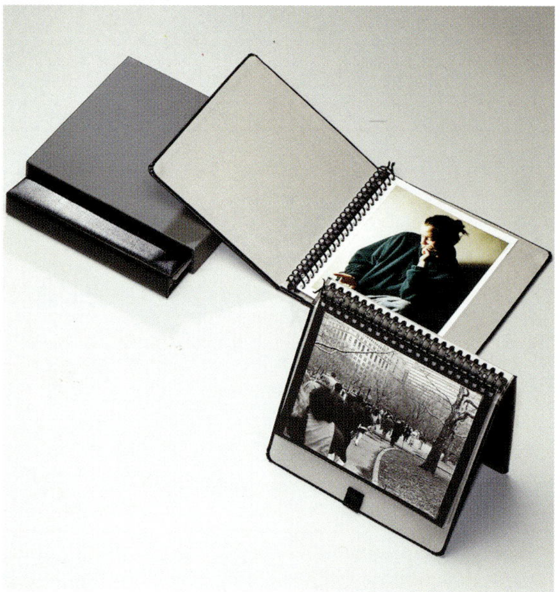

Looking for a classy portfolio presentation? Check out Light Impressions' ProFolio Presentation Kit, which is available for 8x10-inch and 11x14-inch prints. Photograph courtesy of Light Impressions

Prepare a Portfolio

Once you begin shooting glamour photographs, you should start assembling a portfolio containing your best images. A portfolio is important for your new business, because it will show potential clients and models your photographic style and level of technical competence. It also shows the type of photographs you enjoy making and gives people a chance to assess your ability to communicate through your images. Just as you will determine a potential model's talent by reviewing *her* portfolio, she will want to evaluate your talent by reviewing your portfolio. If a model is shown a dozen of your beautiful, sensual images, neatly and professionally presented, she will be interested in working with you. On the other hand, if you present a sloppy handful of out-of-focus or poorly exposed prints, don't be surprised if she walks away.

The most important factor to keep in mind when preparing your portfolio is that quality is more important than quantity. You don't need to show stacks of tear sheets or dozens of fantastic images—few beginning photographers have that ability, anyway. Showing a dozen well-composed and nicely lit photographs is better than displaying 50 images of lesser quality. When you are more successful, you may be able to use a combination of paged slides, tear sheets, and prints.

Presentation is important, but there's no set rule about what kind of portfolio packaging to use. A good rule of thumb is: the simpler the better. You don't want to put your prints in a cardboard box or a three-ring notebook. Most photographers' portfolios I've seen are in binders, with prints placed in acetate pages. Portfolio cases for professionals can cost several hundred dollars or more, but you can get by with a portfolio case similar to those used by models and artists. These cases can be found at any art supply store for under $50. One of the neatest portfolio kits I've seen is Light Impressions' ProFolio Presentation Kit, which is available for 8x10-inch and 11x14-inch prints. It consists of a leather-bound multi-ring binder, 10 pages of acid-free lined Mylar pages, a slipcase, and an easel strap that turns the binder into a presentation easel. If you want to explore a wide variety of portfolio styles, as well as mounting supplies, mats, and other related materials, request a catalog from Light Impressions. The contact information, along with that of other companies mentioned in this book, is located in the appendix.

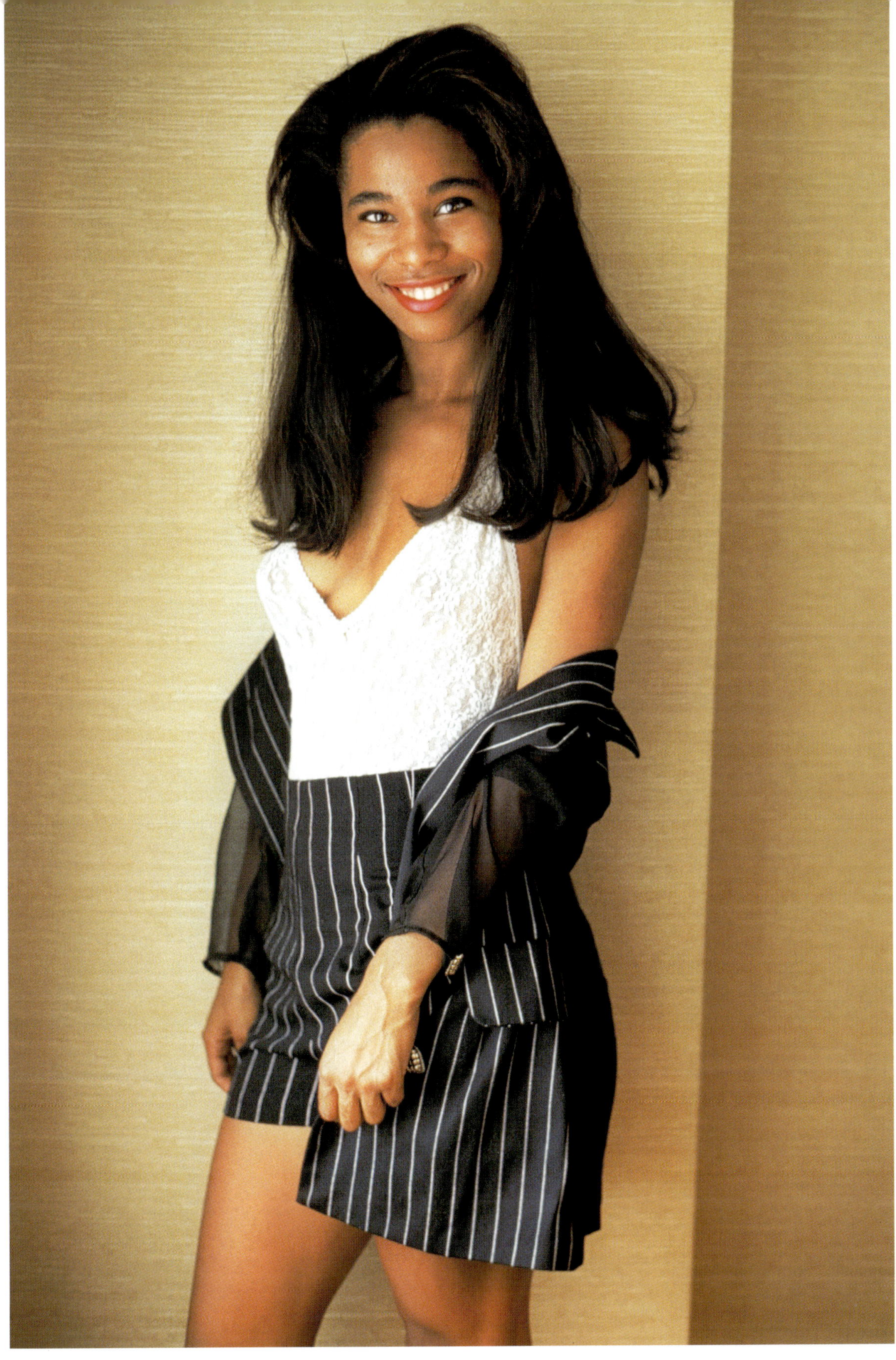

It's not necessary to use complicated lighting or props to create a saleable glamour photo. Here the model is simply leaning against a wall and is lit solely by light from a nearby window. ©Glamour Portfolios

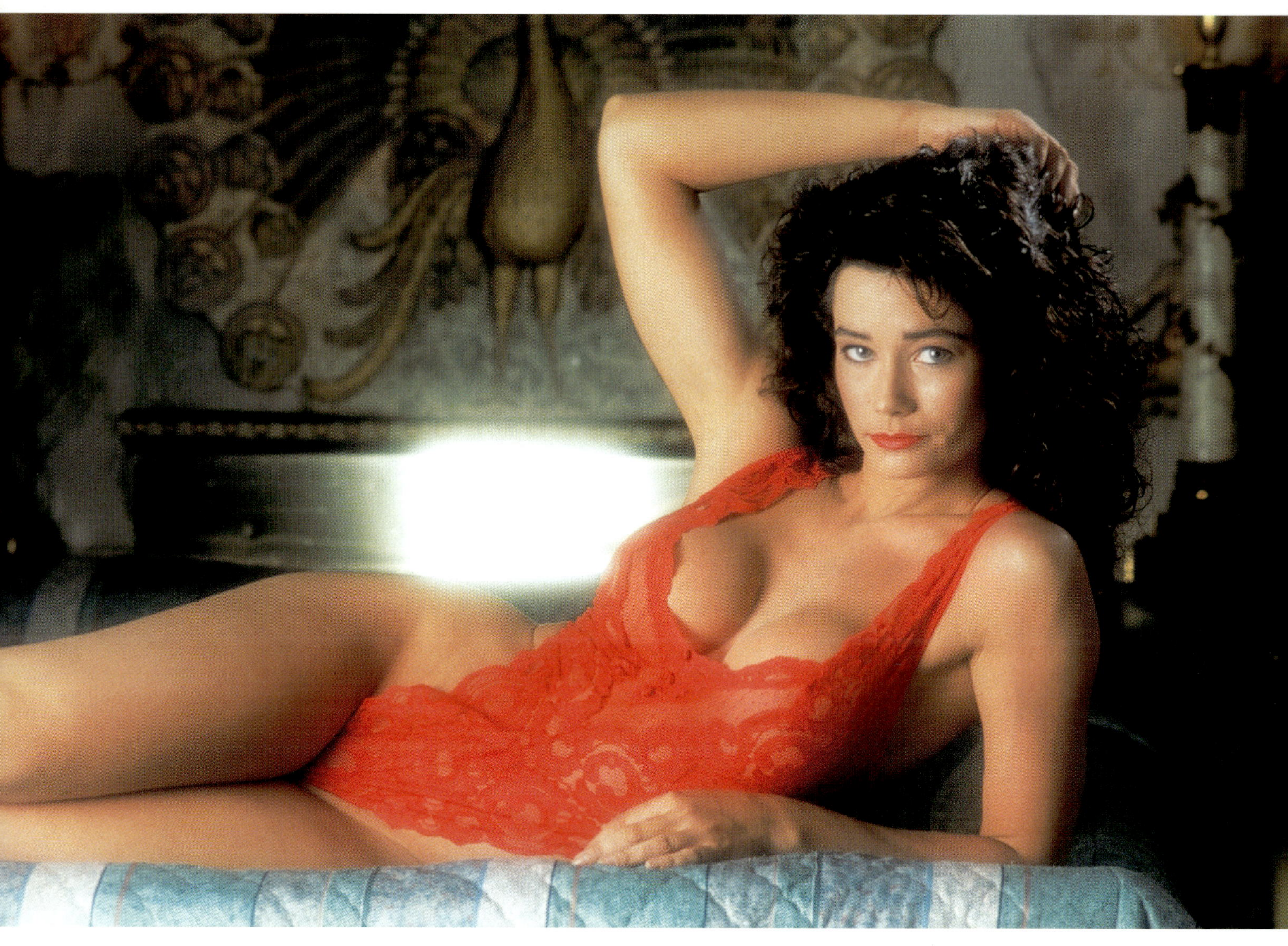

This image combines all of the elements of a successful glamour photograph: an attractive model, an interesting setting, and soft directional lighting. ©Glamour Portfolios

Balancing Your Time

Balancing the time and effort required by your part-time photography along with the demands of your family life and full-time job will be something you need to carefully consider. As anyone who loves photography knows, it can be time-consuming. A typical photographic shoot can last a few hours or an entire day, but there are also trips to the lab, film editing, filing, bookkeeping, and marketing. All of these things take time. If you enjoy doing your own processing and printing, you can spend days in the darkroom producing prints.

If you have a full-time job, you'll probably find yourself shooting on weekends, and since many models you will work with have other jobs, this will be convenient for them, too. You might want to schedule one weekend photo session each month, and see how that volume of shooting affects your work and family life. If the impact is minimal, you might want to increase the number of sessions. Keep in mind that the more you shoot, the more quickly you will build your stock photo library and the more quickly you will see a financial reward from your efforts.

It's a good idea to keep your part-time photography career separate from your regular job. Don't fall into the habit of making phone calls to models or the lab from your full-time job. Avoid approaching women you work with at your regular job when looking for models. As a glamour photographer, you'll be photographing women in swimwear, in lingerie, topless, or nude. Office gossipers will quickly spread the word about how you took sexy photographs of a secretary who happens to work for a senior vice president. Political correctness and sexual harassment are the buzzwords of the corporate world, and it *is* important you consider how your co-workers and employers will view your glamour photography. Pursue your photography, but keep it separate from your regular job.

By now you have a sense that shooting glamour or centerfold photography can become a reality for you. It needn't be difficult or time-consuming. If you manage your part-time photography so it doesn't get in the way of your regular job or family responsibilities, you'll find glamour photography can add a great deal of enjoyment to your life, while providing you with some additional income. How much time you spend shooting and how much money you can make is up to you. By the time you finish this book, I hope you will be on your way to creating glamour photographs part-time and making a full-time income.

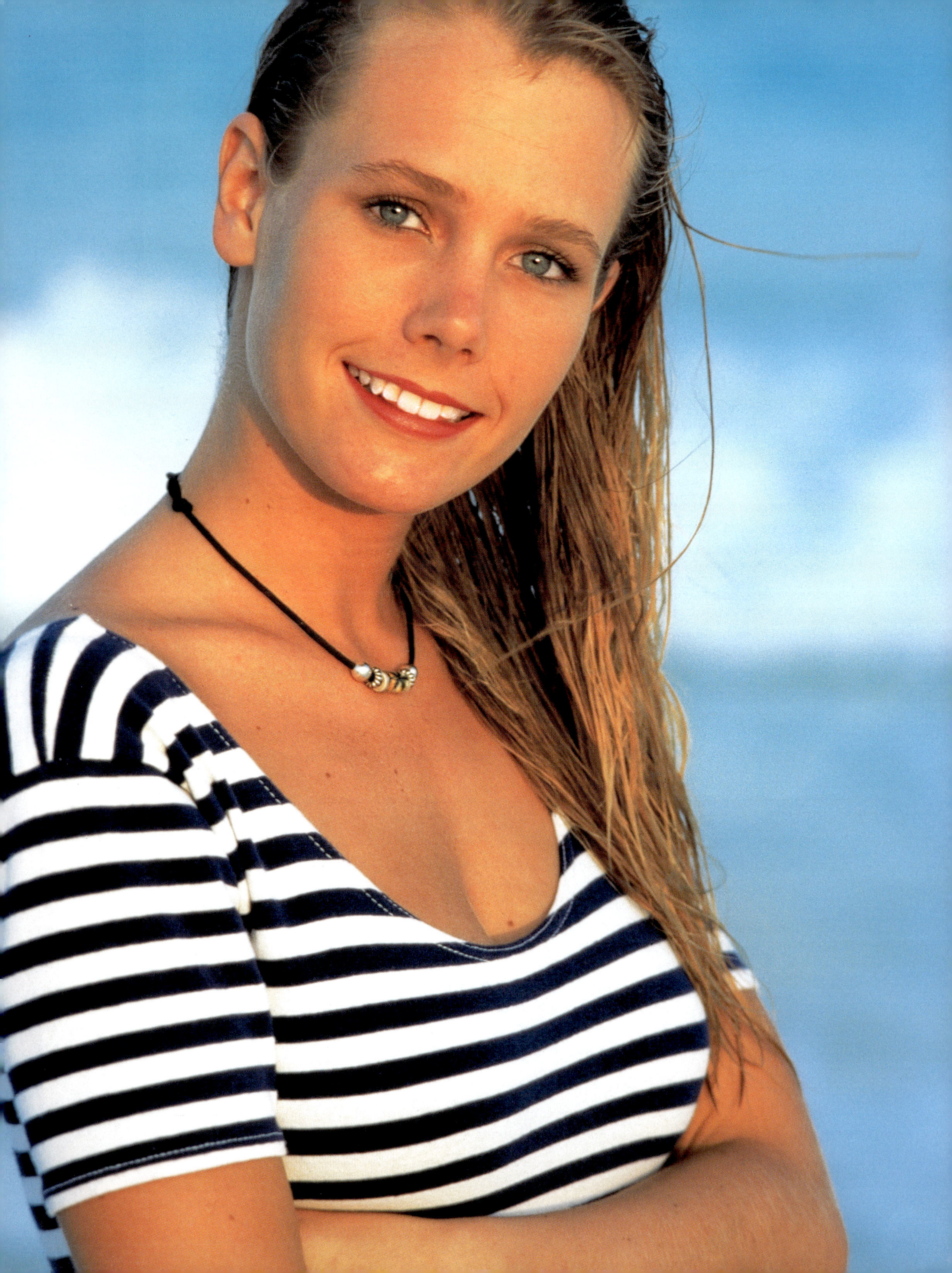

2

How to Find Models

It's not as difficult as you think

Your choice of model can make a huge difference in the success or failure of your photographs—especially their marketability—and is one of the most important elements in glamour and centerfold photography. Many photographers think finding models to pose for lingerie, swimsuit, or centerfold photography is difficult. It's really not. In this chapter, you will find several different ways to find aspiring and professional models. Information is included on how to use classified ads, modeling agencies, nightclubs, "photo days," and even a bikini contest to help find models for your glamour photography projects. One important point to remember in this process is that you must establish your legitimacy in their eyes so that *they* will want to work with *you*.

THE RIGHT MODEL

Let me clear up a misconception many photographers have about working with models: The truth is a good glamour model does not need to have any previous modeling experience. Many successful photographers enjoy working with women who are new to modeling. Beginners are typically enthusiastic and open to your posing suggestions. Experienced models, while skilled at moving smoothly from pose to pose, often have preconceived ideas of how they should look and may try to take over some of the creative aspects of your shoot.

Let me clear up misconception number two: The truth is a good glamour model does not fit any single physical description. Nowhere does the phrase "beauty is in the eye of the beholder" ring more true than for glamour and centerfold photography models. You may prefer to photograph models with beautiful faces, flowing hair, long legs, and shapely breasts, but while that description fits 90 percent of magazine centerfolds, there is no reason why your models have to fit that mold. If you prefer to photograph thin, small-breasted women, or prefer more Rubenesque models, that's OK. If photographing a "biker babe" is more appealing to you than a wholesome "girl-next-door" type, be my guest—the ultimate decision about whom to photograph is yours alone. The most important point to remember is that you should photograph the type of model whose look and style fits your creative vision. Inevitably your choice must be tempered by the reality of the marketplace. If you plan on selling glamour photographs, you must keep in mind that certain kinds of models and images have greater commercial potential than others.

You may be surprised to learn that finding good glamour models does not have to be difficult or time-consuming. With just a small effort on your part, you can have more models interested in posing for you than you can hire. Let me toss another misconception out the window: The truth is you don't have to live in a big city to find attractive women who are eager to pose for your photographs. There is no shortage of beautiful women in this country, and they are just as likely to live in a small town in the Midwest as they are in New York or Los Angeles. The question then becomes how to find them.

Here's a simple outdoor portrait of Shannon, which can be sold repeatedly as a stock image. Shannon has appeared in several issues of *Playboy*. ©Glamour Portfolios

If you are a full-time professional photographer with lots of money to spend for models, you can pick up the phone and call a few modeling agencies, and they will be able to provide you with plenty of models. What if you are a beginner or a semi-pro on a limited budget? Can you find attractive women to pose for you? The answer is yes. Even if you don't have a fancy portfolio or a studio, you can still find good models. All it takes is a little patience, common sense, and confidence.

CLASSIFIED ADS

It sounds too simple, but one of the best ways to find models is to advertise for them. The most obvious and often best place to run a classified ad is in your local newspaper. Even newspapers in small cities have classified ad sections that are read each weekend by people looking for all sorts of work. Beginning models often search want ads looking for opportunities. Start your model search by placing a two- or three-line advertisement in the "Help Wanted" section. Depending on the circulation of the newspaper, this kind of ad usually costs between $20 and $50. Don't waste time and money by running the ad during the week. You will get more value and reach more people by advertising in the Sunday or weekend editions.

How your ad is written is critical to its success. You must choose the words and phrases that you use carefully. Keep track of your response. If your ad is not pulling enough responses, change it! For example, if you write something like the following, you are throwing your money away:

> *Models needed by beginning photographer for centerfold photos. Nudity required. Limited budget. Call Glen at 444-4444.*

While that ad might be accurate and honest, you should not expect it to generate many calls. Instead, you should try something like:

> *Dancers and Models: Needed for posters, calendars, and magazines. Excellent opportunity for beginners. 18+ only. Call Glen at 444-4444.*

To see why this ad would work well, let's review it a line at a time. By using the headline "Dancers and Models," you have placed the ad in a different section of the help-wanted ads where it will be read by more potential models. In most cities, the young women who work as dancers in nightclubs often work topless or nude. Since these women are comfortable working topless or nude, chances are they will consider posing for glamour or centerfold photographs. Even those women who already have jobs scan the want ads looking for new opportunities. Note the ad's emphasis is on the usage, rather than the type, of photographs you will be taking. This ad has been designed to appeal to the model's desire for fame, and answering it might, in fact, be her lucky break. What young model or dancer wouldn't want to appear on a calendar or poster? Even though you may not be shooting for a specific poster, calendar, or magazine, your photographs may end up there. The next qualifier in the ad indicates that this is an "excellent opportunity for beginners." Everyone looking for a job wants a shot at success. You are making your potential model feel that, by calling you, this is her chance. Adding "18+" helps avoid calls from underage models, but you should still check IDs of any youthful-looking potential models.

Jolinda is an amateur model who answered a classified ad in a local newspaper. Glamour Portfolios used her on several shoots, including an assignment in Cozumel. ©Glamour Portfolios

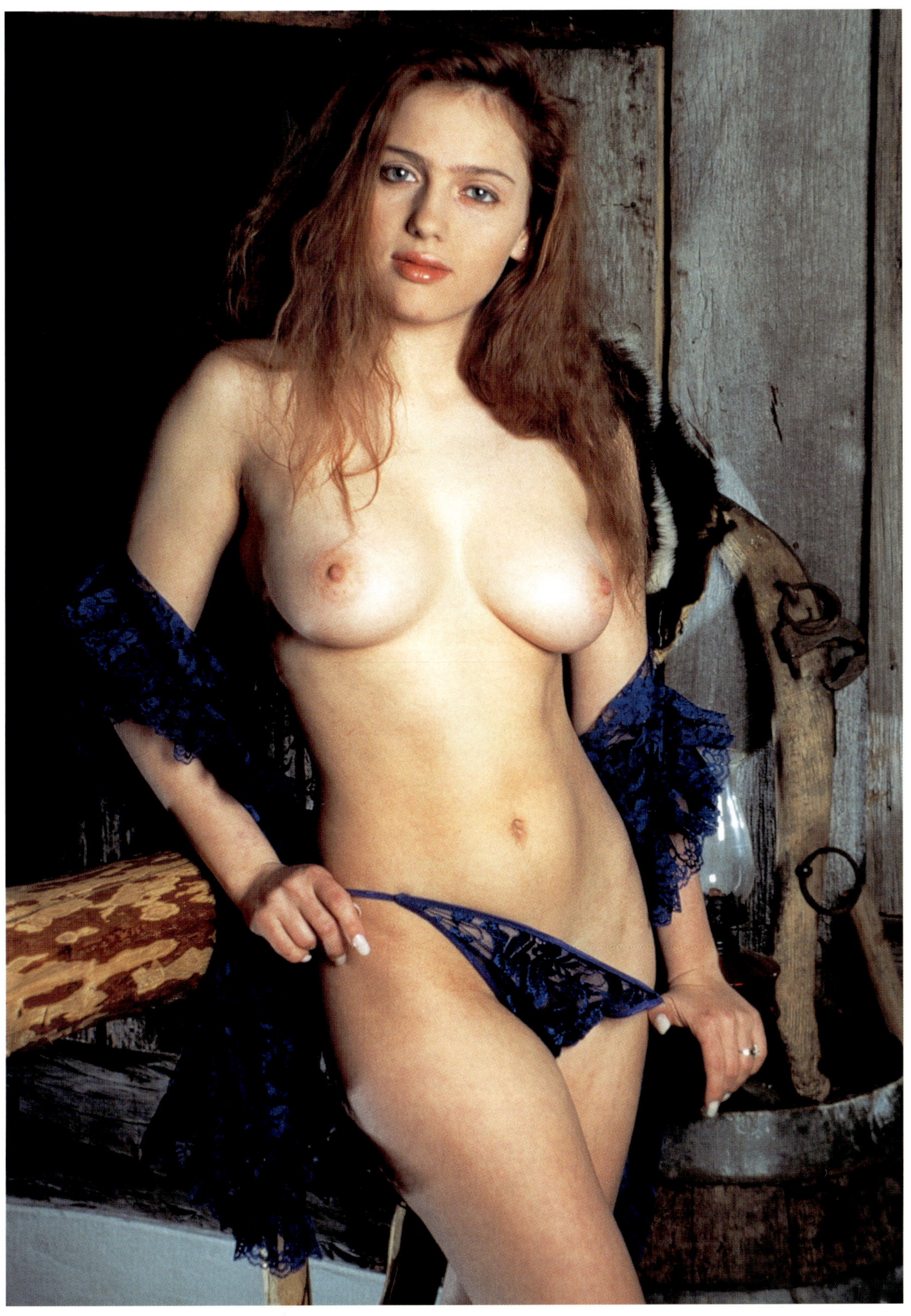

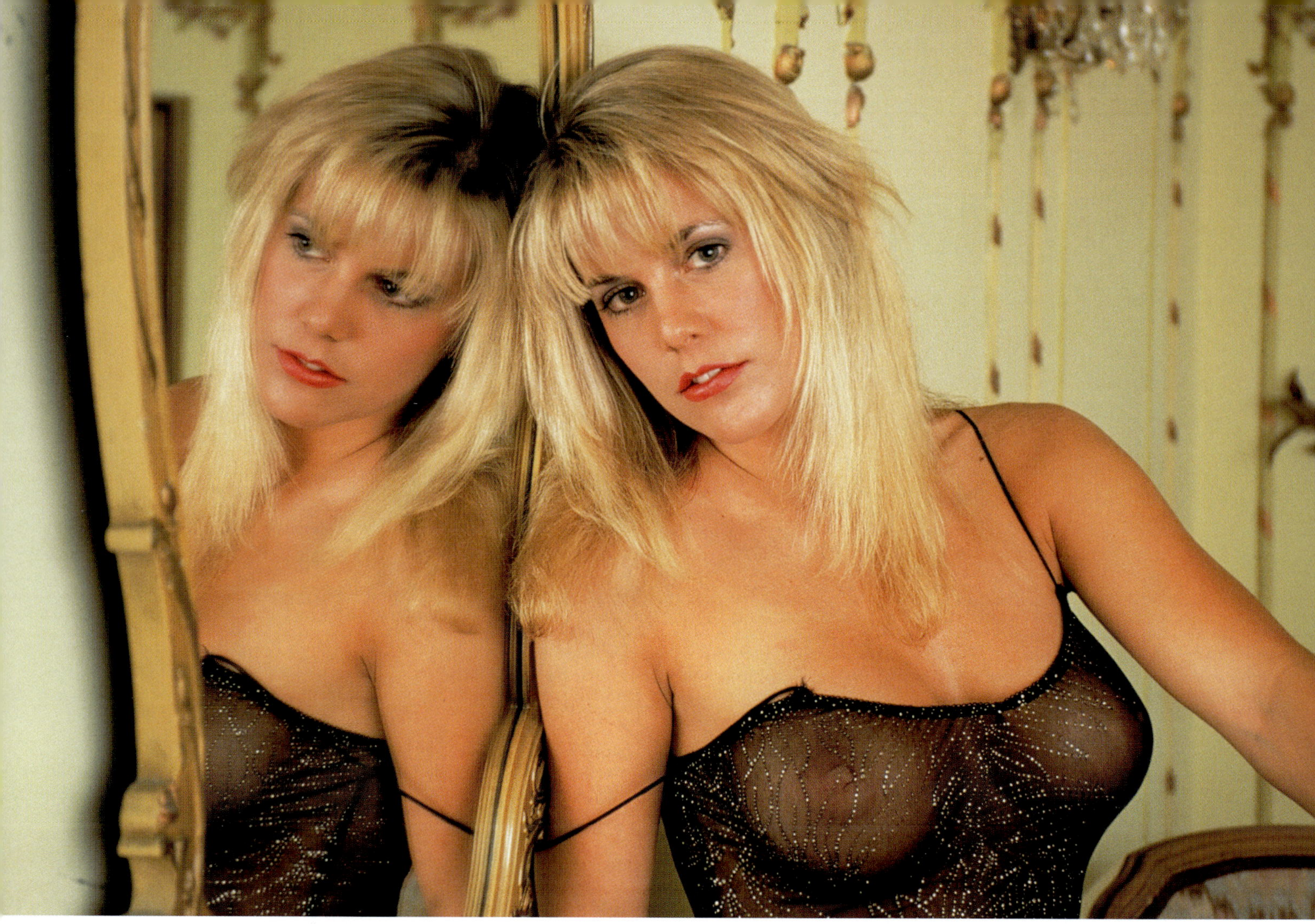

This softly lit portrait of Midi makes excellent use of a mirror to add visual interest. ©Glamour Portfolios

You will notice that the words "lingerie," "topless," and "nude" do not appear anywhere in this ad. The time to discuss those kinds of specific details with potential models is when they call you. Don't hesitate to discuss these details. (All of the information on how to conduct a phone interview is covered in the next chapter.) Another reason for downplaying the kind of photographs you will be making is that there is no need to raise concerns of anyone at the newspaper or anyone else who may be reading the ads. Your goal with the ad is to get as many calls as you can from potential models.

Classified ads let you be as specific or general as you want. If you are not getting enough response, experiment with different phrases to improve the response. No one ad is perfect for every photographer and every situation. You have to be able to write an ad that works for you.

Classified Ad Benefits and Disadvantages

Unless you have the budget to fly models in from distant cities, you need to have models who live within driving distance—the closer the better—of your location. Newspaper ads provide a fast, personal response and allow you to quickly target potential models within a specific geographic area. When an ad appears on Sunday, you will start getting calls on Monday. Usually, potential models will be calling to ask for more details and to check if you are legitimate. You can learn a lot about a person from asking a few questions during the phone call. Are they enthusiastic? Do they sound intelligent and dependable? A few moments on the phone will help you determine a model's experience. A suggested list of questions to ask is found in the next chapter.

Classified ads are relatively inexpensive, and it's usually not necessary to run an ad for more than two or three weeks. Your ultimate response depends on many factors, but you can expect to hear from a dozen or more potential models, which will quickly be narrowed down to a few you will want to interview. Another benefit of a help-wanted ad is that you can quickly change it to fit your requirements. For example, one month you might require blonde models, and one month you might need models over 30 years old.

One of the realities of working with models is that they are not always reliable. When you receive a response from a classified ad, you will be dealing with a stranger. You assume they are truthful and hope they will be dependable, but until you actually meet and work with them, you do not know. If for various reasons, your ad does not pull in the required responses, you may have to run it for a few months, and, depending on the ad rates in your area, it could become expensive. Nevertheless, classified ads remain the most cost-effective and easiest way to find glamour and centerfold models. It's a time-tested method that has worked for many photographers and can work for you.

Jennifer, one of Glamour Portfolios' top models, was discovered when she answered a classified ad in a local newspaper. She's been on several assignments in Mexico and is among the most popular models on their Web site (www.glamourportfolios.com). ©Glamour Portfolios

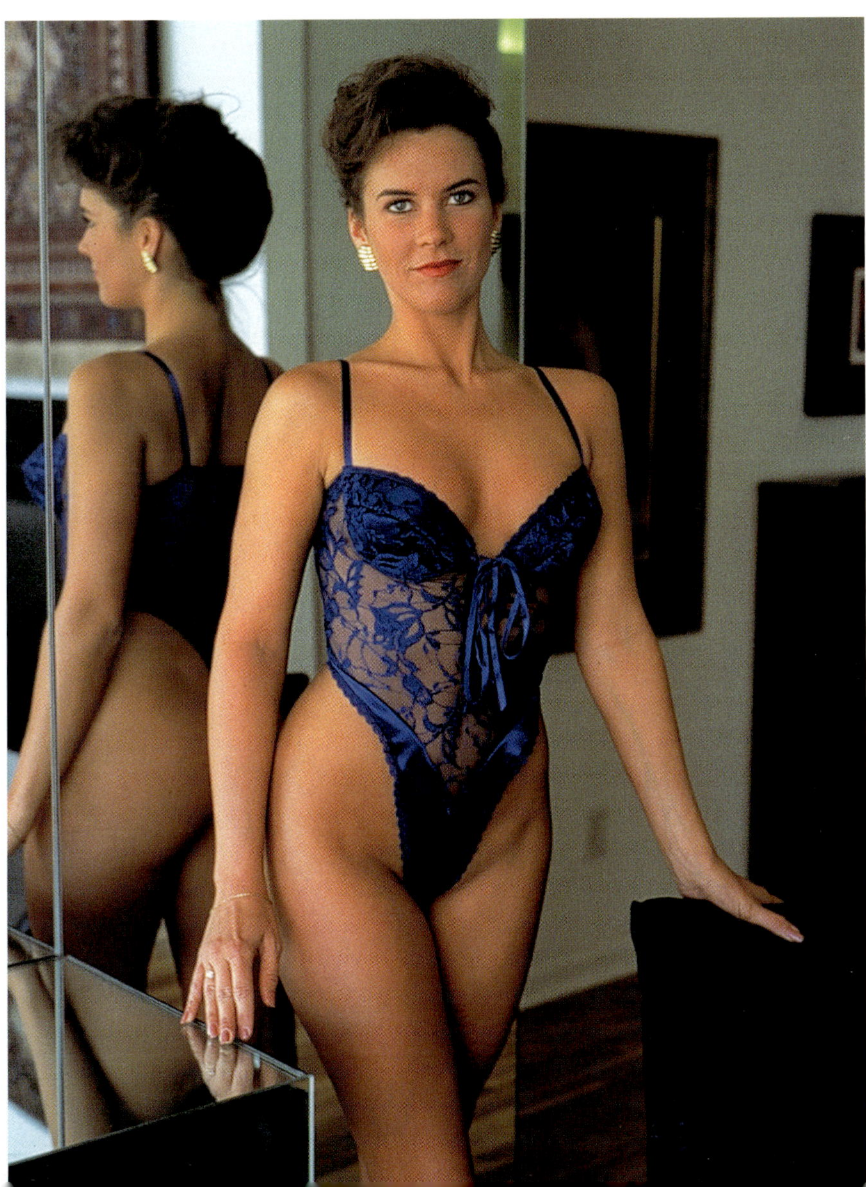

MODELING AGENCIES

Most of the models you see in magazines, catalogs, ads, and TV commercials are professionals, usually represented by agencies. Some modeling agencies, such as Ford or Elite, have worldwide reputations. The larger agencies are based in New York or Paris and usually have branch agencies or associates in smaller cities. There are also hundreds of smaller, less-known modeling agencies.

Because the models they represent expect $150 per hour or more, most agencies will be of little use to beginning or part-time glamour photographers. Agencies want to know who is taking their models' photographs and how the photographs will be used. When you mention the words "swimwear," "lingerie," "topless," or "nude" to an agency, you can easily be quoted an hourly rate much higher than $150—with the assumption you are shooting for a specific client. If you mention that you want an unlimited model release, you will politely be told to go elsewhere. The "blockbuster" or unlimited model release is critical to the success of the part-time glamour photography concept and is explained in the next chapter.

Nevertheless, don't not let any of the above statements discourage you. If you are an aspiring professional photographer with a good portfolio, you should investigate your local modeling agencies—some agencies may be looking for photographers to work with their models to help them build their portfolios. In smaller cities, you will find some agencies that need more assignments for their models and might be open to your needs for models to pose in swimwear or lingerie. Beginning models need portfolio shots and, for that, they need a photographer. Even if your budget is limited, you still have something important to offer a beginning model—good photographs. Perhaps you can barter, exchanging portfolio photographs for modeling time. This is a traditional way for beginning models and photographers to work together to their mutual benefit.

How to Approach a Modeling Agency

Modeling agencies are careful about where they send their models. That's why it's important that you look and sound professional at all times when approaching an agency. For example, do not even think of calling an agency unless you already have a portfolio. If they don't know you, they will want to see samples of your work and possibly references. If you don't have any sample images, they will assume you are an amateur photographer—or worse. Assuming you have a portfolio, the first step is to call, introduce yourself, and inquire about the possibility of working with the agency's models. A typical phone call might go like this:

Good afternoon, this is XYZ Models, may I help you?

Hello, this is Jack Jones. I'm a photographer and am working on projects that will require models. I have a limited budget, but I don't mind working with beginning models.

We'd love to meet you and can set up an appointment, but first, can you tell me a little more about the assignment?

I'm working on a swimwear and lingerie project right now. It's a calendar, but the photographs will probably end up on a CD-ROM. I also do tasteful figure photography and need models who do nudes. Do you represent any?

There's no problem with swimwear, however we don't have many models who do lingerie and few who will do nudes. Are you working for a particular client?

Actually, I produce most of my own projects and then market photographs independently or through a stock photograph agency.

Hmmm... well, we generally book our models for specific assignments and usually need to know clients and usage before quoting a price. Perhaps we can work something out with some of our newer models. We have two new models who have no experience or photos, and we're anxious to get their portfolios going. Why don't you come in, show us samples of your work, and we'll see what we can do.

There are two things modeling agencies hate: low budgets and unlimited model releases. Unless you have good budgets and specific clients, modeling agencies will not jump through hoops to supply you with models for glamour and centerfold photographs. When you look at things from their perspective, you will understand why: They do not want to send their models on jobs where they make less than their regular hourly rate, and they don't want photographs of their models ending up in the "wrong places."

Let me present a hypothetical but realistic scenario. You photographed a model named Judy when she was starting out. She was not with a modeling agency when you met her. You did some tasteful nudes and had her sign an unlimited model release. Three years later, you sell some of her nude photographs for a calendar. Judy has moved and is unaware her photographs are being used in the calendar. She has had some success and moves to New York, where she is represented by a major modeling agency. Just as she is being considered for a national cosmetics account, the nude photographs you took appear. The cosmetic company's owner hears about them and tells the agency he doesn't want anyone who appeared nude to represent his company.

Even if Judy did not appear nude, there can be other conflicts. Perhaps you sold a head shot of Judy for use in a pimple cream ad. The cosmetic company wants "exclusive beauty and hair industry" rights and will not consider her, since she is appearing in another industry-related company's advertising. Nevertheless, this situation is not *always* the rule. Glamour or centerfold photographs do not always hurt a model's career, and many superstar models and actresses choose to appear in *Playboy* to give their careers a boost.

The good news for glamour photographers is that a growing number of agencies specialize in models who pose for swimwear, lingerie, and nude photography. Due to the growing number of topless and nude cabarets and nightclubs, the number of glamour-oriented model agencies and talent representatives is increasing. These agencies specialize in booking dancers and exotic entertainers in nightclubs. However, they will also book their dancers for a variety of glamour projects and are typically less restrictive about model releases. That does not mean they will allow their models to sign an unlimited release, but they will be more open to glamour-oriented projects. Of course, as with any agency you deal with, make sure you are dealing with legitimate professionals to avoid unforeseen problems.

Agency Pros and Cons

There are several benefits of working with an established agency rather than dealing with the model directly. One of the most important is that agencies are dependable sources of models. You are dealing with experienced professionals who are interested in making money. It is in their interest to find suitable models and to make sure they show up for the sessions.

A good agency will be able to supply a wide selection of models. Modeling agencies in large cities can represent several hundred models, and even agencies in smaller cities have many models available. The agency will send or deliver a directory containing photographs of their models, along with information on height, hair, eye color, and clothing size. Any special talents or restrictions are listed. Also, modeling agencies are able to provide models quickly. If you place a call to an agency today, you will probably have head shots on your desk by the afternoon or next morning and, after making your selection, a booking for the following day. To a glamour photographer, this can mean the difference in the success or failure of a last-minute shoot. One of the best reasons for using an agency is

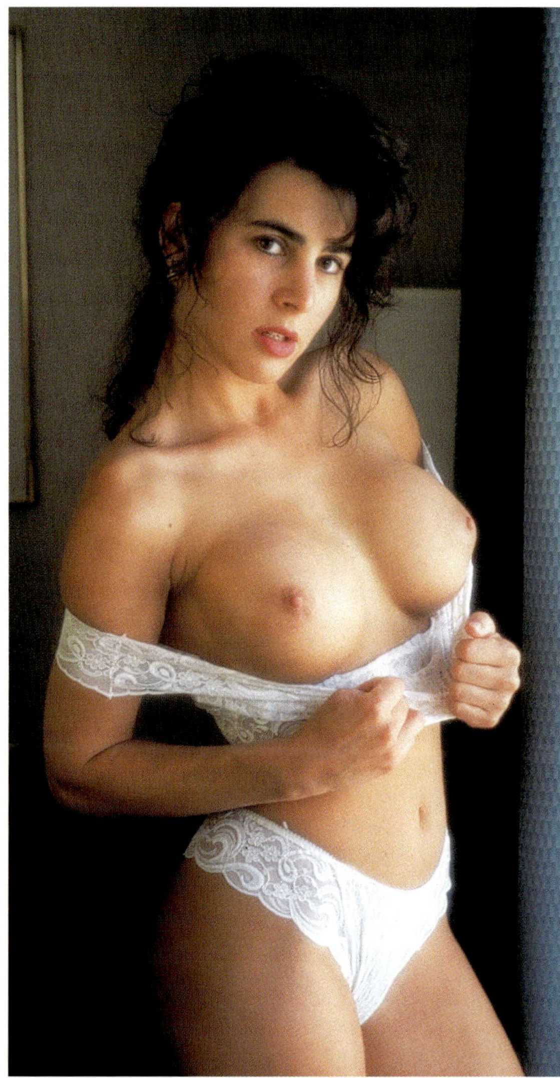

Bonnie is a perfect example of why working with an agency is beneficial. For a Las Vegas shoot, Glamour Portfolios had booked another model through a Los Angeles agency. The model never showed, and the agency quickly sent Bonnie, a capable substitute. Since that first shoot, Bonnie has worked with Glamour Portfolios several times and assisted them in locating other models and locations. ©Glamour Portfolios

the agency's ability to provide substitute models if there is a "no-show" or last-minute cancellation. Few things make photographers more nervous or angry than booking a model for a shoot, only to have the model cancel or come late. On some commercial photography assignments, budgets can be in the tens of thousands of dollars. If the model doesn't show, you can't do a shoot!

There are some drawbacks to working with agencies. Finding models through an agency costs more than all of the other methods discussed in this chapter. It's rare that a model booked through an agency will work for less than $50 to $100 per hour, and that's at the low end. Some models expect between $250 and $500 per hour for nude photography, and only for a specific assignment. Agencies typically won't let their models sign unlimited releases and prefer to book their models for specific assignments for one client. Model agencies tend to be cautious about lingerie, topless, and nude assignments. Unless you are well known and have excellent credentials, it can be difficult to find glamour models through a traditional modeling agency.

NIGHTCLUBS

A local nightclub can be an excellent place to find models. Some clubs feature dancers and adult entertainers who dance topless or nude. While some adult-oriented businesses have the reputation of being seedy, there are "gentlemen's clubs" with better reputations and a more upscale clientele.

Before approaching a dancer at a club, you should visit the club a few times and meet some of the people who work there. Get to know the manager or DJ—it wouldn't hurt to know the bouncers, too! That kind of relationship can come in handy. Do not approach a dancer while she is performing—it is a mistake to walk up to a dancer while she is on stage and hand her a business card or start a conversation. The big strong hand you feel on your shoulder will soon be leading you out the front door. Instead, wait until the dancer is on her break. Often, dancers relax between performances or look for customers for private dances. Bring a small portfolio with you, which could consist of a group of 3x5-inch prints with your name and phone number printed on the back. Tell her you are looking for models, and, if she's interested, you would like to tell her more about your photography. Be sure to tell her that these are *paid* assignments. Dancers are usually in the business for one reason—money.

At some clubs, if you discuss business with a dancer, you may find a manager or bouncer will quickly interrupt you. If that's the case, meet with the manager first and show him a few examples of your work. Propose a barter arrangement or offer a finder's fee if he or she will help you find models. Clubs often need promotional photographs for their own use. You can suggest doing their promotional, advertising, or calendar photographs at no charge or for expenses in exchange for helping you find models.

There are many advantages to finding models in nightclubs. The most obvious advantage is you can see what potential models look like. It's almost like inviting a few dozen models to a casting session. Not all dancers will be interested in your offer—perhaps only a few will be. If a young woman will dance nude for strangers, she will probably be open-minded enough to pose for a tasteful glamour or centerfold shoot. Many dancers will tell you that one of their goals is to become a centerfold model. That's why there is a natural synergy between dancers and glamour photographers. Also, as covered in chapter 5, nightclubs can be great shooting locations.

One way to find models is to visit local nightclubs and hand out business cards to dancers. Offer a $50 finder's fee if they help you find models. A dancer handed Traci one of Glamour Portfolios' cards, she called them, and they've worked with her several times. ©Glamour Portfolios

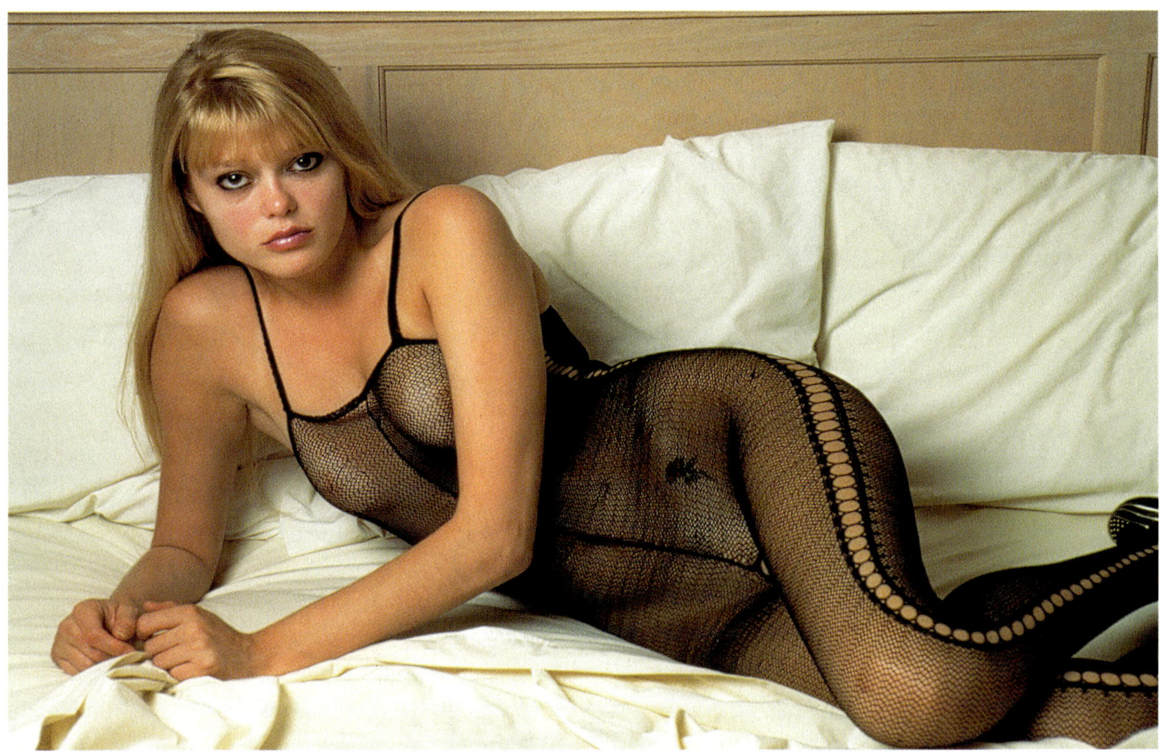

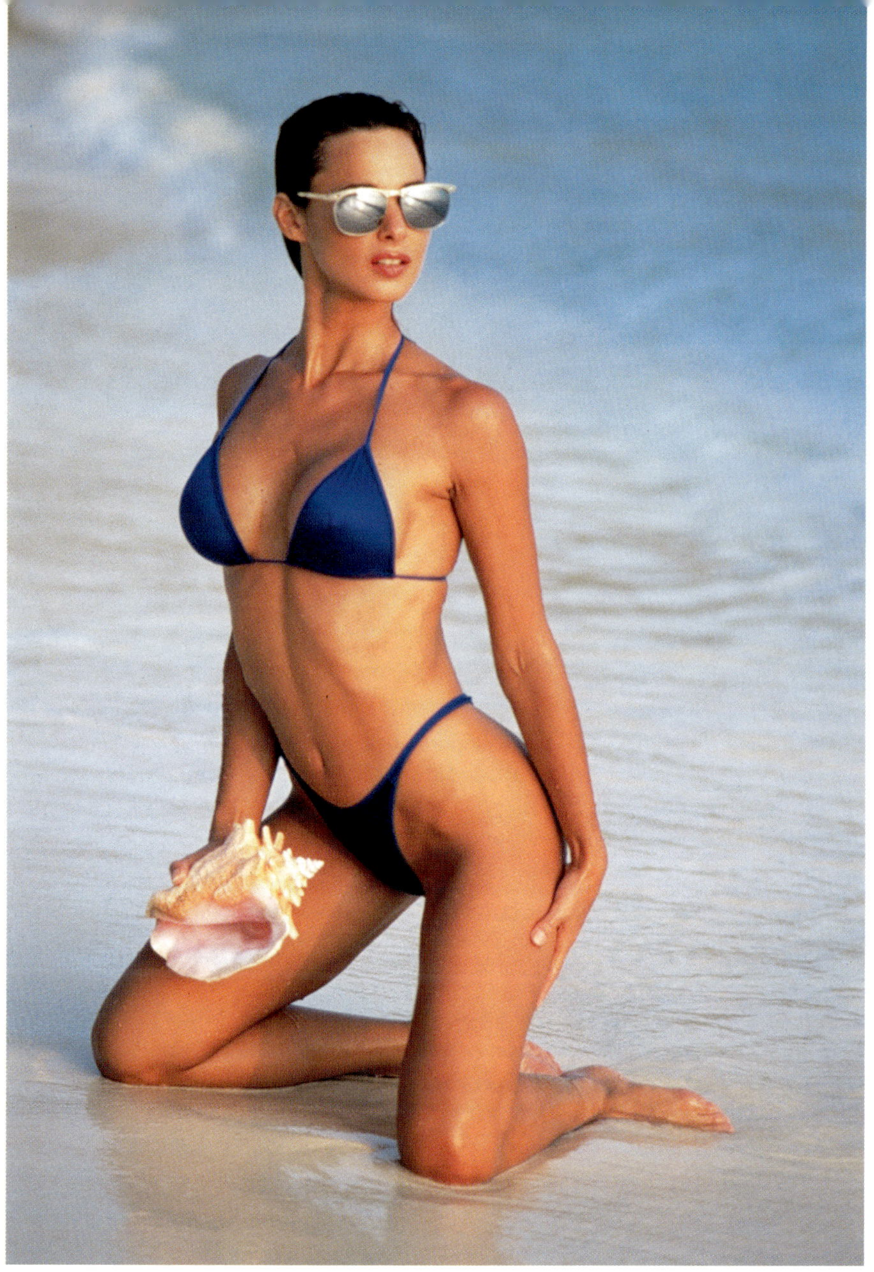

Wendi was one of five models who won a "Caribbean Portfolio Modeling Contest" held at a nightclub. Sponsoring a contest can be a lot of work, but in this case the effort paid off nicely. ©Glamour Portfolios

There are some disadvantages to finding models in nightclubs. The first is that you cannot assume the dancers will want to model for you—or anyone. Some nude dancers work far from their hometowns, and family and friends are not aware of how they are making a living. Dancers are often young women in need of money, and dancing may be a quick fix to a financial dilemma. While some dancers will accept a legitimate glamour assignment, others may be afraid that photographs of them will be published where a family member might see them. Be aware that even if a dancer seems serious and suggests that you call her to set up a photography session, there is a chance she will change her mind later.

Be careful with whom you deal. While most clubs today are reputable, you still need to be careful. Before you become involved with club owners or managers, take time to check them out. Has the club had legal problems? You don't want to become involved in someone else's problems. You're just looking for models—not headaches.

FINDING MODELS IN DAILY LIFE

Once you start working with different models, you may start getting calls out of the blue saying, "I saw some photos you took of my friend, and I'd like to work for you, too." Such referrals are the most cost-effective way of finding new models, and with some experience, it will happen to you. Of course, it depends on how good your photographs are and how easy you are to work with. If your photographs are lousy, you do not pay well, and are rude to models during shoots, you will get another kind of reputation, but not the kind that will have models calling you!

Everyone has heard stories about top models or actresses who got their big break when they met a photographer or casting agent on a bus or in a restaurant. Believe it or not, this kind of pleasant accident does happen! When you go to a mall or to a movie, keep your eyes open for potential models. If you are a shy person, you may feel uncomfortable about approaching a stranger and starting a conversation. The old "you-should-be-a-model" line is one of the all-time classic pick-up lines and might not be taken seriously. A casual introduction might be well received if you use a low-key approach and have a business card handy. The location in which you speak with a potential model can sometimes determine whether or not you will be taken seriously. If you're standing at a bar with a beer in one hand, there is a good chance you're not going to be well received. On the other hand, if you're in a supermarket or mall, for example, your intentions might be perceived as genuine and professional.

Asian and other minority models are often in great demand by clients. Serena was introduced to Glamour Portfolios by another one of their models. ©Glamour Portfolios

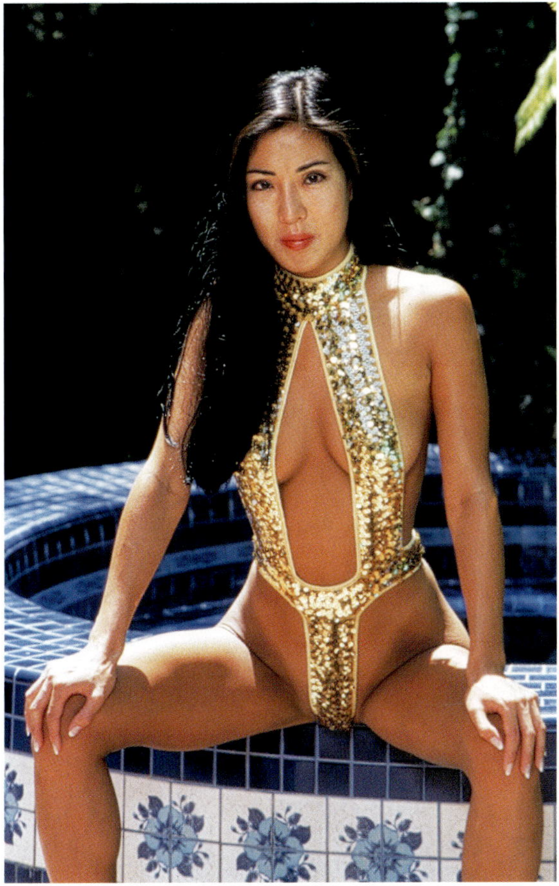

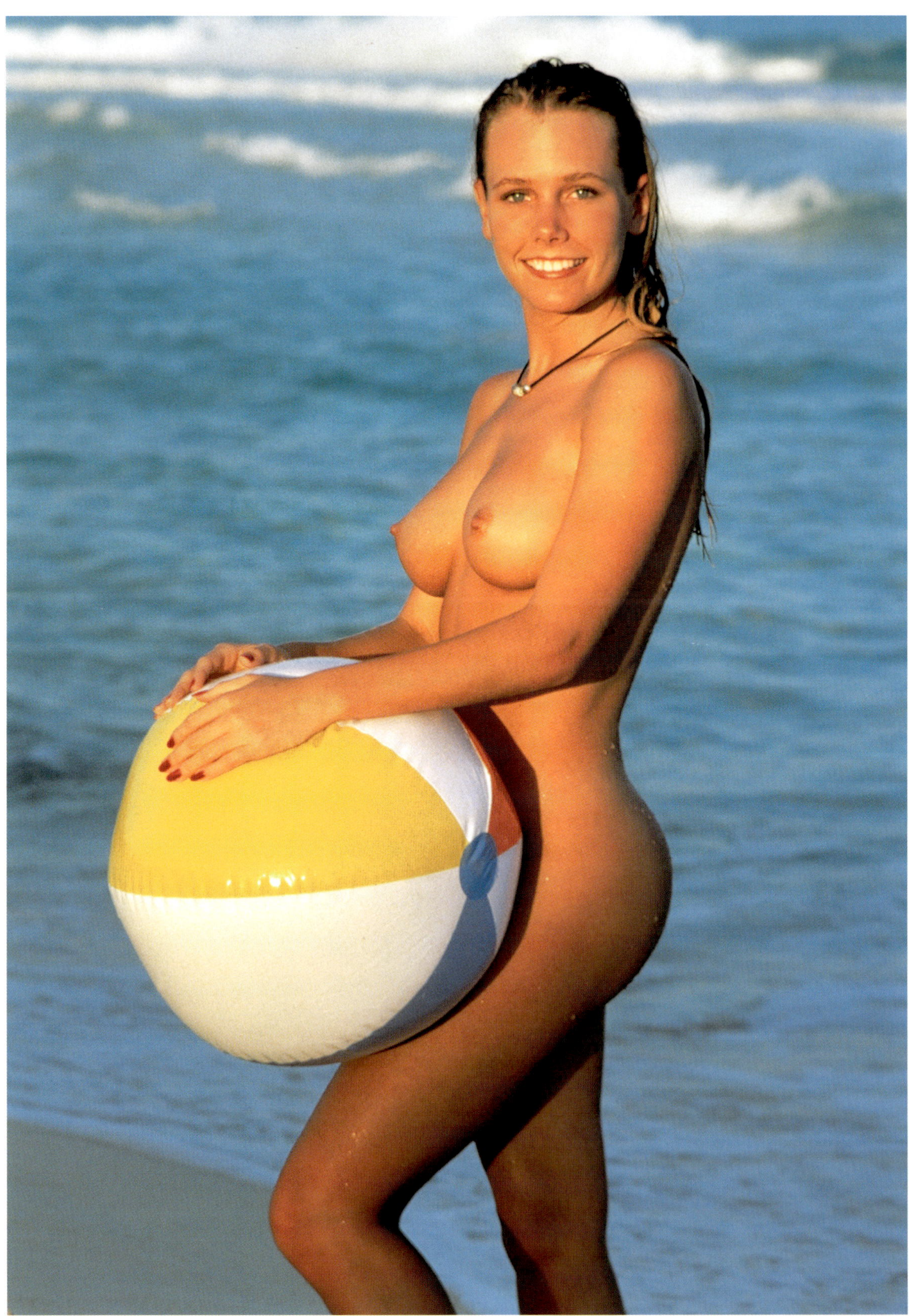

Still not sure? You might want to try an approach such as this: *"Excuse me, I'd like to give you my business card. I'm a professional photographer and use models in my work. You are attractive, and if you'd be interested in discussing a modeling assignment, please give me a call."*

Most women are flattered when politely told they are attractive. If you act professionally, there is a good chance they will inquire about your work. If asked, describe the kinds of projects you work on. At the initial meeting, you might want to concentrate more on your non-glamour, swimwear, or lingerie projects. Since you do not know anything about this person, immediately discussing topless or nude photographs is unwise. You should ask her to come by your office or home for a casting session and to show her your portfolio. To set her mind at ease, suggest she bring a friend or relative to the meeting.

"PHOTO DAYS"

Depending on where you live, there might be an easy way to find models and locations for your glamour photography. Often called "photo days," glamour shoots, or photography workshops, these are events staged by sponsors that feature anywhere from a half dozen to 50 or more models who participate in hopes of building their portfolios, meeting photographers, earning a modest modeling fee, or winning cash prizes. Many events take place in California, but there are promoters in other states, too. When I lived on the East Coast, I attended several glamour shoots sponsored by local and regional camera clubs. A list of typical photo day event sponsors appears at the end of the book.

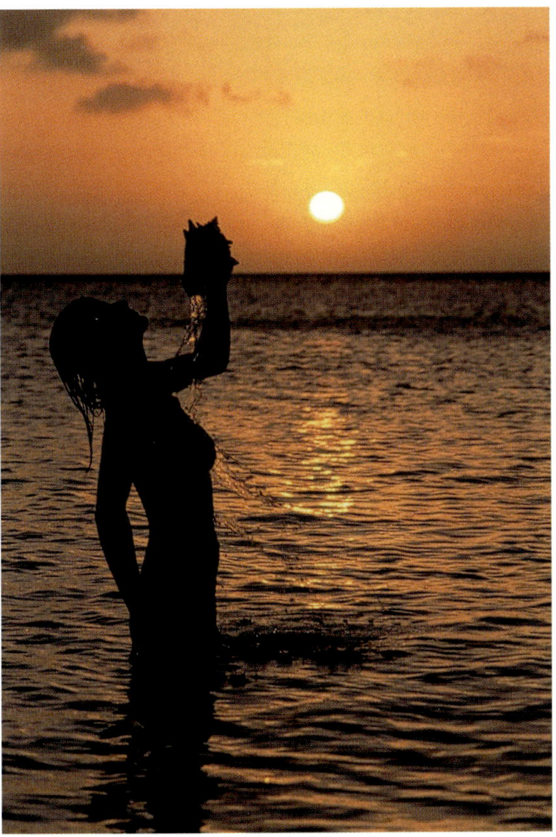

Sometimes models just find you. When Len Kaltman was on a shoot in Curacao, a young hotel employee kept hinting she wanted to be a model. She didn't have the look he wanted, but Kaltman was able to photograph her in a creative way. This was one of several marketable photographs he took as she tagged along on the shoots. ©Glamour Portfolios

Glamour Portfolios found Shannon, one of their top models, when an amateur photographer sent them e-mail about her. He had photographed her at a local camera club and thought she had potential for bigger and better assignments. Glamour Portfolios agreed and booked her for a shoot. ©Glamour Portfolios

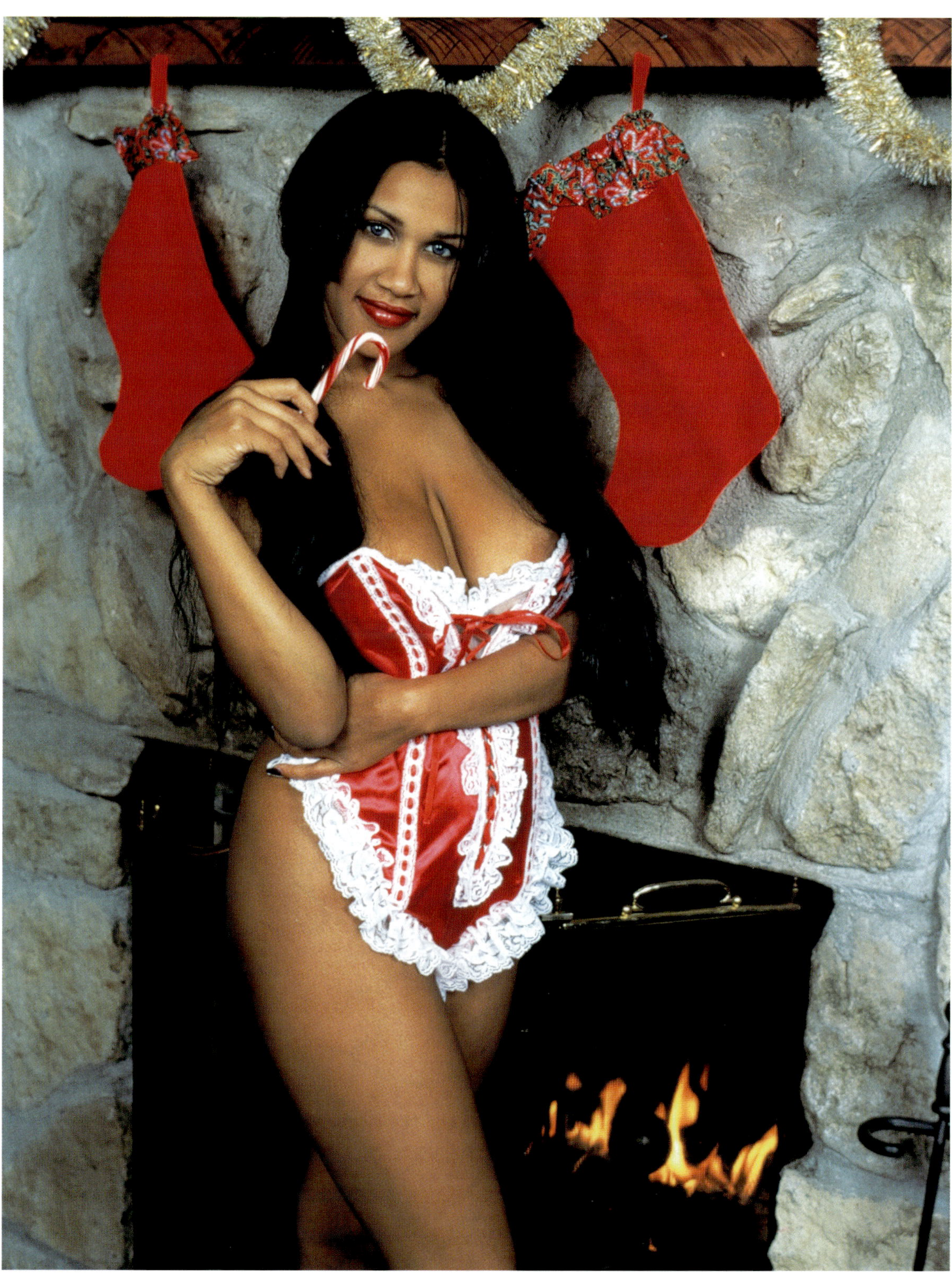

Glamour Portfolios noticed Ebony at a photo day event held in the Midwest. She was with five models but stood out from the rest. She agreed to release the photographs taken at the shoot for a fee and was booked for another shoot, during which this photograph was made. ©Glamour Portfolios

There are generally three types of sessions: fashion, glamour, and nude. At fashion shoots, the models range in age from 14 years old and up and appear fully clothed. They bring their own wardrobe, but the sponsor may provide some of it. In glamour shoots, the models are 18 years old and older and appear in swimsuits and lingerie. Nude or "figure" shoots provide models who pose totally nude. More than anything else, photo day shoots are one of the best ways for the beginning photographer to build a portfolio of glamour images.

Pre-registration is usually required for glamour or figure events so the promoter can hire an appropriate number of models. Once registered, you'll be given directions to the shoot. Locations vary, but usually these events take place at a large house, or an interesting and private outdoor location, such as a farm, private park, or ranch.

When registering, you are sometimes asked to sign a form indicating that the photographs are for your personal use only. Any photographs you take are *not* model-released, so you cannot sell them. Nevertheless, many models who participate in these events are open to negotiation. If you meet with them during a quiet time of the shoot or contact them at a later time, you can probably get the photographs released by paying an additional fee. It's a good idea to discuss the topic of releases with the event's promoter. He or she can probably save you time by indicating which models regularly release photographs and which never do.

The events can take on a whimsical atmosphere as hordes of amateur photographers, draped with top-of-the-line Nikons and Canons, surround those models wearing the least amount of clothing. If the event is well planned, there should be enough models so that you can get time to shoot "one on one," or at least with a smaller group of photographers around you. When I attended workshops sponsored by the New England Council of Camera Clubs, I was able to speak with models after the official sessions to ask them to join me for a semi-private session later in the day.

If you want to find models for photo shoots after the event, remember to bring plenty of business cards to hand out. If you have a good portfolio, bring that along, too. Models at these types of events are used to amateurish photographers and are usually eager to work with better photographers—when they can find them. Having a good portfolio and a professional attitude will attract the models you want.

In addition to contacting local camera clubs for information on these types of photography events, it's a good idea to subscribe to one or more glamour photography magazines or newsletters. The quality of these publications varies widely, but they are inexpensive and often provide useful technical tips as well as a classified section for you to place ads for models.

SPONSOR A CONTEST

Another way to find a large number of potential models is to become the sponsor of a bikini or beauty contest. Sometimes they are called beauty pageants or exhibitions, but the theme is usually the same. Young women compete for prizes by wearing a skimpy bikini or wet T-shirt. There are similar national contests sponsored by magazines or suntan lotion companies. Often there are large prizes and extravagant settings, but there is no reason you cannot have your own contest, pageant, or exhibition on a smaller scale.

There are federal, state, and local regulations regarding all types of beauty contests. Who may run a contest, how the prizes are awarded, and where the contest is held all have legal implications. You need to do some research before producing a contest, and, whatever you do, consult an attorney.

An easier alternative is to find a business or organization that is experienced in running a contest, perhaps a nightclub, modeling agency, fitness club, or swimsuit retailer, and offer to

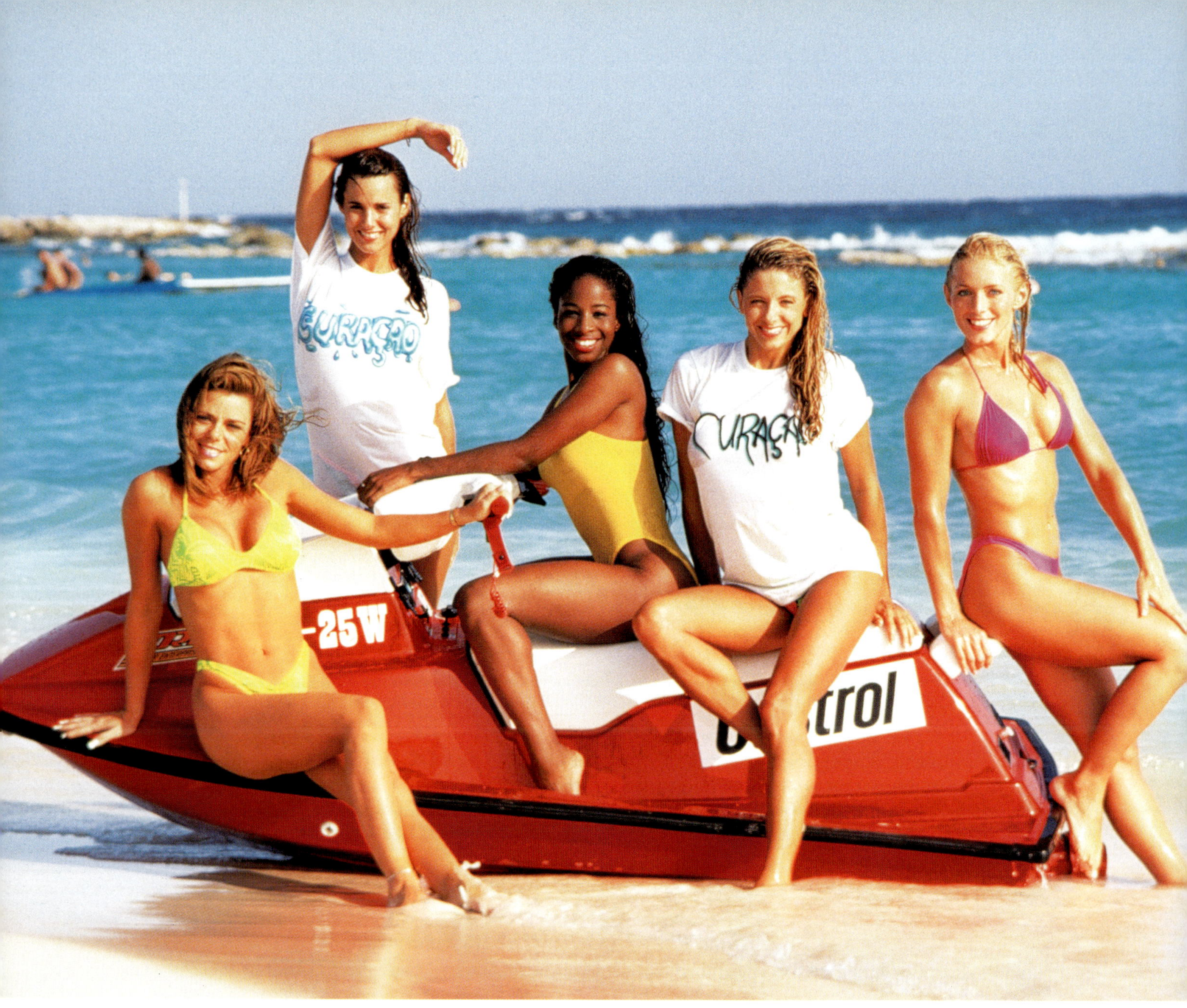

Here all five winners of one of Glamour Portfolios' modeling contests—Patty, Wendi, Nikki, Kim, and Chris—pose on the beach in Curacao, a beautiful Caribbean island. ©Glamour Portfolios

become a judge or sponsor. You are typically required to provide cash or a prize in exchange for being a judge. One prize that will appeal to the organization and the participants of any modeling or talent competition is a complete photographic portfolio for the model. Your portfolios may be valued at $1000 or more, but the actual cost is just your time and the cost of film and processing. With out-of-pocket costs so low, it's a good idea to offer a portfolio to the winner and all of the runners-up. You can almost hear the master of ceremonies calling you up to the stage as he says...

How 'bout a big round of applause for one of our judges and sponsors, ‹your name here›, who is providing over $5000 worth of professional modeling portfolios to our grand prize winner and runners-up. Make sure to pick up one of his business cards on the way out.

Just think about the contestants who entered and did not win. They might want portfolios, too. So in addition to the exposure and access to all the models, you will probably boost your portfolio sales.

At the event, it's important that you maintain a low profile and don't make it appear that your only reason for being a judge is to find models. Avoid the temptation to run around, passing cards out to everyone, suggesting that they call you the next day. There will be time before and after the contest for you to meet and talk with the contestants, and you should suggest that they contact you about some work you might have for them. It is important that you remain impartial and never appear to favor any contestant—after all, you're one of the judges!

FINDING MODELS ON THE INTERNET

A relatively new way to find models for your glamour and centerfold photographs is to search for them on the Internet. Later in the book, you'll find information about marketing your photographs by using the Internet, but you'll also be glad to know that it is a great way to find models. The Internet is international in scope while, at the same time, inexpensive, convenient, fast, and discreet. Yet because there is so much information about so many people, places, and things, it can be overwhelming. You might want to check your library or bookstore for books focusing on the many aspects of being on-line.

An increasing number of models and modeling agencies post photographs and information about their services on-line. Models are looking for traditional fashion and commercial assignments, but there are also many who specialize in—and actively pursue—glamour and centerfold assignments. One of the most useful types of Web sites is the kind produced by individual models, in which they list complete information about themselves along with portfolio samples. Often you'll find complete résumés, references, and a variety of other useful information. Some of these Web sites are run by famous models who use their sites as on-line fan clubs; these sites will be of little use to aspiring glamour photographers, because it's unlikely these superstars are using their sites to seek assignments. There are, however, a growing number of Internet models who use their sites *specifically* to find assignments, and these are the sites that will be of most use. Here are just a few samples of the hundreds, if not thousands, of modeling sites that you can find on-line:

http://www.angelfire.com/oh/shelby
Shelby is a model in the Midwest whose Web site includes modeling rates and booking information. You'll also find a portfolio of 10 glamour images, along with an e-mail link that lets you communicate directly with her to schedule a shoot in your area.

http://www.theinternetgirl.com
Lisa Marie lives in the Midwest. Her site is traditional-looking, but well designed. It includes her résumé, portfolio photographs, links to photographer's sites, and contact information.

http://www.annalieb.com
Anna Lieb is a model from Sweden who has quickly become one of the most popular models on the Internet. She lined up assignments for a recent U.S. tour by using bulletin boards, her own Web site, and e-mail.

http://www.angelfire.com/oh/rochelleandfriends
Rochelle uses her Web site to showcase her portfolio photographs, snap-shots from shootings, and products in which she appears, including a CD-ROM and video.

You will also find Web sites operated by traditional model agencies, such as Ford, Elite, and a number of other large and small agencies. Typically you will find head shots, booking information, e-mail addresses, and phone numbers. Although the Web sites might be attractive and show many models, they are just an extension of the model agencies' traditional promotions and will probably be of little use to you if you are not already working with that agency.

Another useful type of Web site is one that includes a database of freelance models. Here there is greater potential to find glamour models, for several reasons. The database is usually searchable by location and/or model specialty. You can find models who are interested specifically in glamour photography and who live in your area. Once you have selected models who show potential, contact information is usually listed, as well as a link to her own Web site if there is one. One of the most useful on-line model databases can be found at http://www.glamourmodels.com. Dave Hall, a top glamour photographer in upstate New York, operates it. What makes his site worth visiting is that he features photographs of over 150 models who are specifically seeking glamour assignments; he also lists links to dozens of model and photo industry bulletin boards. It is a great place to start your on-line search for glamour models.

A growing number of photographers have their own Web sites. And, if you review the ones who do glamour and centerfold photography, chances are they will have photos of models, as well as links to the models' sites. It's the nature of the Internet that most sites have link to other sites. You may feel uncomfortable calling a photographer you don't know to recommend glamour models, but it's easy to check out his site to see models he has photographed and visit their corresponding Web sites.

Bulletin Boards

Modeling or photography industry bulletin boards are among the most useful Web sites you can visit. Photographers looking to hire models post messages about themselves and the particulars of the assignments they are offering; models looking for jobs post messages about themselves and the particulars of the assignments they are seeking. Most bulletin boards are set up so photographs can be posted within the body of the message (as long as the photo is on-line at another Web site and can be linked), so you can see a photo of the model as you review her message. Here's an actual message from a model in the Midwest who was recently seeking some additional assignments:

Hello, my name is Rochelle. I'm 23 years old and live in Ohio. I am looking for paid jobs and enjoy working with creative photographers. I specialize in swimwear, lingerie, and figure assignments. To review my photos and modeling rates, please visit my Web site: http://www.angelfire.com/oh/rochelleandfriends. I look forward to hearing from you.

What makes bulletin boards so useful is that often, with the message, there will be a photograph of the model, an e-mail address, and a link to the model's Web site. So you can read the message, review a photo, and immediately send her a letter or visit her Web site for samples and information. One of the most popular model industry bulletin boards is called the Webmodels Professional Forum and can be found at http://www.webmodels.com.

Using the Internet, Glamour Portfolios' Len Kaltman said he was able to find six models for a planned photo shoot in Mexico, review their portfolios, negotiate the details of the trip, and book them for the job, all without picking up the phone and making a single call. Everything was done on the Internet and using e-mail. He even used the Internet to find the house he would rent in Mexico.

The Other Side of the Net

As attractive as this high-tech world may sound, it's important that you realize that things don't always work as smoothly on the Internet as you would like them to. There are pitfalls, scams, phonies, and other things to watch out for as you begin your search for models. Here are some things to be wary of.

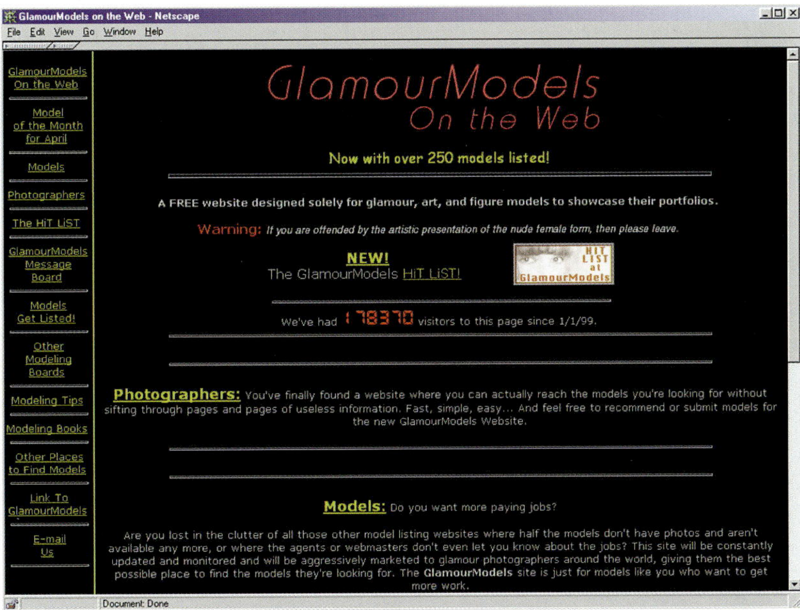

Glamourmodels.com is one of the Web sites you can visit to find models. ©1999 GlamourModels-Dave Hall

There is a huge amount of pornography on the Web, and often when searching for "models" using an Internet search engine (a database which allows you to find Web sites by entering keywords), you could get a list of perhaps five million (no kidding) Web sites that have a lot more to do with X-rated photos than models who are looking for legitimate assignments. To find models on-line, you may want to avoid using search engines and concentrate more on the kind of Web sites previously described.

Be aware that you need to determine the credibility and reliability of models who post information on-line. Keep in mind that many "model" sites are commercial sites set up to look as if models run them. With some experience, you will be able to tell if the model who runs the site is actively seeking assignments or really just trying to sell you her latest CD-ROM, print sets, or autographed 8x10s. In fact, you need to assess the credibility and reliability of almost everyone with whom you do business on-line. You can do that by carefully judging several factors, including how long it takes someone to respond to your e-mail, the content of the response itself, references, and your own "gut feeling."

If you spend some time learning how to use the Internet to locate models, you will find that it provides options not available through any other media. The Internet could soon become your primary method of finding models for your glamour and centerfold photography.

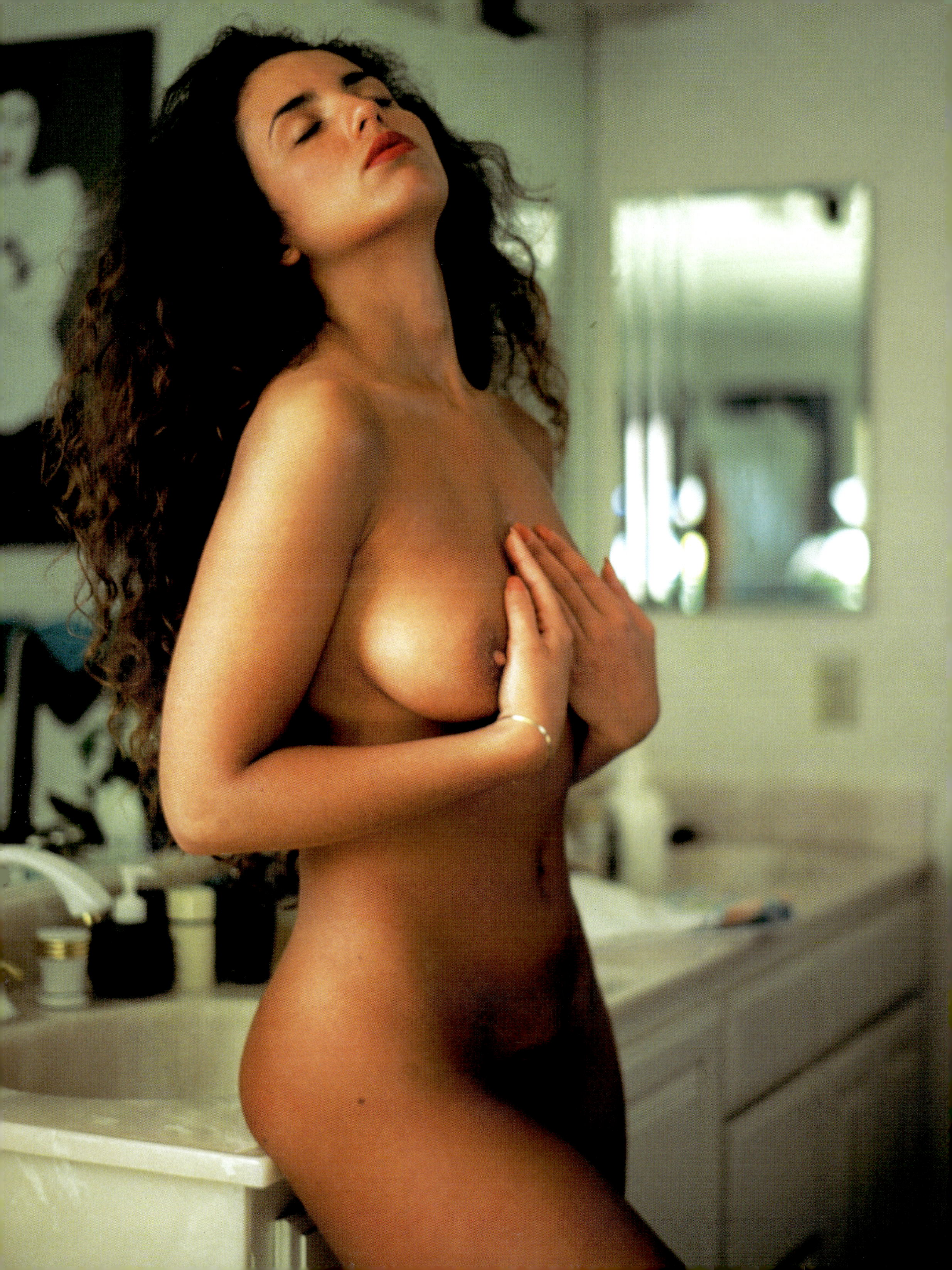

3

Working With Models

What do you say to a naked model?

The number one question most photographers have about working with nude and centerfold models is how to talk to them. They want to know the best way to communicate honestly and effectively with models in order to have them pose with confidence. This chapter takes you through the steps necessary to give you confidence in how to select the right model and how to give posing instructions that will produce saleable photographs.

If you expect to produce marketable photographs on a regular basis, you need good models. Once you have found them—or they have found you—you need to be able to communicate with them effectively. Many of the models you hire will be amateurs who know little about modeling and even less about the business of photography. That's why developing a good working relationship with your models is one of the major keys to success as a glamour photographer. Building this relationship begins from the first time you talk with or meet a potential model. What you say, how you act, and the manner in which you treat your models are important factors that will help determine your success as a glamour photographer.

THE TELEPHONE INTERVIEW

If you followed the advice in the previous chapter, after you place a classified ad in your local newspaper, your phone is going to start to ring. What do you need to do next? Before you answer the phone, you can safely assume that 75 percent of the potential models calling you will be women between the ages of 18 and 30 years old. They will have little or no modeling experience, think they are attractive, and are nervous about posing in lingerie or in the nude. Chances are good they have never heard of you and wonder if you are a legitimate business. The photographer with a storefront location will have less to explain about his business to a new or aspiring model, but if you are a part-time photographer working out of your home and looking for models to pose in swimwear, lingerie, or nude, what you say and how you say it becomes very important.

Glamour Portfolios' model Francoise was new to modeling. She took the photographer's direction well and moved effortlessly from pose to pose. She was photographed in a large house that was rented specifically for the shoot. ©Glamour Portfolios

Remember that this initial phone call is really a two-way interview. The model is calling to learn more about you and the job that you advertised, and you are trying to decide whether to invite her to a formal casting session. Start by being prepared with a few basic questions. Here's what you should ask:

What is her age?
What is her physical description?
Does she have any modeling or dancing experience?
What types of modeling assignments will she consider?

When asking potential models what they look like, you may only get bits of the truth over the phone. The reason to ask the question at all is to eliminate someone who is obviously not right for the kind of photo sessions that you will be shooting. You should already know the typical profile for the kinds of models your target market is looking for. If the model misses that mark, you will have to politely decline.

Before you get to ask her any more questions, she will probably want to know more about you and the assignments you will be giving her. The first question she will want answered is: Are you a legitimate business? At this point in your conversation, it's important to set the model's mind at ease, and let her know you are not trying to sell her anything. Young, attractive women are often exposed to modeling agency scams, and perhaps she has already run into one or two. You want to assure the caller that she will be *making* money working with you—not spending it. Then she will probably be curious about the type of photographs you will be making. Lastly, but maybe just as importantly, she will want to know how much money you are paying.

Be prepared for these questions. You should have a standard speech memorized that answers all of these questions; it's something you are going to say each time a potential model calls. You should be ready to provide her with some information about yourself, the kind of photography that you do, and the kind of assignment she is calling about. During this initial call, you do not have to give specific details. Like most stock photographers, you will not often know in advance how any of your photographs will be used. At the same time, you should never say, "I'm going to shoot sexy photos of you and don't yet know how I'm going to sell them." That's not the way to get any woman to model for you!

If this sounds complicated, it's not. After interviewing models on the phone several times, you will quickly develop your own criteria about whom to reject and whom to invite for a casting session. When in doubt, invite them to your office for a face-to-face interview.

The Answering Machine Dilemma

Depending on where you live and how many people see your newspaper ad, you might get fifty or more phone calls. If you are busy or working at your full-time job, you may not be able to answer the phone. Here's how one part-time glamour photographer in the Midwest solved this problem. The key to his approach was using an answering machine that could record more than one outgoing message. The main message says, "If you are calling about my casting ad, press 2 now." Remember, ad answerers can also choose to hear your other outgoing messages, not just the one about the casting ad, to try to learn more about you. When they "press 2," callers hear the following message:

"Thank you for calling. I'm a photographer presently working on several assignments and am looking for five models between the ages of 18 and 30. Experience is helpful but not required. You should have a good figure and clear complexion. In addition to using modeling agencies, I often look for new talent by running classified ads. I'm not associated with any modeling agency or school and have nothing to sell you. All assignments are totally legal, and you will be paid for each one. You will also receive photographs for your portfolio at no charge. The photos I take of you will be sexy, but in good taste. Some of the assignments will be photographed locally. Each year I shoot calendars and posters in Mexico and will be reviewing models for that assignment, too. If you are interested in attending a free casting session, please leave your name and phone number along with your age, height, and hair color. Please describe any modeling or dancing experience you have. Don't forget to leave your phone number and the best time to return your call. Thanks for calling. I look forward to talking with you and meeting you at a casting session in the near future."

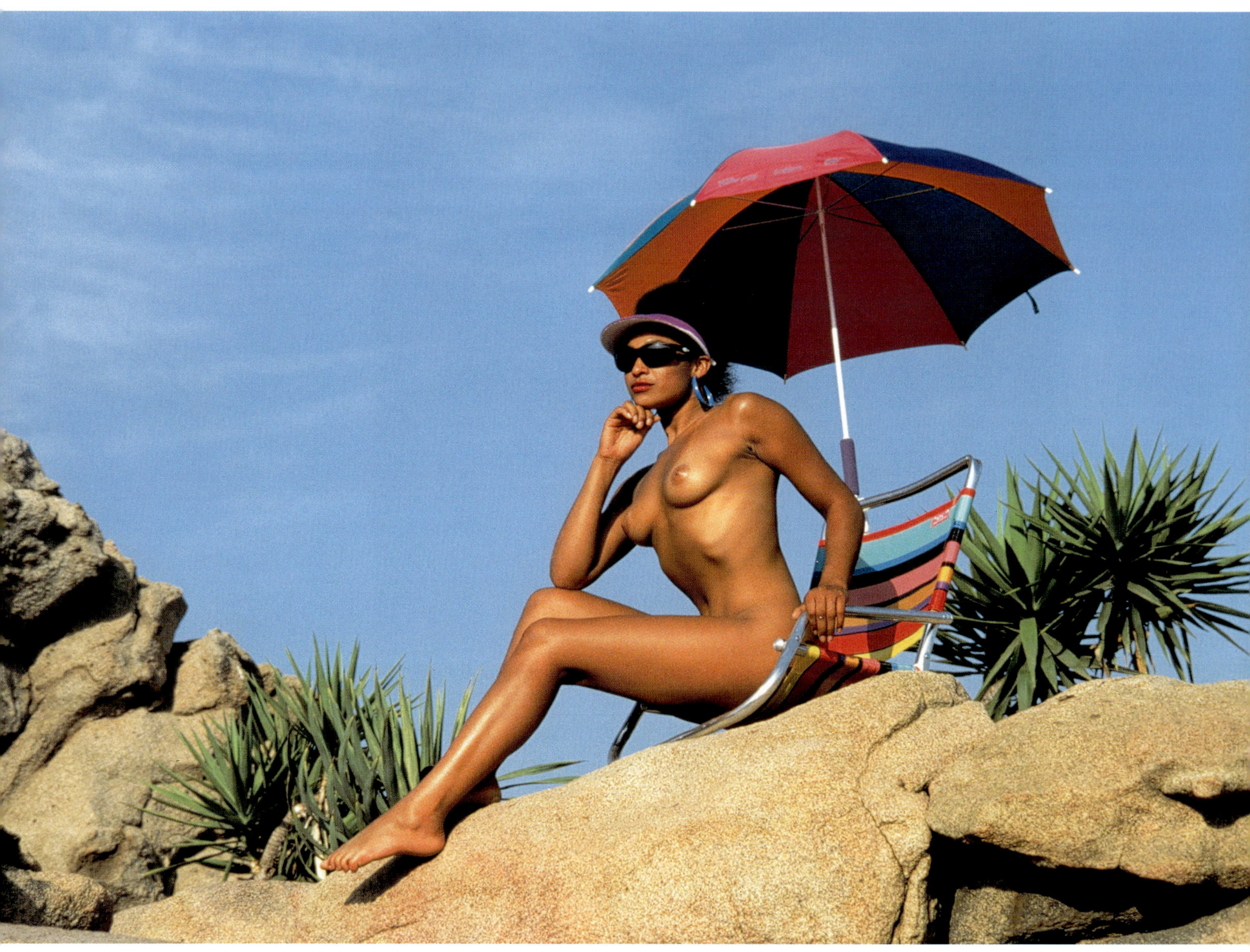

Nikki came up with the idea and props for this shot, taken in the desert outside of Los Angeles. Glamour Portfolios booked half a dozen models for the shoot. There is always some risk when you shoot outdoors, but everyone was careful as they moved around the rugged hills, and there were no twisted ankles or bruised shins. ©Glamour Portfolios

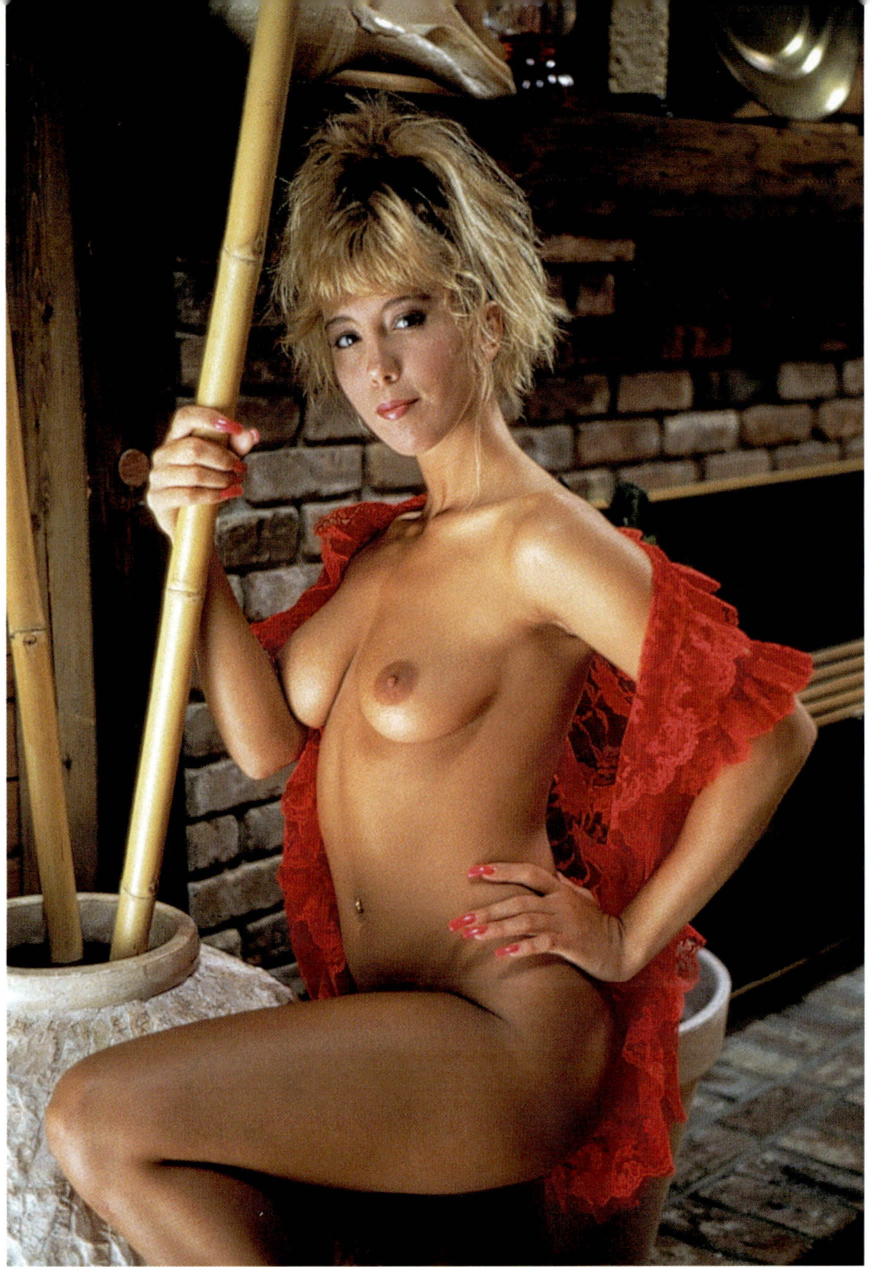

Denise was introduced to Glamour Portfolios by a "photo day" promoter. For this shoot, eight models were hired and a large house was rented. In this photograph, you can see how a few interesting props can add atmosphere to the photograph. ©Glamour Portfolios

THE CASTING SESSION

After your ad appears and you've conducted many telephone interviews, within a few days you may have a dozen or more models scheduled to attend a casting session. At these sessions, you will get to meet potential models face-to-face, review their appearance and qualifications, and determine if you would like to use them for future shoots. Keep in mind that you have invited a stranger to come to your home or office. Not only should you be cautious, all she knows about you is that you are someone who would like to take photographs of her. Until you convince her that everything about you and your assignment is legitimate, she may be a little suspicious.

Here are a few suggestions to help set your model's mind at ease and help your presentation appear more professional. When answering the door, act friendly and shake her hand. Immediately introduce yourself and thank her for coming. Invite her in, take her coat, show her a place to sit down, and offer a soft drink or coffee. If she brought along a friend, you should make that person feel comfortable, too. You should dress appropriately for every casting session. You don't have to wear a suit and tie, but you shouldn't walk around in ripped jeans, a T-shirt, and no shoes. You need to look professional and make your potential models feel comfortable at the same time. Make sure your office and house are clean. Even if your house is not impressive-looking, it should be neat and tidy. Have one room set aside as an office, and conduct all of your interviews there. If you have tear sheets or portfolio photographs, have a few of them framed and up on the walls to show potential models what your work looks like. Also, if you have a Web site, you may want to show it to her.

If possible, *never* be alone with the model. Always have a family member or friend in the house with you. You never want to be accused of behaving in less than a professional manner, and having someone around will reduce the chances of this happening.

The Casting Form

When both of you are comfortably seated at a table or desk, it's time to start the casting session. A typical session includes several steps. The first step involves the use of a casting form, which is the easiest way to get information about a model for reference purposes. It includes the kind of basic information you will need in your files if you plan on using the model in the future. If you would like to see the kind of information that is typically found on a casting form, see the sample form shown on page 132. Have the model fill out the form, then review it with her to make sure all of the questions have been answered. It's important that you keep a casting file or book containing information about all the models you meet. File the forms by model type, alphabetically, or whatever suits the style of glamour photography you're interested in. After she completes the form, you should be ready to show her a few samples of your work, nicely presented, and explain the kinds of assignments you have in mind.

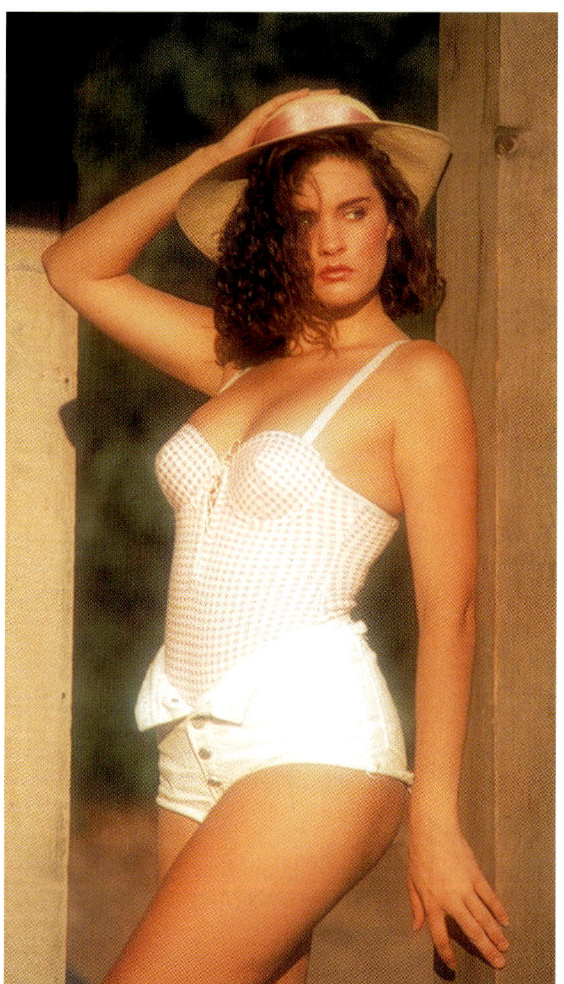

It's always a good idea to let your models use and interact with props. The model will be more comfortable than just standing doing nothing, and you'll come away with a more interesting photo. ©Glamour Portfolios

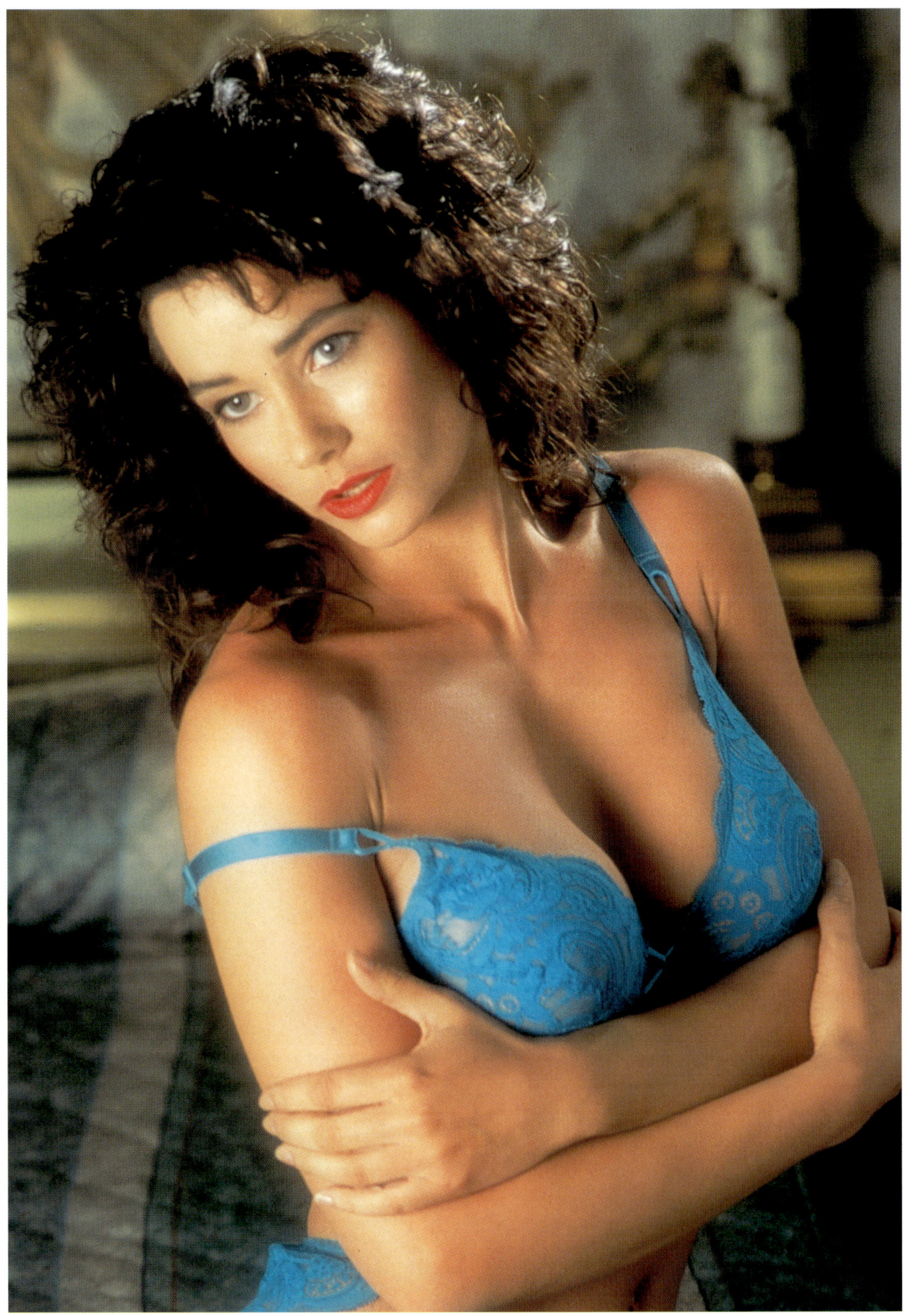

Your Portfolio

Photographers are judged by the quality of the images in their portfolios. Never make excuses about your photographs. If they are in your portfolio, they need no explanation. Avoid saying things like "Oh, that would have been better if the light weren't so dim" or "I like this shot but wish the model had a better expression." If it's not a good photograph, it doesn't belong in your portfolio. If your photographs are professional-looking and well presented, the model's first impression will be positive, and she will probably want to work with you. On the other hand, if your photographs are poorly lit, in poor taste, or just plain bad, she'll be hesitant to work with you.

While she is flipping through your portfolio, watch her expression and pay particular attention to any comments she might have. For example, if she is looking at a tasteful topless or nude photograph and says, "I would never pose like that," you'll know she is not interested in that type of assignment. If she seems more enthusiastic about your topless and nude photographs, she's probably more open-minded. At Glamour Portfolios, models have to walk through a small hallway on their way to the chief photographer's office. To get there, they have to pass 16 framed photographs and tear sheets hanging on the walls. Models usually ask the photographer, "Did you shoot these?" Nothing sets a model's mind at ease more than seeing tasteful photographs nicely presented. Often women who, on the phone, would not consider posing nude will change their minds when they see models stretched out on a beautiful deserted beach. It's all part of the fantasy and one of the reasons they choose to do this kind of work.

Soft sidelighting from a lightbank is a simple yet very effective way to illuminate your portraits. It's a very flattering light that is classic and attractive. ©Glamour Portfolios

Explain How You Work

Assuming you are interested in working with the model and she appears interested in accepting an assignment, now's the time to tell her how you work. Start by explaining that you produce and sell the photographs yourself and that you are not shooting for a particular client. While doing so, make it sound interesting and exciting to her by giving her examples of previous shoots. What is most important in this session and in all future dealings with the model is that you must be truthful in your description of all assignments. For example, always tell the model how you plan on using the photographs, including your intention to sell them as stock photos—if that's what you plan to do. Never tell a model the photographs are for your own use or portfolio and then sell photographs of her.

Many part-time glamour photographers and full-time pros are really stock photographers, but shooting stock images is not a concept that is familiar to people who are not in the business. That's why it's important that you explain to the model exactly what stock photography is. She may expect to be hired for one specific job and that her photographs will only be used once in a limited fashion. Explaining that you intend to sell her photographs over and over may make her nervous—unless you go about it the right way. Tell her that some of the photographs you take of her could wind up in a calendar, poster, or even a national ad. Avoid exaggerating how your photographs will be used or what the potential exposure may be. Tell her that if you are shooting a simple nude of her on a wicker chair, it's doubtful the photograph will appear as a national ad. On the other hand, if you are shooting sexy images on a beach, it's easier to imagine the photographs may appear in a calendar, poster, or album cover—which can be an exciting prospect for a beginning model.

If you have a specific use in mind for the photographs you are discussing, say so. For example, many photographers create their own CD-ROMs, Web sites, posters, or calendars. If you take the time to describe specific usage and explain future potential uses, she will be able to understand the concept of stock photography.

At this point during the casting session, it's important to take a Polaroid (or maybe digital) photograph of the model. After seeing perhaps a half dozen or more models, you will have trouble remembering what each one of them looks like. Most photographers just stand the model next to a wall and take a Polaroid shot. No one is going to see the casting photograph except you (unless you wish to share it with other photographers), so it does not have to be a great shot. Clip or staple the photograph to the casting form.

Hailey insisted that Glamour Portfolios hold off on any print usage of her photographs for three years so as not to ruin her chances of appearing in *Playboy* magazine. Instead, the photographs were used for several digital products, making the shooting session profitable. ©Glamour Portfolios

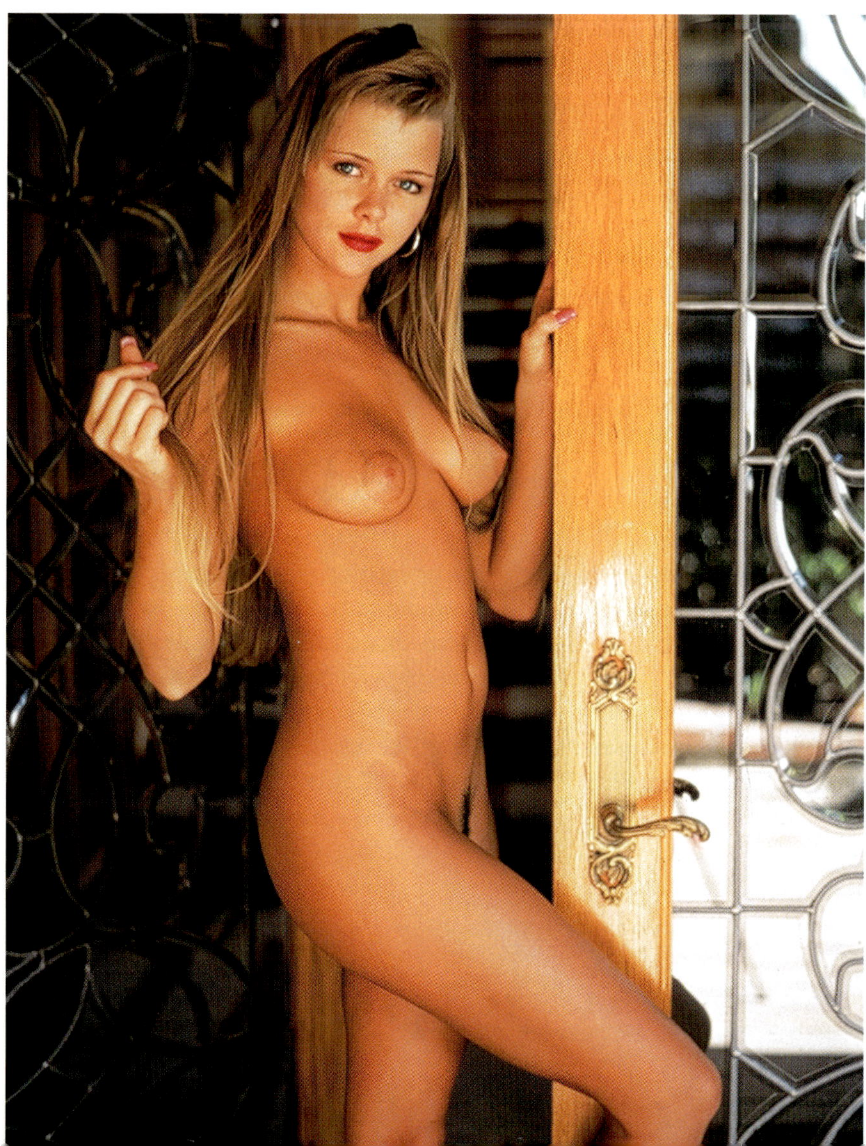

At this time, it's also a good idea to take a critical look at your model from head to toe. Many clients like "smiley" shots, so don't forget to check for a good smile. If you plan on photographing her in swimwear or lingerie, there is no need to see her nude. If you are planning on booking a model for a nude shoot, it is more than a good idea to see her totally nude before the day of the shoot. A woman's figure can change dramatically depending on what she is wearing. You will want to review her general appearance and figure, looking for any cosmetic defects, such as scars and tattoos, that might require retouching. If a model has some unusual or wild tattoos and you are able to market that kind of image, that may not be a problem. Tattoos, however, unless they can be easily retouched, generally minimize the commercial viability of a photo.

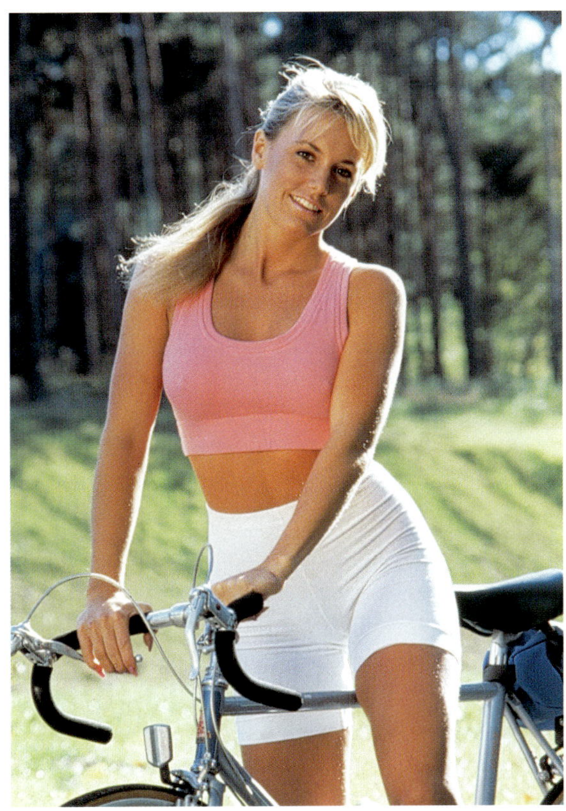

Here's a simple yet very marketable photo; it can be sold time and time again for a wide variety of uses. Notice the model is wearing clothing that won't become outdated. ©Glamour Portfolios

"I didn't notice* that *during our casting session!"

Here's what one photographer told me about why he insists on seeing his models totally nude before the shooting session:

"I was planning a shoot in Jamaica and was looking for a model with a good figure. The photographs would include tourism-oriented stock photographs, as well as glamour and figure photos. I was working with a model I met during a catalog shoot and thought she would be a good choice. At the casting session, I asked her to disrobe, and when she came out of the changing room, she was topless, but wearing black tights. When I asked her to remove them, she told me that she had a dance class immediately after the casting session, and they were hard to get off and on. Even with the tights on, I could see her legs were attractive and didn't ask her to remove them. I booked her for the shoot. The day of the shoot arrived, and when I got to the beach location, she was in the water, wearing a bikini. She looked beautiful, and I felt my choice of models was excellent. When she came out of the water, I saw a large scar on her right leg. I couldn't believe it. How could I have missed seeing that during our casting session? Then I remembered the black tights. Obviously she knew if I saw the scar, I never would have booked her for this assignment. I've learned my lesson: If I need to photograph a model nude, I need to see her totally nude ***before*** *the shoot."*

HOW MUCH TO PAY?

When meeting models, it's best to have a pay scale in mind. There is nothing wrong with trying to stay within a budget, but remember the adage, you get what you pay for. When booking inexperienced models who do not have portfolio shots, some photographers will only consider a barter arrangement. The photographer and model both offer their time and talent and no cash is exchanged. Usually, the photographer will supply the model with portfolio photographs at no charge. I have found it's much better to pay models for their time, particularly if you expect to develop a good reputation. If a model knows she is going to make a few hundred dollars working for you, chances are much greater that she will turn up for the shoot! Offer a model too little, and do not be surprised when she is a "no-show."

If you are booking a model through a modeling agency, they will inform you of the model's hourly rate, which is usually between $100 and $250 per hour, depending on the nature of the job. Most agencies I have worked with keep 25 to 35 percent of the fees paid to models as a commission, but I have heard figures as high as 50 percent in some parts of the country. By booking models directly, you can save money. You should be able to find attractive models who will work for less, with the fee open to negotiation. Here are some typical rates you might want to consider paying:

	Hourly	Day Rate
Fashion/Swimwear	$20 - 50	$100 - 250
Lingerie	$30 - 75	$200 - 300
Topless/Nude	$50 - 100	$250 - 500

After you have met a model you want to photograph, explain the type of photographs you will be taking. It's very important to be very truthful when discussing modeling fees. Always tell your model three things before the shoot: how much you are paying for the job, how she will be paid, and when she will be paid. Be specific and matter of fact. She should get the impression that this is your standard rate and is not open for negotiation. If you are offering too little, she will ask for more. Some beginning models are topless or nude dancers. Depending on where they work, they could be making $200 - $400 per day or more just in tips. Knowing this, don't expect a model to get too excited when you offer her $50 for an assignment. As you find and work with more models in your area, you will get a feeling for the going rate. Generally, the market rates for models in cities such as New York or Los Angeles will be higher than those for models living in smaller cities.

MODEL RELEASES

A model release is a printed document signed by the model in which, among other things, she authorizes you to sell the photographs you have taken of her. If you plan on using, distributing, or selling any of these photographs, you must have a model release. If you don't get a release, use of the photographs will be primarily limited to your portfolio. There are various kinds of releases, but many professional glamour photographers use one that is similar to the sample shown on page 133. This type of release is often referred to as a "blockbuster" release, since the scope of the permissions granted are so sweeping.

It's important during any discussions with the model before the shoot that you explain to her the need for a model release. How you present the release and describe why you need it will determine whether a model signs it reluctantly or with confidence. The last thing you want to happen is to have her refuse to sign a release after the shoot has been completed. Since some releases may contain a lot of legalese and sound a bit scary to a beginner, it's a good idea to go over a sample release with a potential model during your initial casting session.

When discussing and using model releases, be sure to describe the form as your standard release form. Have a three-ring binder or file folder with signed model releases nearby, and take a blank release out of the binder or folder when presenting it to the model. Let her see that many other models have already signed the same release. Make sure your release is clearly printed and in a typeface that is easy to read. On the top of the page in a large font, type the title "Standard Model Release." It's a good idea to briefly describe the shoot within the release. This way there will never be a question about which photographs are covered. For example, just above where the model signs, you can have her write "this release is for all photographs of me taken at..... between the dates of ..... and ...." Ask the model to read the release and offer to answer any questions she may have about it. If she asks why you need a release, explain calmly and completely that you cannot use any photographs that you make of her without her permission. If she seems reluctant to sign, do not get defensive or agitated. This may be the first time she has ever seen a model release. Ask her what her concerns are, and then discuss them.

After the model signs the release, check the name she is using, date of birth, and signature against a driver's license or other identification. This is particularly important when working with dancers, who often use stage names and don't think twice about signing their pseudonyms. If possible, have a witness sign the model release. This is useful in case a dispute arises regarding the release. You don't need a witness to make a release valid, but it never hurts to be prepared.

Even if you photograph a model several times, be sure to get a separate release for every assignment. You should pay the model and have her sign the release just before the start of the shoot. This way, all the legal details are completed, and both of you can relax and enjoy the shoot. Always keep the original release in a safe place, and make extra copies. If you sell a photograph and the client needs a copy of the release, never send the original.

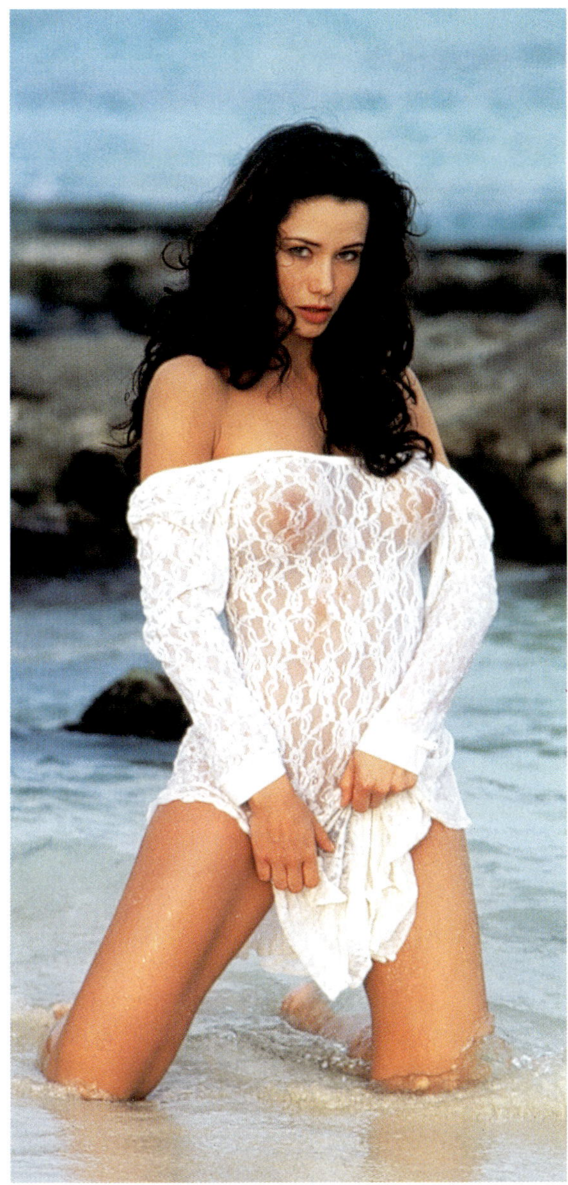

Balancing the needs of both photographer and model is a key to a good working relationship. Carolyn is a professional model and actress. She insisted on restricting the usage of her photographs so that nude images could not appear in print but could be used for digital products, like CD-ROM discs. ©Glamour Portfolios

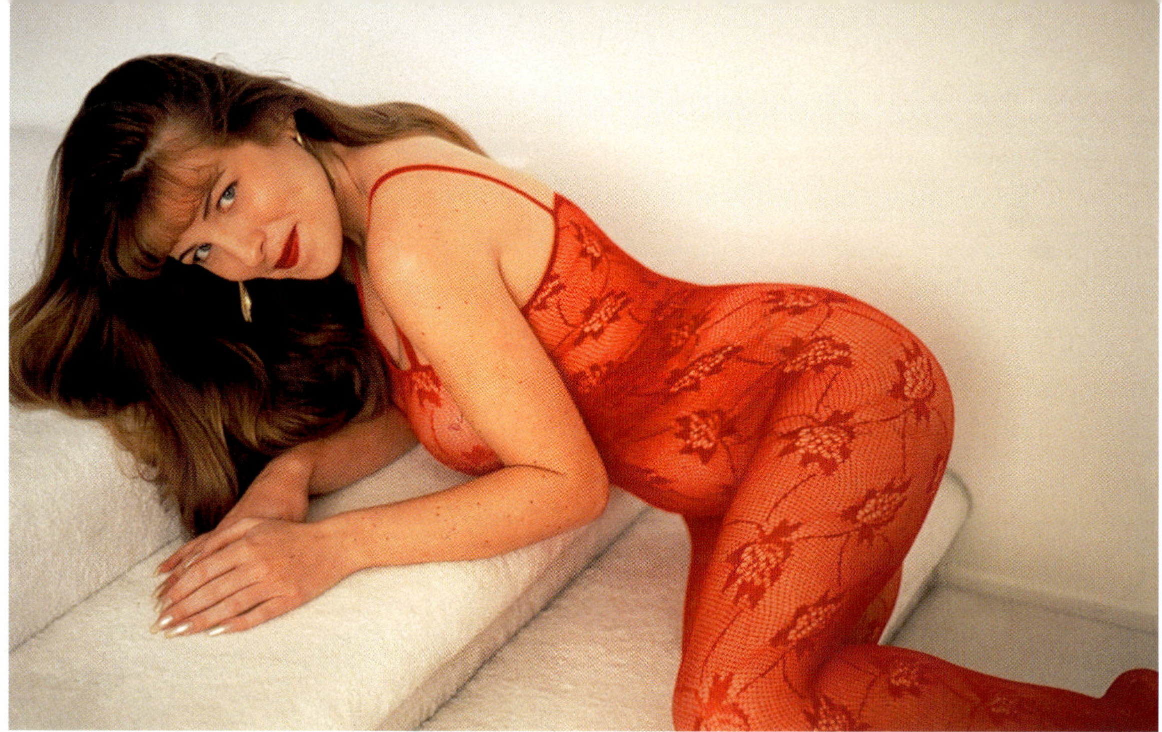

Suzi is a West Coast model. The clothes she brought with her to the shoot ranged from mink coats to ripped jeans and T-shirts. Note the simple background—no props necessary here. ©Glamour Portfolios

DURING THE SHOOT

The process of developing a good working relationship with your model begins from the first moment you meet at the casting session. Nowhere will your personality, working style, and communication skills be more helpful than when you have a model in front of your camera.

Before you start the session, tell the model about the kind of photographs you have in mind. Explain the kind of shot you are looking for, tell her the type of attitude you want her to express, and share any other information that will help her do a good job. If you can get the model involved at the start of the shoot, you will always get better results. If you have done a shot similar to the one you are working on, show a print from that session to her.

Always respect a model's privacy. Start by giving her a private place to change and do her makeup. Do not hang around or be nosy when she is changing her clothes. When working with models, particularly beginners, give her some additional time to "warm up." This might be a new experience for her, and many beginners will be a bit clumsy or awkward at first—particularly during shoots that involve nudity. Some photographers even pretend to put a roll or two of film in the camera and actually shoot without film for a few minutes while the model warms up. Still, film is relatively inexpensive when compared to the other costs associated with a session—I think you are better off using film during the warm-up, but process it only if you think you got some good shots.

One rule of thumb is that you can never compliment a model too much during a shoot. While it may seem obvious, never shout at a model. If she is not doing what you want, you should calmly explain what you have in mind. Without being excessively forceful, guide her into the pose you want. The last thing you want is a model who feels uncomfortable or insecure with you. When taking glamour shots, you may want to do a series of photographs showing the model disrobing. (This approach to a session will be explained in more detail in chapter 7, "How to Pose Your Models.") Talk her through the steps as you are shooting, and once she gets the idea of what you want, you can easily repeat the series again with different garments or props.

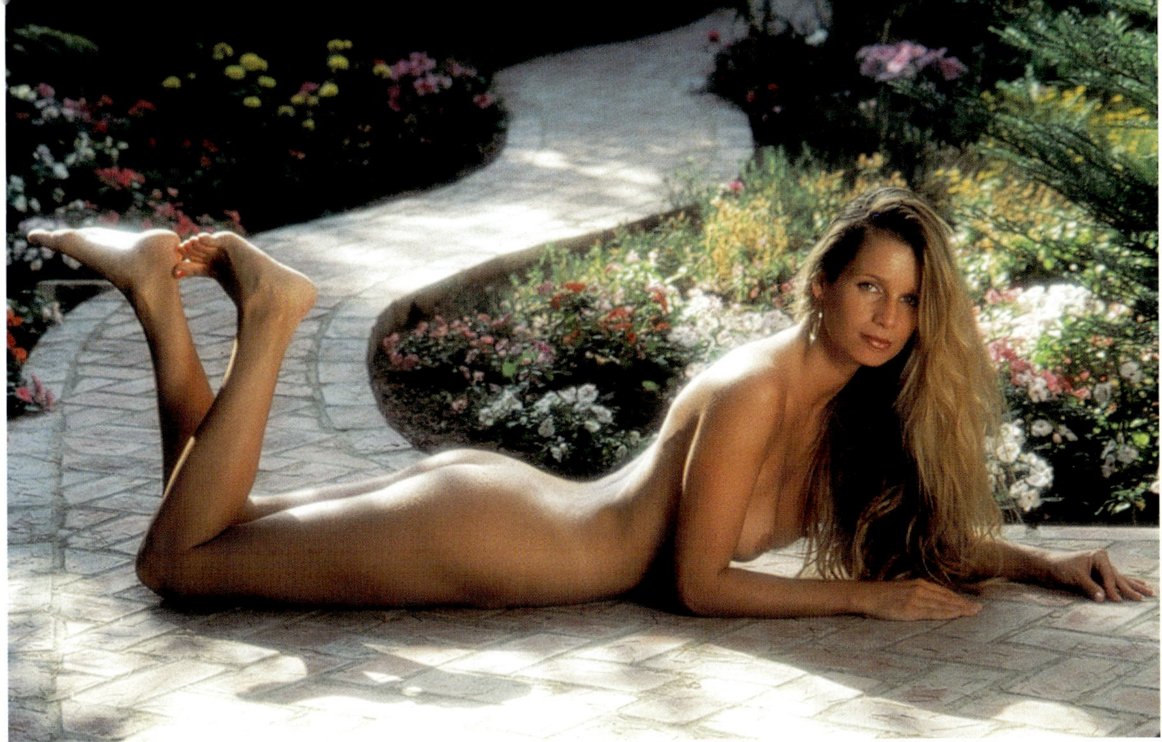

This particular model felt uncomfortable with full frontal nudity. Because this was discussed before the shoot, the photographer knew to pose her in a way that would accommodate her wishes. ©Glamour Portfolios

Another important rule is never, under any circumstances, touch a model. If possible, always have her adjust her own garments. If it's absolutely necessary for you to do so, you should ask permission first, but try to have her do it. Some photographers—I have noticed this in some wedding shooters—are used to touching their portrait subjects to place them in a pose. They get into this habit because of the high pressure and time crunches under which most weddings are photographed, when there is never enough time to talk people into poses. In centerfold or nude photography, touching models is unthinkable. If you need to show a specific pose, show her by putting yourself in the pose so she can see what it looks like.

Since you and the model are collaborators, you must try to establish a climate of respect for her talents and skills. That's why you also should avoid off-color jokes or stories, no matter how amusing you may think them to be. How you act ultimately establishes the atmosphere for the communication that must happen between photographer and model to create successful images.

If you are doing a shoot in which the model is wearing lingerie or is nude, respect her privacy by offering a "closed-set" environment where only the minimum number of people will be watching her. Work quickly and professionally to minimize the time she spends waiting for you to get ready. If you are fiddling with lights and seem unorganized or clumsy, the model will lose her enthusiasm for the shoot and become bored. This boredom will show in the photographs and make the session a wasted one.

With experience, every photographer will develop his or her own personal style of working and communicating, but let common sense be your guide. Treat each and every one of your models politely, professionally, and with respect.

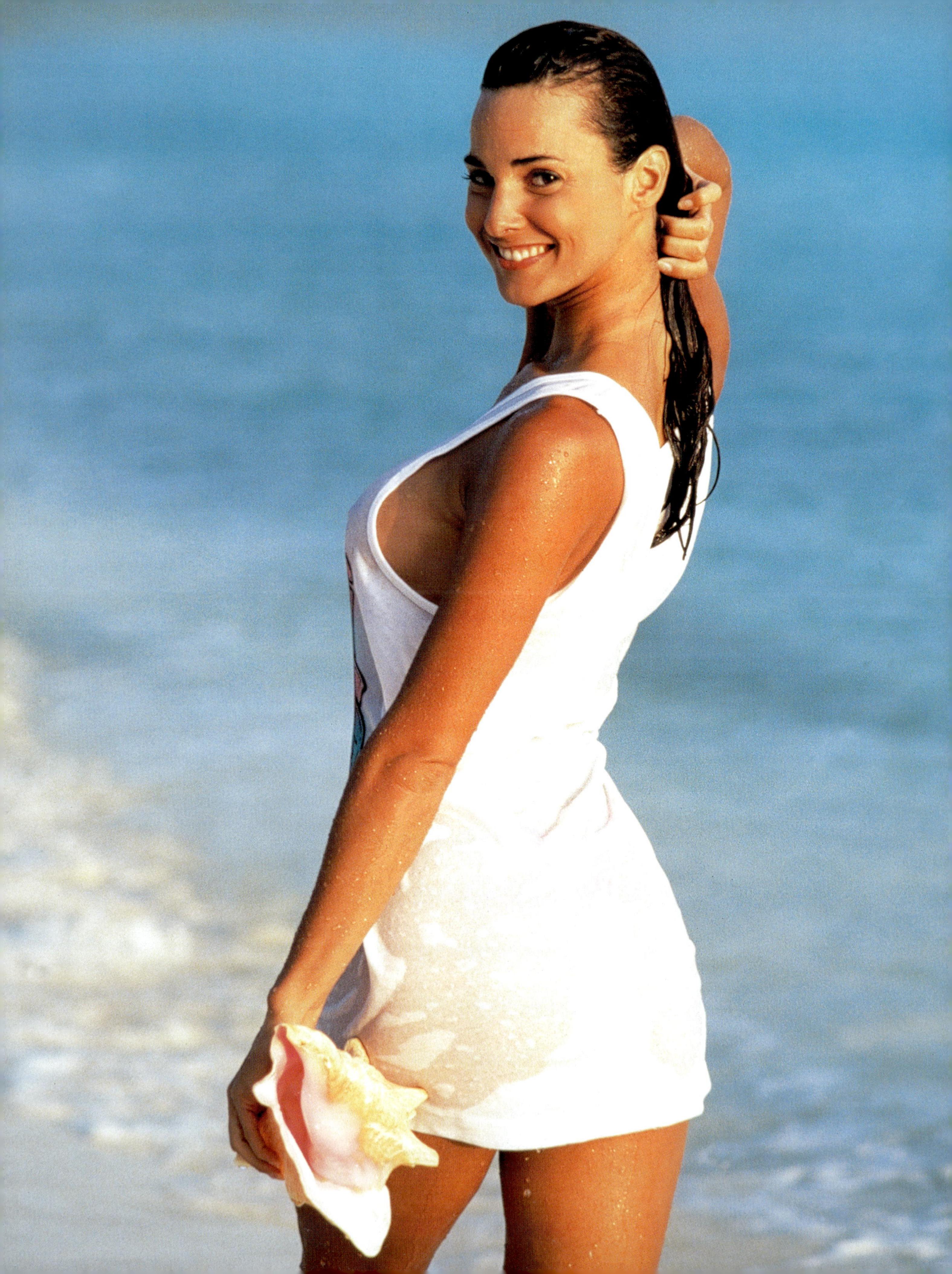

4

Keep Your Shooting Easy

Create beautiful, dramatic, and marketable images by concentrating on the basics

This chapter is not intended to be a technical treatise on shooting glamour photos; it would take an entire book to do that. Instead, I want to introduce you to the tools that you can use to take your glamour and centerfold images. In this chapter you will discover how to create attractive and marketable glamour images using only natural light and a minimum of photographic equipment. Sound easy? That's because it is.

Many beginning photographers often become so involved with the hardware and tools of photography that they lose sight of what should be the ultimate goal of any professional photographic session—to create attractive images with commercial value. You need to hone your technical skills to the point where using your tools becomes natural and intuitive. What is important is that you feel confident in your ability to use your equipment to create top-quality photographs that are aesthetically pleasing as well as technically excellent.

KEEP IT SIMPLE

Nowhere does the adage "keep it simple" hold truer than during a glamour or centerfold photographic session. While there's nothing inherently wrong with using complex lighting setups, lots of props, and extravagant hair and makeup styles, you will quickly find that you can create beautiful, dramatic, and marketable glamour photographs by concentrating on the basics. You just need an attractive model, an elegant pose, simple lighting, and relatively simple equipment.

Many aspiring photographers, after seeing the latest *Sports Illustrated* swimsuit video, think they need the latest top-of-the-line SLR, along with half a dozen lenses, professional-quality strobes, meters, reflectors, and all the other paraphernalia of some professional photographers. The good news is that you don't have to take out a second mortgage to buy a minivan full of photo gear. Instead, take your cue from photojournalists who stuff all the gear they need into a single camera bag.

Your Camera

For the aspiring glamour photographer, any reasonable-quality 35mm SLR will work fine. Every camera manufacturer offers a variety of cameras ranging from point-and-shoot models to top-of-the-line, built-like-a-tank professional models. The one you choose might be more a matter of how much you want to spend rather than what "bells and whistles" you really need. While shopping for equipment, don't ignore the used market There are mail-order dealers who specialize in pre-owned photo equipment, offering excellent buys on a wide variety of photographic equipment from most manufacturers.

For your glamour photography camera, all you need is the ability to use interchangeable lenses, full manual and automatic control, and a PC connector that allows the camera to be used with electronic flash units. Beyond these minimum features, all 35mm single-lens-reflex cameras have a wide range of features, most

The soft, directional lighting from the setting sun was all that was needed for this simple yet sexy, lighthearted photo of Wendi. ©Glamour Portfolios

of which might be helpful but are not really necessary. For a look at what different camera models and lenses are available, pick up a copy of *Shutterbug's Photography Buyer's Guide.* The main guideline to follow when purchasing new or used cameras is that you shouldn't spend more than you can afford. Stay within your means, keep your overhead low, and you can upgrade to newer, more expensive gear later on.

A Few Good Lenses

Once you select a camera body that meets your budget, it's time to consider which lenses you need for glamour and centerfold photography. The good news is that you will probably find yourself using two lenses most of the time. They are a medium telephoto lens in the 135–180mm range and a shorter lens, either 50 or 85mm. That's it! You'll use your telephoto lens for any sort of head shots or close-ups of your model, and it is great for outdoor photographs where you want to separate your model from the background by using a shallow depth of field. For indoor photographs where space is limited and you may be working closer to the model, you'll need shorter lenses. Try to get the best-quality, fastest lenses that your budget permits, because you may find yourself working under lighting conditions when an *f/*2.8 lens is better than a less-expensive *f/*3.5 model. If the *f/*2.8 or *f/*2.0 lens is too expensive, don't forget they are available used.

You may also want to consider using a zoom lens. Zooms are very practical, and modern zoom lenses are usually of excellent optical quality. When using zoom lenses, there are a few trade-offs you will quickly notice, especially greater weight and slower speed. While fixed-focal-length telephotos often have a maximum aperture of *f/*2.8 or even faster, a typical 85–210 zoom might have a maximum aperture of *f/*4.5. Depending on the type of film you use and lighting you need, that may be restrictive to your shoot. Nevertheless, with a little planning and research, you should be able to strike the right balance between lens speed, focal length, and cost.

The Filter Factor

Filters are small but useful additions to any camera bag. Although there are dozens of different kinds, glamour photographers typically use three particular filters to creatively add effects to their photographs to increase sales.

Soft-focus filters, which do what their name implies, are particularly useful when photographing a model who may have less-than-perfect skin. They can also make a photo look more pastel, dreamy, and romantic by taking the hard edge off the details. Soft-focus filters come in varying degrees of strength. Tiffen's Soft/FX filter lets you retain overall image clarity while softening unwanted details, such as facial blemishes. Soft-focus filters generally have little effect on exposure, and if you're using a handheld meter (see the next section), you won't have to compensate for exposure.

Warming filters are useful for creating a more pleasing skin tone, particularly when working in cool light (such as open shade) or when using electronic flash (that might have a bluish tint). Unlike a red or yellow filter that is often used with black-and-white film to darken blue skies, a warming filter has only a slight amber tint and just adds a touch of warmth to the photo. Warming filters have minimal effect on exposure, but a strong one might require an exposure increase of about 1/3 of a stop. If you're using a built-in meter, you won't have to compensate. If you're using a handheld meter, take one reading normally and one with the filter placed over the meter's light sensor to see if there is any difference.

By changing the cropping of your images as you shoot, you can create numerous photographs of the same model and outfit. Here the photographer started with a tight head shot then zoomed out to get mid-length and full-length shots. ©Glamour Portfolios

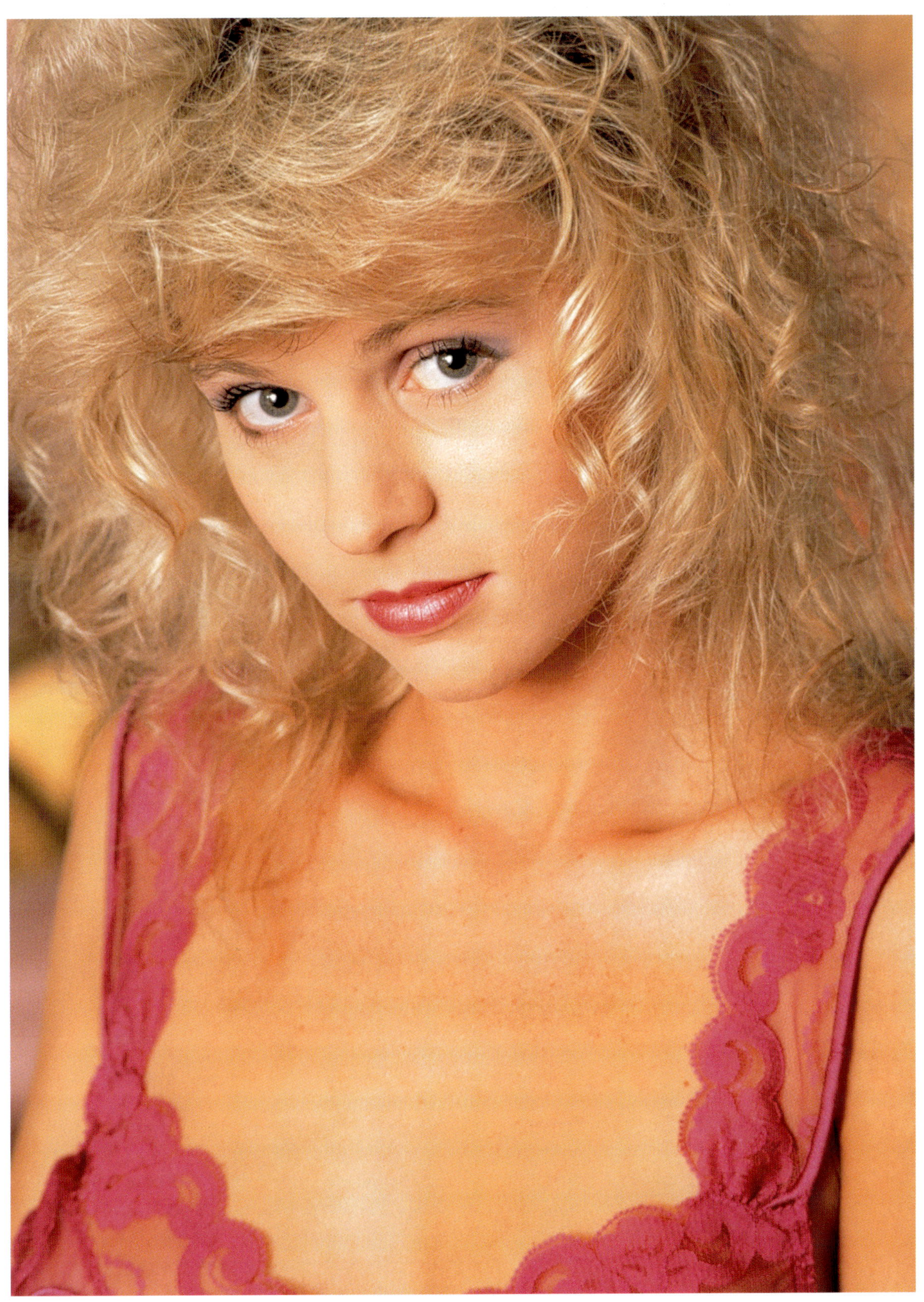

Polarizing filters are useful for reducing reflections and can turn a rather plain sky into a very dramatic one. Try experimenting with a polarizing filter when you are photographing models outdoors, particularly during midday. By rotating the filter while looking through the lens, you'll see the contrast between sky and clouds increase dramatically. This effect is very pleasing and dramatic, yet looks totally natural. Polarizing filters always require some adjustment to your exposure, so be careful to compensate if you're using a handheld light meter.

Although there are dozens of other kinds of filters available, I've only mentioned those that are of most use for glamour photography. If you have a special effect in mind for a particular shot, you can take advantage of prism filters, multiple-image filters, star filters, sepia filters, and many others.

Filters usually come in two types. The first, *screw-in filters*, are usually made of glass mounted in a threaded, metal holder. You just screw them onto the front of your lens. As

Soft-focus filters can erase an image's hard edges, make skin tones look smoother, and give highlights a soft glow. ©Glamour Portfolios

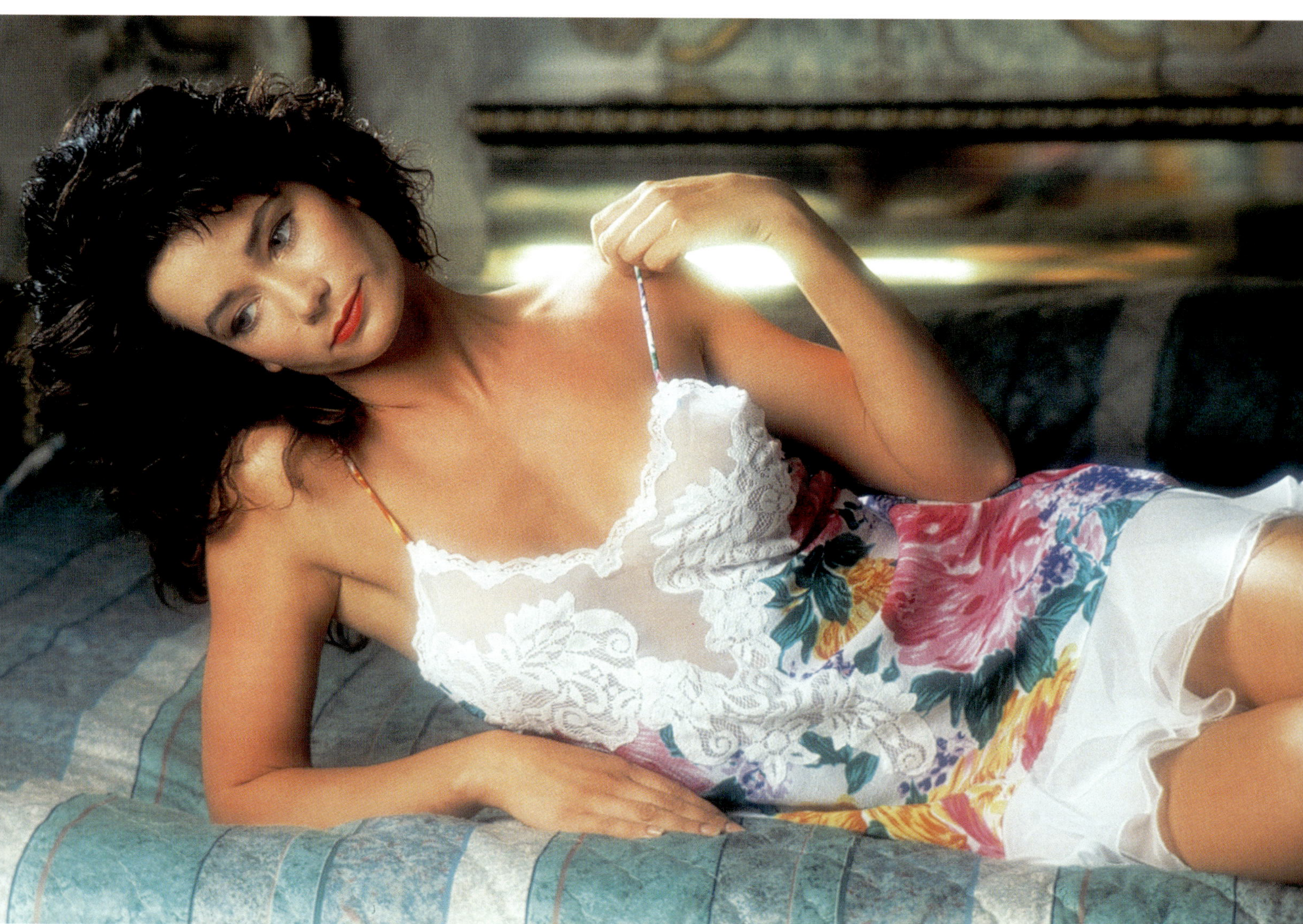

Protective Filters

While not everybody agrees with the concept, many photographers like to place a UV or skylight filter on every lens they own. I find a haze or skylight filter provides extra protection when shooting outdoors. A skylight (sometimes called "1-A," "sky 1-A," or "KR") filter will also absorb UV light and provide a slight warming which I like for films that tend to be on the cool side. A skylight filter can also be useful when shooting outdoors in the shade or on overcast days. Haze, sometimes called UV, filters are designed to reduce blue haze caused by UV light. A good-quality skylight filter absorbs 45.5% of the UV light, while a haze filter provides 71% absorption. Photographers who live at high altitudes or shoot marine scenes may want to use a haze 2 filter to absorb virtually all UV light. As an alternative to haze or skylight filters, Tiffen offers a "clear" filter that's designed for protection only; it's made of clear optical glass.

you add equipment to your system, you can easily find yourself with lenses that have different diameters. Unfortunately, camera manufacturers no longer standardize the filter size of most of their lenses, and you may have to purchase several of the same filter types in different sizes or use an adapter ring.

With the second type, *modular filters*, you can purchase one filter size for all or most of your lenses. These filters are designed to fit a standard filter holder and use various-size adapter rings to fit different lenses and even different camera formats. All you need is a single, inexpensive adapter ring for each of your different lenses' thread sizes.

Light Meters

If you're serious about producing high-quality images, one of the best investments you can make is a high-quality light meter. While these days almost every camera made has an internal light meter, you'll often be better off using a handheld light meter that can measure both flash and daylight.

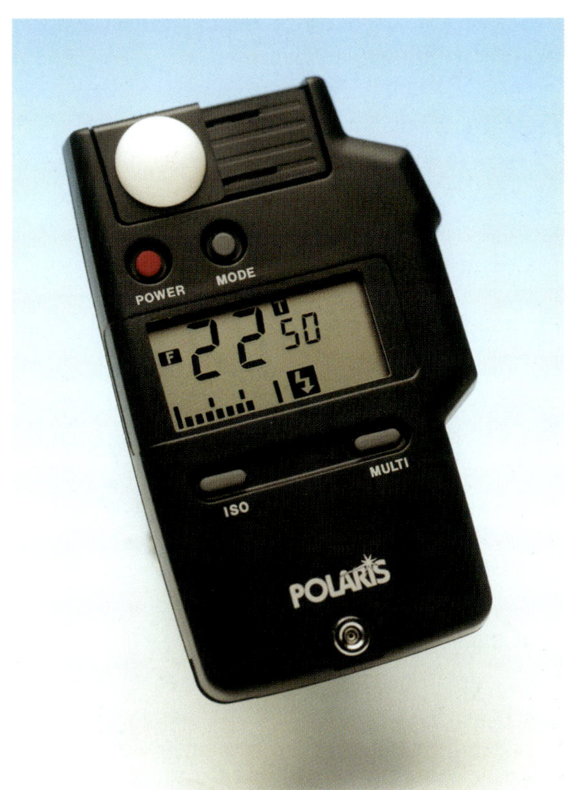

The Polaris digital flash meter features an oversized LCD display in a sleek, lightweight housing with ergonomically designed controls. Photograph courtesy of The Tiffen Company

Metering devices sense light in two different ways. Most handheld and in-camera meters have been designed to take a *reflected* light reading by measuring the light that is being reflected off the subject. A second way of measuring light is called the *incident* method, which measures the light that is falling onto the subject, not light being reflected from the subject. Most professionals prefer to use incident light meters, although many meters have the ability to measure both reflected and incident light. An incident meter uses a small, translucent dome over a light-measuring device to measure the light falling on a subject. To use this type of meter, all you need to do is set the speed of the film, hold the meter up to the subject's face, and take a reading. By pointing the meter toward the camera, you will quickly and easily get an accurate exposure reading.

There are times when you'll find yourself under extreme lighting conditions, such as at the beach. Here, a spot meter can be a useful tool. A spot meter's one degree of coverage lets you place the "spot" where you want to measure the subject (not the surrounding area) exactly in the viewfinder.

Lighting Gear

When I first opened my own studio many years ago, Denver photographer Jim Carlson gave me this advice: "Light is light." It doesn't matter if the lighting equipment you are using is the latest state-of-the-art gear or a dusty electronic flash that you bought used from a photographer who was upgrading his equipment. Both units put out the electronic equivalent of daylight—the only difference may be the amount of light output or the flash unit's controls. What you do with the light is more important than the equipment you use.

If you plan on using only natural light, you may not need an electronic flash unit at all! I know a successful portrait photographer who only works with natural light. If you want to shoot indoors or have total control of lighting outdoors, electronic flash units should be your next investment. As with cameras, you'll find a wide range of lighting equipment available—from small, semiprofessional units to high-powered, multi-feature studio models. Most part-time shooters are well advised to use inexpensive, lightweight, portable units.

There are pros and cons to both monolights and power-pack-style electronic flash systems, and your decision of which to use must be based on whether you do more work on location or in a studio. When using monolights, you have more control over the light output of each head. Also, by using self-contained monolights, you only have to take the exact number of lights you'll need; remember, as a location photographer, the ability to travel light is important. What's more, if a monolight malfunctions while on location, you can always finish the job even though the lighting setup may have to be revised to be somewhat flatter and perhaps less exciting.

Power is an important consideration, especially on location, and most monolights have relatively low AC requirements. If you need to spread the load, simply plug each light into different circuits. Just remember to bring some good extension cords.

The amount of light that any flash can put out depends on its ability to store energy. Being able to generate more light output means more weight, heavier brackets, and bigger light stands. With few exceptions, self-contained monolights are of moderate power—by design. Since monolights are usually lightweight, the amount and type of accessories (which can get heavy) are more limited.

If you are working outdoors at midday, consider having your model toss her head back to keep hard shadows off her face. ©Glamour Portfolios

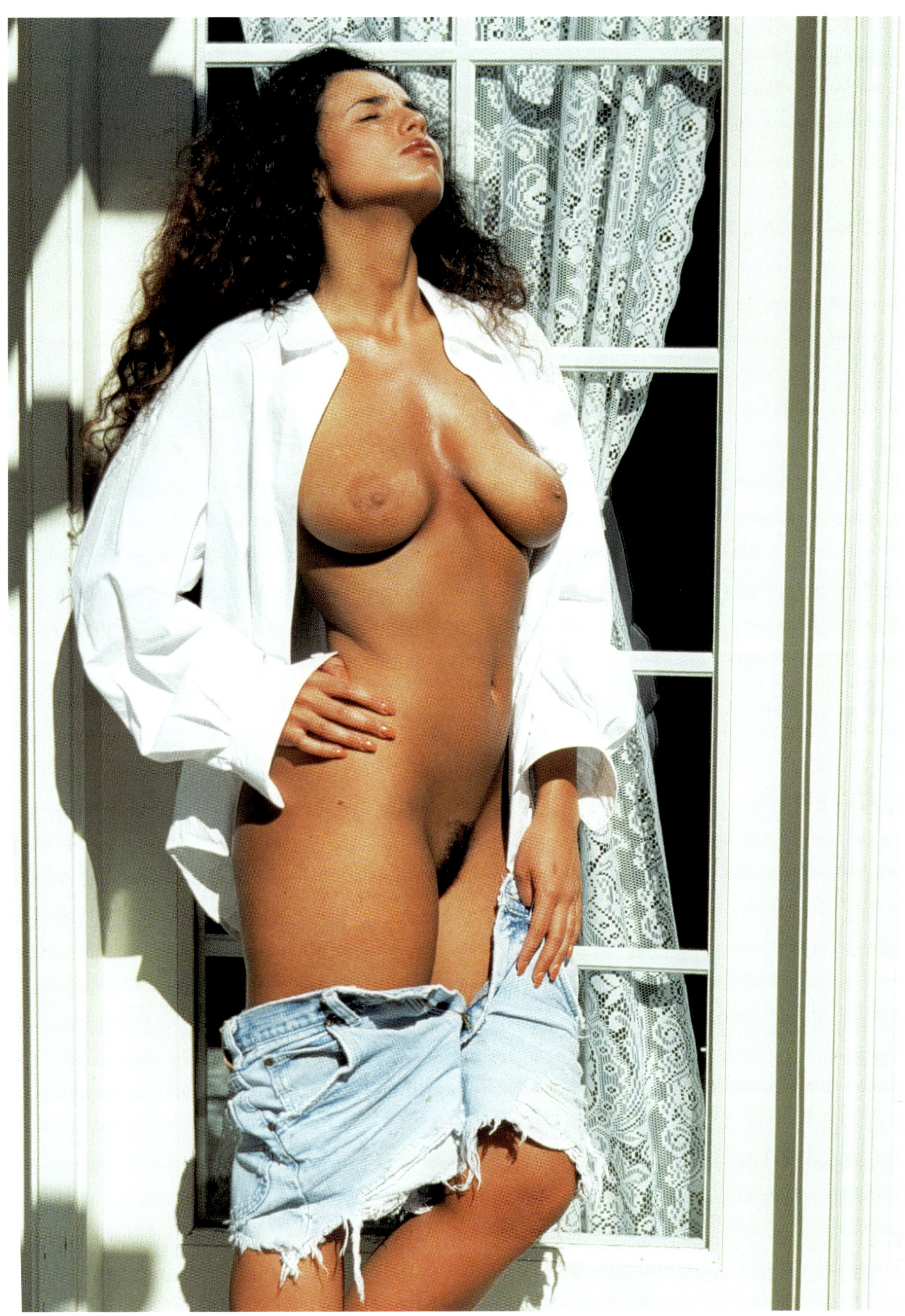

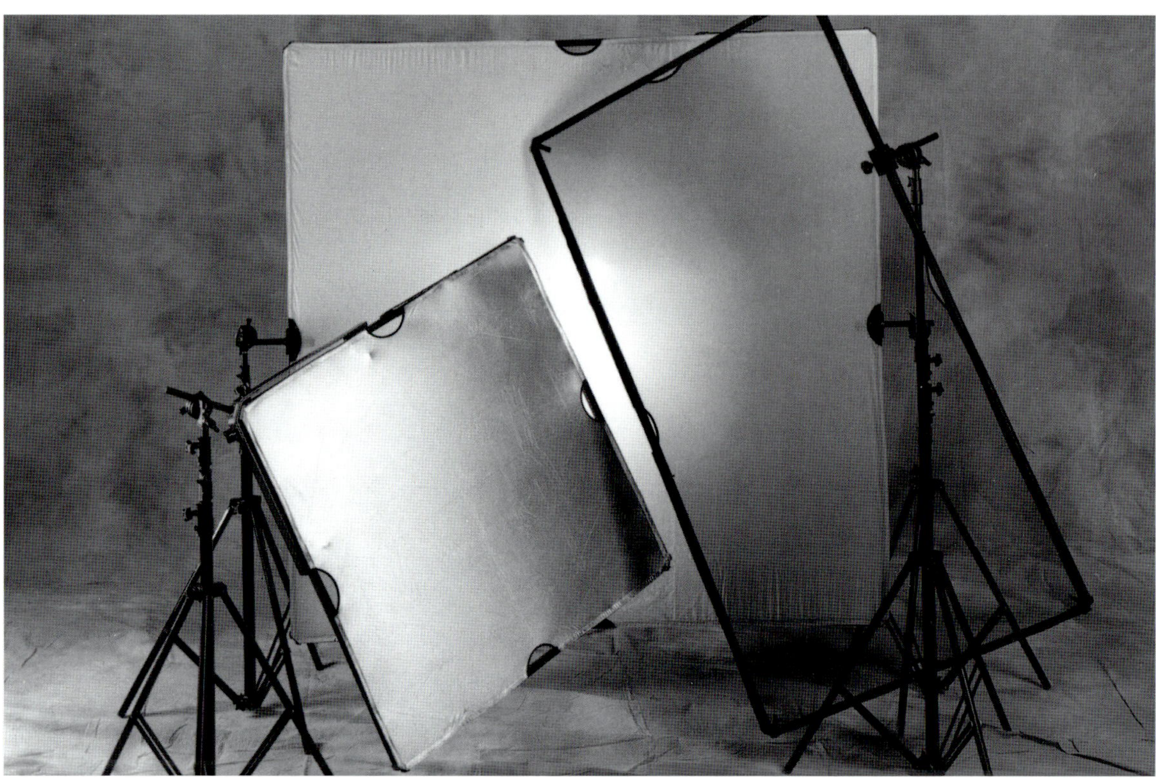

F. J. Westcott's Scrim Jim system consists of collapsible diffusion and reflector panels. The modular frames come in three sizes, and various fabric types are attached with Velcro fasteners. Photograph courtesy of F. J. Westcott Company

There are other factors that make it difficult to compare the two different types of strobes. Most power packs are designed to recycle faster with a single head than a monolight can, but every monolight has its own individual charging system. In a comparison of recycle times between three monolights versus a power pack with three heads of the same capacity, the monolights could win! Costs of the equipment vary more by manufacturer than by type.

Flash output is measured in units called watt-seconds. Typical portable flash units range from 400 to 1600 watt-seconds, and two or three heads are sufficient for most glamour photography situations. Don't get hung up comparing cost per watt-second between the two different styles. There are expensive monolights and some low-priced power pack/head systems. To add further confusion, there's really no effective standard measurement of power. Some flashes use the familiar watt-second, while others use guide number or BCPS (beam candle power seconds) as a standard. When you buy your new system, use your trusted flash meter and shoot a test to see how much light actually hits the film.

Rounding out your basic camera and lighting outfit will be various kinds of reflectors. These come in handy for manipulating and controlling natural and artificial light. They can bounce light to illuminate shadows, keep unwanted light off of your subject, and prevent light from falling onto your camera lens. Reflectors are usually white, silver, or gold, although other types are available from companies such as F. J. Westcott and Photoflex. In general, white or silver reflectors will be the most useful, but gold reflectors can be used to add warmth to your glamour photographs. Reflectors are relatively inexpensive, so you may consider purchasing several different kinds in various sizes and colors. I like to use the collapsible LiteDisc reflectors from Photoflex. Their 22-inch round reflector, for example, fits into a slim 8-1/2-inch case and costs under $30.

Umbrellas & Lightbanks

To a newcomer unfamiliar with photographic lighting techniques, questions about when to use a lightbank or an umbrella can lead to confusion. There appear to be as many different ways to modify the light from electronic flash as there are different types of flash units.

Umbrellas are less directional and more forgiving of where they are placed, and nothing is quicker than popping open an umbrella. They are available in different colors, such as white, silver, gold, and blue, and you can buy a 45-inch umbrella for under $32. Some are available with a removable cover. Having the cover in place prevents light from escaping out of the umbrella's back. When the cover is removed, you can turn the umbrella around and fire a flash through the umbrella. This way you get the same kind of direct, diffused lighting effect that lightbanks produce. Lightbanks wrap around an electronic flash to prevent more light loss, but umbrellas are less expensive.

When do I use lightbanks? I use them when I want soft, yet directional light. Remember the old photographic rule that the closer the light source is to the subject, the softer the light will be. While similar light quality can be obtained by placing an umbrella close to the subject, a lightbank can seem less psychologically threatening to a model than an umbrella. Lightbanks also produce fewer reflections in eyeglasses, glass tables, and windows.

Choosing a size of lightbank took me a while to get used to. While a 45-inch umbrella works well for a head shot or 3/4 length pose, you may prefer to use a small lightbank (16"x22") for head shots, a medium lightbank (24"x32") for mid-length poses, and a large lightbank (36"x48") for full-length shots.

KEEP YOUR GLAMOUR LIGHTING SIMPLE

If you are shooting outdoors or indoors with sufficient available light, chances are you won't require any sort of artificial lighting. In this kind of situation, you can probably get by without any equipment other than your camera and a light meter. If you need to fill in some shadows or soften the light falling on your model's hair, you can use a reflector to add light or a scrim to soften the intensity of light.

Keeping things simple will do more than save you time. By taking advantage of natural light, you'll also enhance the photograph's marketability. That's because a few years from now a clean, natural-looking lighting scheme won't look dated. Just as trendy fashions or hairstyles can date a photograph, so will a lighting scheme that calls too much attention to itself. Any review of fashion or photography magazines over past years clearly shows this. For example, ring lights that produce flat lighting with odd catchlights in the eyes were once popular, but no more. Strong sidelighting, spotlights on faces, and even Hollywood-style glamour portraits with deep shadows and multiple hairlights are all lighting styles that, although acceptable at the time, tend to date a photograph. Having a natural look to your lighting will help to insure that the glamour and centerfold photographs you make today will be saleable for years to come.

Even if it's necessary to use electronic flash to illuminate your glamour photographs, you can still keep your lighting simple and natural. Avoid harsh lighting by using an umbrella or a lightbank to diffuse direct flash. If you're in a room that has white walls, consider bouncing your flash off of the ceiling or walls to create an indirect lighting effect. There's generally no need to use more than two lights—three at the most—unless you have a special location that demands it. By keeping your lighting setups simple, you'll be able to concentrate more on your model, her expression, and pose.

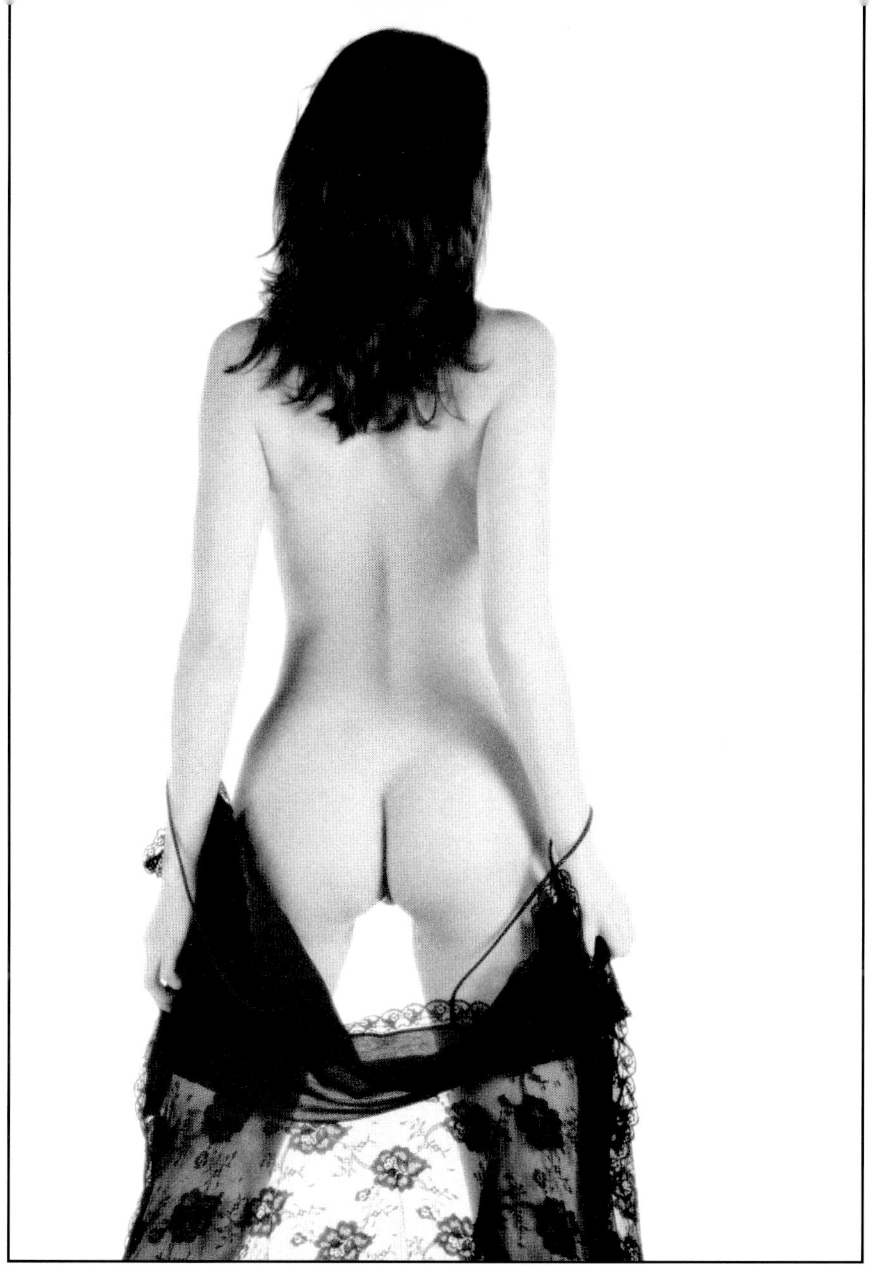

Black-and-white images have a dramatic and somewhat nostalgic feeling. Try experimenting with different types of film to heighten creativity and change the look of your photographs. ©Bob Shell

THE FILM

Whenever two or more photographers get together, one question usually asked is, "What kind of film do you use?" Film choice is based on personal preference as well as commercial reality. Every photographer has his or her own favorite film but usually also shoots a few other kinds—even different brands—to achieve a special effect or when lighting conditions are less than perfect.

The most important consideration when making a decision about whether to shoot slide or negative film is how your photographs will be reproduced. If your primary goal is to produce fine-art prints, you should choose negative film. Negative film is also best if you're shooting glamour photographs and selling them to your models as boudoir portraits. Because the dynamic range of color negative film matches the dynamic range of digital images on a Kodak Photo CD disc, I prefer to make most of my images on negative film if I know they will be delivered in digital form. Other photographers prefer to shoot on slide film because it gives them more versatility. You can place images from transparencies onto a Photo CD disc just as easily as images from negatives, and if you plan to sell your photos to commercial markets, such as advertising and publishing, you should shoot slide film. Most advertising agencies, printers, and publishers prefer working with transparencies rather than negatives, and using industry-accepted practices helps to show that you are a "pro."

One of the benefits of shooting negative film is that you have more latitude in exposure. If you underexpose your film by up to a half stop or overexpose it by as much as a full stop, you can probably still get a good print or digital image. For usable end results, slide film requires that your exposures be accurate. That's why it's important to learn how to take accurate light meter readings or bracket your exposures. Bracketing is a procedure in which you take several photographs of the same shot, changing your exposure setting each time you expose another frame of film. A typical bracket might include shooting at one stop overexposed and one stop underexposed. Some photographers prefer bracketing in $\frac{1}{3}$-stop increments. After the "correct" metered reading has been shot, they shoot $-\frac{1}{3}$, $-\frac{2}{3}$, -1 stop. Then they go the other way, $+\frac{1}{3}$, $+\frac{2}{3}$, and +1 stop. I prefer to use a "biased bracket" system in which you use the computer in your head to determine that the best exposure will be either over or under the meter's stated reading. That way I save film and get more usable images from a smaller number of bracketed frames. Many new cameras can be set to take a series of bracketed exposures when the shutter release button is pressed.

If you have been shooting one type of film for a while, you might want to experiment with a few different films during a particular shoot to see how the results differ. Some slide films might be a bit warmer, while others might be cooler. Faster films, those with higher film speeds, will usually be grainier than slower films. That's why many professionals who shoot 35mm film prefer to use film with an ISO of between 25 and 200, although they might use films with ISOs of 800 or more for a grainier effect. I could write an entire book covering the wide range of film options, but the only way to find out which film is right for you is to experiment.

A warning: Although some amateurs use bulk film to keep their expenses down, this isn't recommended for the part-time glamour photographer. One tiny speck of dust in a bulk loader can ruin a lot of images. To save money when buying film, check out ads in photography magazines for professional supply houses where you can find prices up to 50 percent less than what you pay locally. It's also a good idea to buy a large amount of film (with the same emulsion number) at one time so you can test that particular batch for color and be able to produce consistent results from several different shoots. Nothing is more frustrating than getting a roll of slide film back from the lab only to see your model's face with a greenish tint.

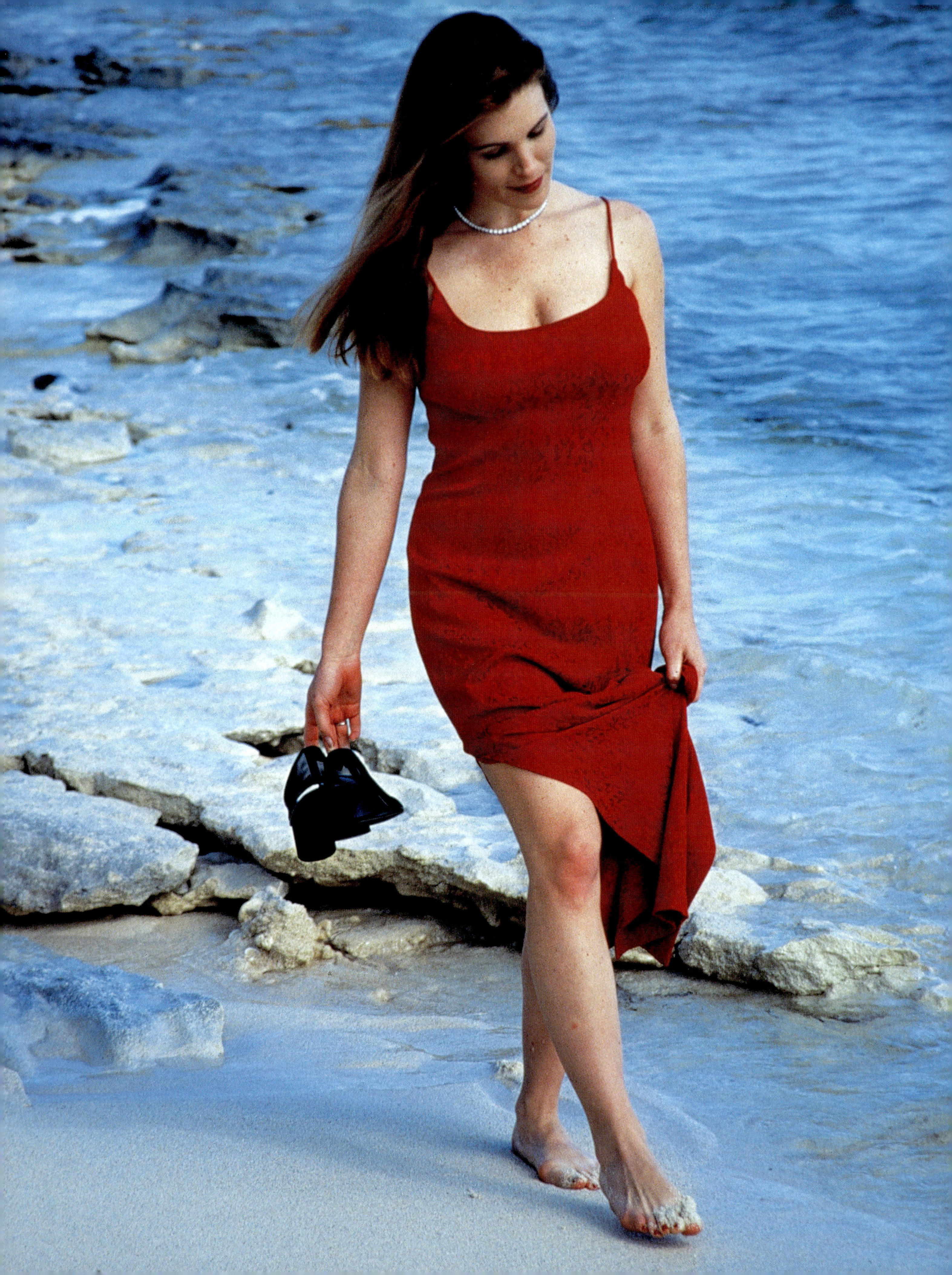

5

The World is Your Studio

You don't need a studio—the world is your studio

For the glamour photographer, choosing the appropriate location to make photographs is just as important to the ultimate success of the final image as the selection of a model. You may have a beautiful and elegant model for your next shoot, but if your background and props are not selected with care, your photographs may not turn out as well as you expected. In this chapter, you will discover how to find interesting and attractive backgrounds and locations for your glamour and centerfold photography shoots.

WHERE TO SHOOT?

Beginning and part-time photographers often think that in order to create professional-quality glamour and centerfold photographs, they need a dedicated studio facility. One of the biggest advantages of being a glamour and centerfold photographer is that you do not need to own or rent a studio. While many full-time professional photographers operate a studio in which they regularly shoot images for clients and conduct their business, glamour shooters, much like photojournalists or nature photographers, can get by without one.

Just take a look at any issue of *Playboy*. Sure, some of the layouts are photographed in a studio setting, and the centerfold is almost always made this way, because Hugh Hefner insists the centerfold image be shot in 8x10 format. But as you review other photographs in the magazine, you will notice many are made outdoors or in other non-studio settings, often using just natural light or relatively simple lighting techniques.

When you take the time to look around, attractive and dramatic locations can be found everywhere. The locations you choose will depend, of course, on the photographs you have in mind. If you want to shoot outdoors, you can choose from parks, beaches, farms, backyards, pools, city streets, country roads, and an endless variety of other suitable locations. If an indoor setting is desirable, why not shoot in an attractive private home, office, loft, or health club?

Do these alternatives mean you shouldn't shoot glamour photographs in a studio setting? Of course not. Great images are created in photographic studios every day. The decision on whether to shoot in a studio or not should be just one of many creative choices you make, but you should never consider a studio an absolute requirement for producing high-quality images. Whatever decision you make, there are advantages and disadvantages to the types of locations typically used by glamour and centerfold photographers.

Always be on the lookout for interesting and unique locations. After finding this small stretch of beach, the photographer envisioned this shot and returned with a model, wardrobe, and props. ©Bob Shell

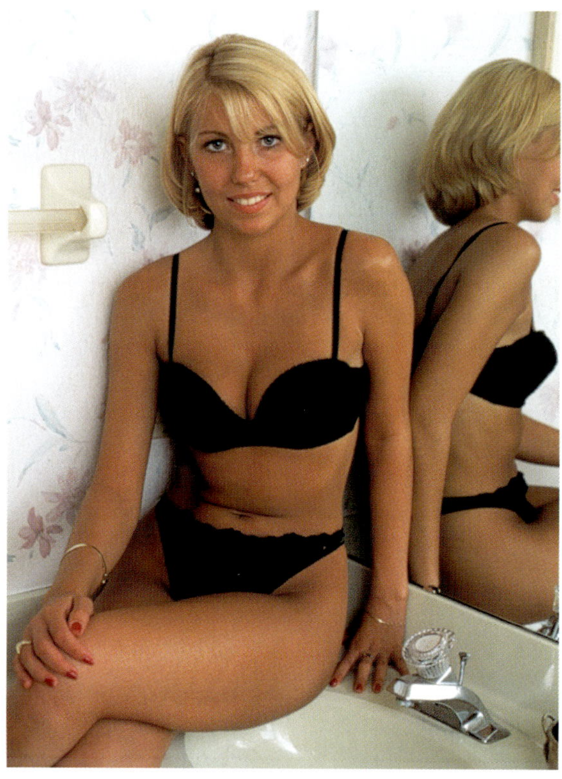

Don't have a studio? If you check around your house, you'll probably find suitable locations that you may have overlooked. Here's a photo of Tarah that the photographer took in his own bathroom. ©Glamour Portfolios

THE STUDIO SHOOT

If there is one word to describe the primary advantage of shooting in a studio it is *control*. Shooting in a studio gives you complete control over every aspect of the photograph. You can control the lighting, background, props, and mood. It may be a bright sunny day outside, but in the studio, you can create a soft and dimly lit portrait. If it's pouring cats and dogs outdoors, your model can stay nice and dry on your studio set. If the wind—a big problem depending on where you live—makes a beauty shot difficult, perhaps you can use a soft breeze from a fan in your studio. No matter what is going on outside, it will have little or no effect on a photograph made in a studio.

Since a studio is self-contained, shooting is highly efficient. Everything you need for the shoot is just a few steps away, including camera and lighting equipment, makeup and hair supplies, props, telephones, food, changing rooms, even a bathroom and shower. Another important benefit of shooting in a studio is privacy, especially important when shooting centerfold photographs.

Yet there can be drawbacks to shooting in a studio. The biggest problem for many part-time and aspiring professionals is that operating a studio is expensive. Far too many beginning photographers make the leap and rent a studio before their income from assignments can support the additional overhead. According to noted photographer and lecturer Don Feltner, moving from a home-based operation to a studio before sufficient cash flow exists is the number one cause of failure for new photographic businesses. Instead of using the profits from assignments to build a more impressive portfolio and hire better models, these photographers spend too large a percentage of their income paying rent and utility bills. Another drawback is that some studio photographers use the same backgrounds, props, and lighting styles over and over again. Before long, they can find themselves lost in a creative rut that may be difficult to break out of. This cookie-cutter approach to photography can lead to boredom and can kill creativity. As a visual artist, you want to strive to consistently create fresh and interesting images.

OUTDOOR LOCATIONS

There is something special about being outdoors on a beautiful day taking photographs. Whether shooting a landscape or a beautiful nude model, there is nothing better than feeling the sun on your back as you click away, knowing you will bring back some beautiful photographs. There are just some advantages of nature that cannot be duplicated indoors.

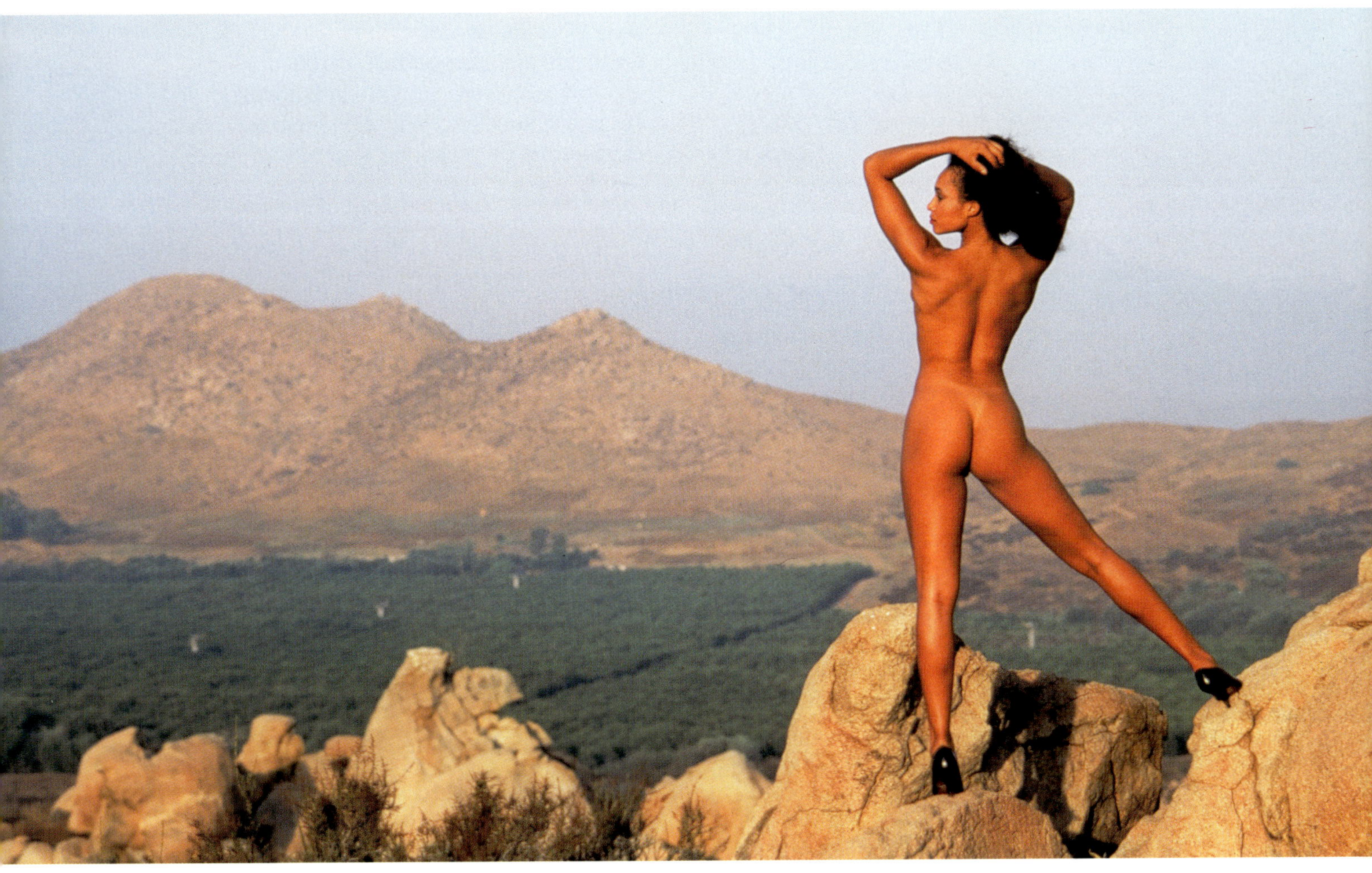

There are few things more exciting for a photographer than being in a beautiful location with a good model. Photographed near Riverside, California, this image shows why the nude in a landscape is a recurring theme for so many photographers and artists. ©Glamour Portfolios

There are many reasons why so many photographers enjoy working on location: the endless variety of natural and man-made settings; the incredible variation in lighting from sunrise to sunset; the sounds, smells, and visual excitement. The location you choose might be as close as your own backyard. Or you might have access to a mountain lake or seaside beach. Regardless of where you live, there are plenty of potential shooting locations for you to choose from. As you make your decisions on where to shoot your images, you should also try to consider the potential disadvantages inherent in whatever location you choose.

Just as a permanent studio offers complete control over your environment, once you head outdoors, you are completely at the mercy of the weather. Perhaps you envisioned shooting on a beach with the setting sun's golden light sweeping across your model. Instead, as you wait patiently, the sun has disappeared behind some large, dark, and ominous-looking clouds. The golden rays of light you had expected have deteriorated into an overcast haze that destroys your chance of creating the image you had envisioned.

When shooting on location, there can be potentially far more troublesome conditions to overcome before you can get the photographs you planned. For the glamour photographer, privacy is one of the most critical issues to consider when choosing an outdoor location. If your model is wearing lingerie or something less, you can forget about shooting images where there will be people walking by. It's also unprofessional to place your model in such a situation, and it might be illegal in your area. That does not mean you cannot shoot glamour images outdoors, but it does mean you are going to have to be creative about where and when you shoot. Perhaps you will need to walk a bit farther down the beach or into the park to give your model the privacy she deserves.

It is important that you keep up-to-date on the laws regarding public exposure wherever you are shooting. Just as in all aspects of glamour photography, it pays to use common sense and be discreet. Interestingly, while it's now legal for a woman to sunbathe topless in New York City's Central Park, it's illegal to photograph a topless model there.

Safety is another important consideration when shooting outdoors. While a photograph of your model standing on top of a rocky cliff may appeal to your sense of style, don't lose your common sense when it comes to getting her safely up and down that cliff! If you would like to photograph your model walking in shallow water along a tropical beach, don't forget that there may be sea urchins hiding there. Before you have a nude lie down in the beautiful bed of wild flowers, pause to consider that under those flowers there might be poison ivy.

Unfortunately, the greatest threat to safety might not come from nature. It's important that whenever you shoot outdoors, you keep an eye out for people who could cause problems. Just as shooting in a controlled studio environment keeps out bad weather, it also keeps out troublemakers. When you are shooting outdoors, it's always a good idea to take the following precautions:

Have an assistant keep an eye on you, the model, and your equipment at all times.

Carry a cellular telephone with you, great to have in the event of an emergency.

Keep a well-stocked first aid kit in your car or camera bag. Even if you only use it to bandage your own finger, it's a good idea to have a first aid kit handy—just in case.

Always let someone know where you are going and when you expect to be returning.

SHOOTING IN HOMES AND HOTELS

One of the easiest ways to get interesting backgrounds for your photographs is to rent an attractive home or hotel suite for your shoot. Many catalogs, advertisements, and movies are photographed in locations ranging from small, casual homes to large, elegant mansions. While the fees charged to use a home for a shoot might be $500 to $2000 per day, with a little research and a few phone calls you can often find a suitable location for a fraction of that amount. In fact, you might be able to use a friend or relative's house for free. Whenever you shoot at a house or other private property, it's usually a good idea to get a property release. The American Society of Media Photographers' (ASMP) book *Professional Business Practices in Photography* contains a sample property release form that should provide all of the legal protection you need. Contact information for ASMP can be found in the appendix at the back of the book.

Upscale homes make great glamour photography backgrounds. Glamour Portfolios' staff photographers rented a house for $250 per day and made extensive use of its numerous rooms, as well as a large yard and pool. In this photograph, Katrina is shown in the dining room and is lit by natural light coming through a large window. ©Glamour Portfolios

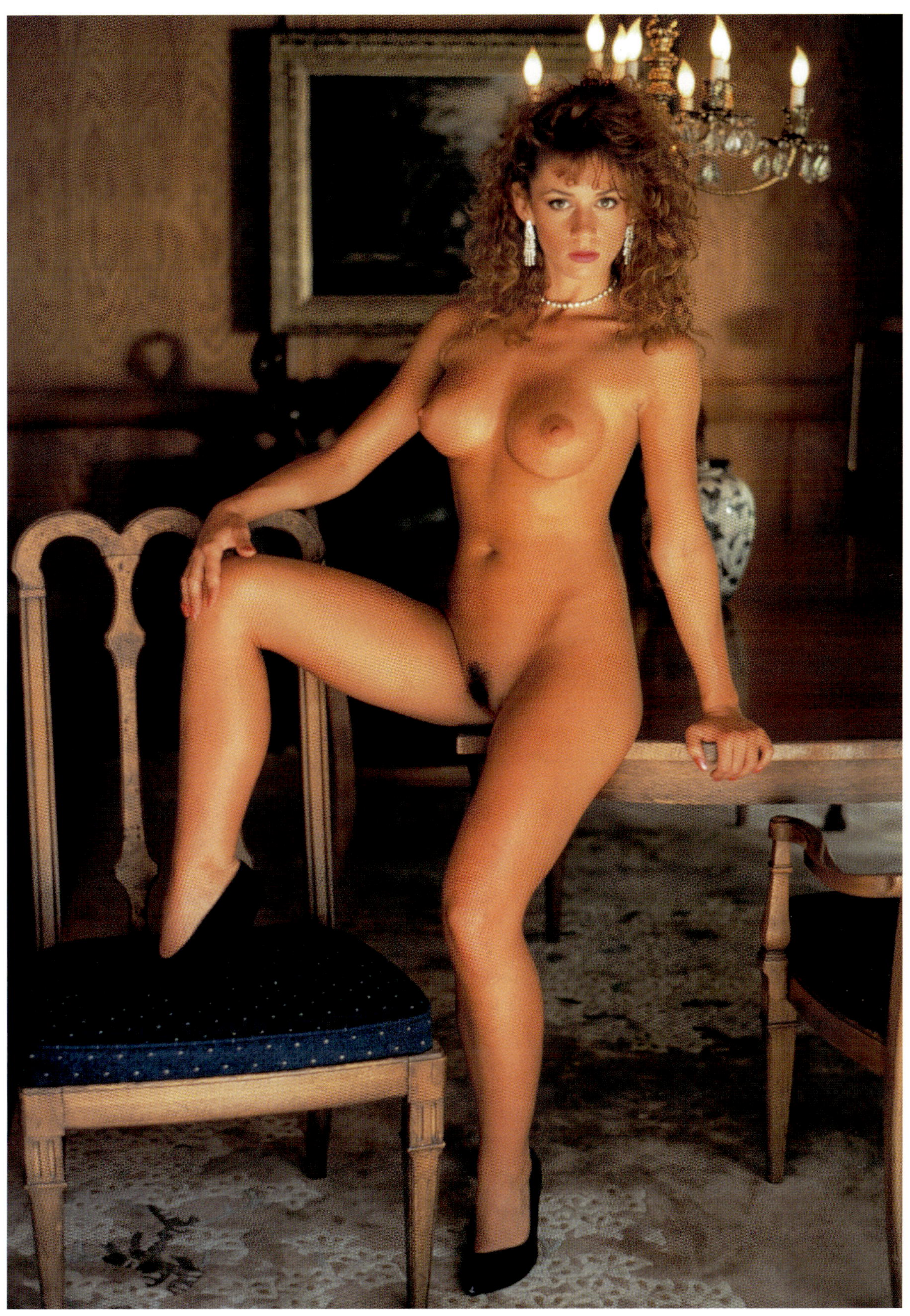

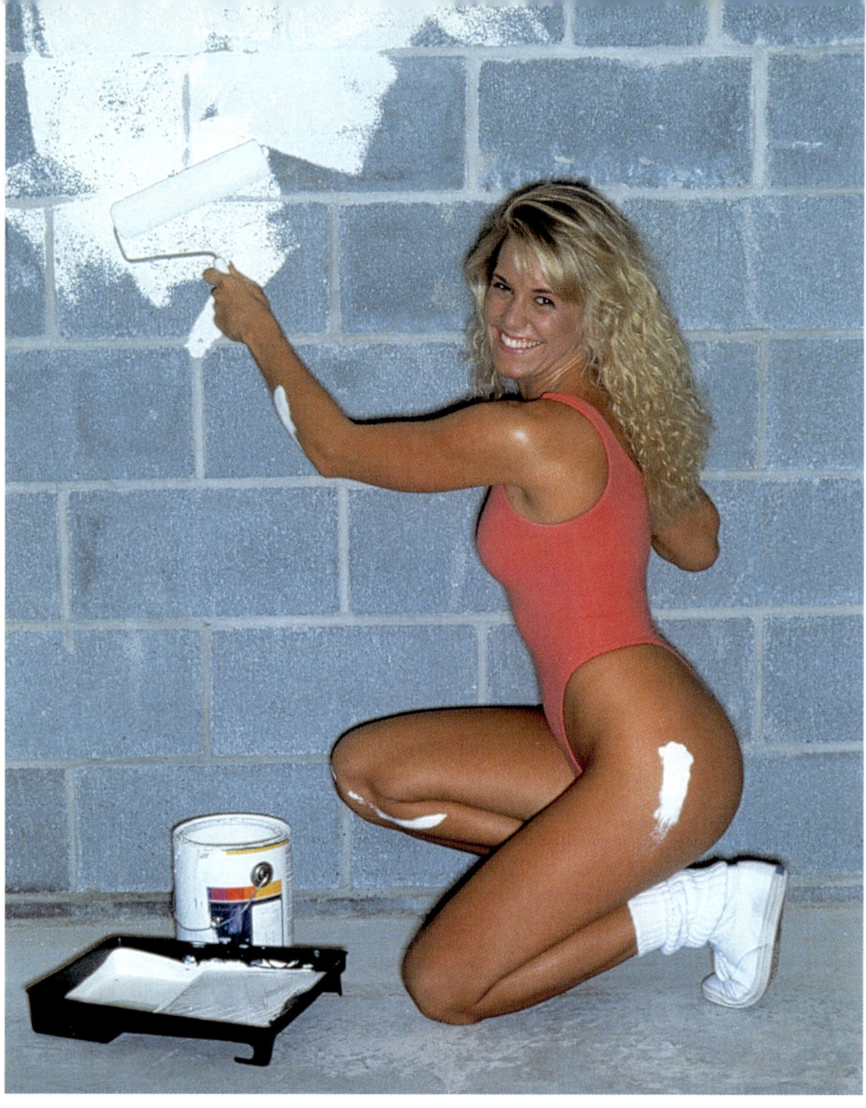

You don't have to look far to find good locations. This photograph of Midi was one of several taken in an unfinished basement. Don't overlook locations right at home—basements, living rooms, bedrooms, even bathrooms might be suitable backgrounds for your photographs. ©Glamour Portfolios

If you don't have friends or relatives who own houses suitable for your glamour shoots, you might want to ask other photographers if they know of available locations in your area. In major cities, there are often professional location scouts who will have a large selection of available homes. A better choice might be your state or city film commission. They maintain a list of freelance people and equipment rental options; it's a good place to start when looking for interesting, possibly unusual, available locations.

Although some homeowners might not want their houses used as locations for a glamour shoot, most will not care what you shoot as long as you don't break anything or make a mess. For an eight-hour shoot, you could probably rent an average-size house for $250 to $400. If you are friendly with a real estate agent, he or she might suggest clients who are selling their homes who would be willing to rent them out for a morning or afternoon photography shoot.

If you cannot find a house to rent, consider renting a hotel suite. It shouldn't be difficult to find a hotel in your area that has attractive rooms and suites suitable for shoots. These accommodations can vary from upscale honeymoon or executive suites at a large hotel to a beautifully decorated suite in a bed-and-breakfast. Some hotels catering to honeymooners and romantic couples have fantasy or theme suites that make interesting locations.

When you shoot at a hotel, it's important to get permission from the management and a property release. Depending on the hotel and the type of shoot you are doing, you might be turned down when you ask. Don't be discouraged. If you have a good portfolio and present your ideas in a professional manner, management usually won't mind your using the hotel as a location—especially midweek when there are many empty rooms. While talking with the manager, you might want to inquire if the hotel needs photographs for a new brochure or other use. If so, perhaps you can barter for the room in exchange for your photography skills. Some photographers just book a hotel room and shoot without permission, but if the room you are shooting in is unique and easily recognizable, that's not a good idea. You could find yourself at the wrong end of a legal action if your photographs are published in a magazine and a hotel executive recognizes the room.

Whether you are shooting at a home or a hotel, it's important that you be discreet, low-key, and careful not to damage anything. This may seem obvious, but it's worth remembering that you will be held responsible for anything that breaks. That's why it's a good idea to move valuables or fragile items out of the shooting area. At a minimum, make sure your models and others with you are aware of things they should not bump into. When using extension cords for your lights or long PC cords for your camera, be careful. You do not want people tripping over those, either!

Sometimes renting a suite at an upscale hotel provides numerous locations and props. All this photographer needed was a beautiful bed to serve as a background for his model. ©Glamour Portfolios

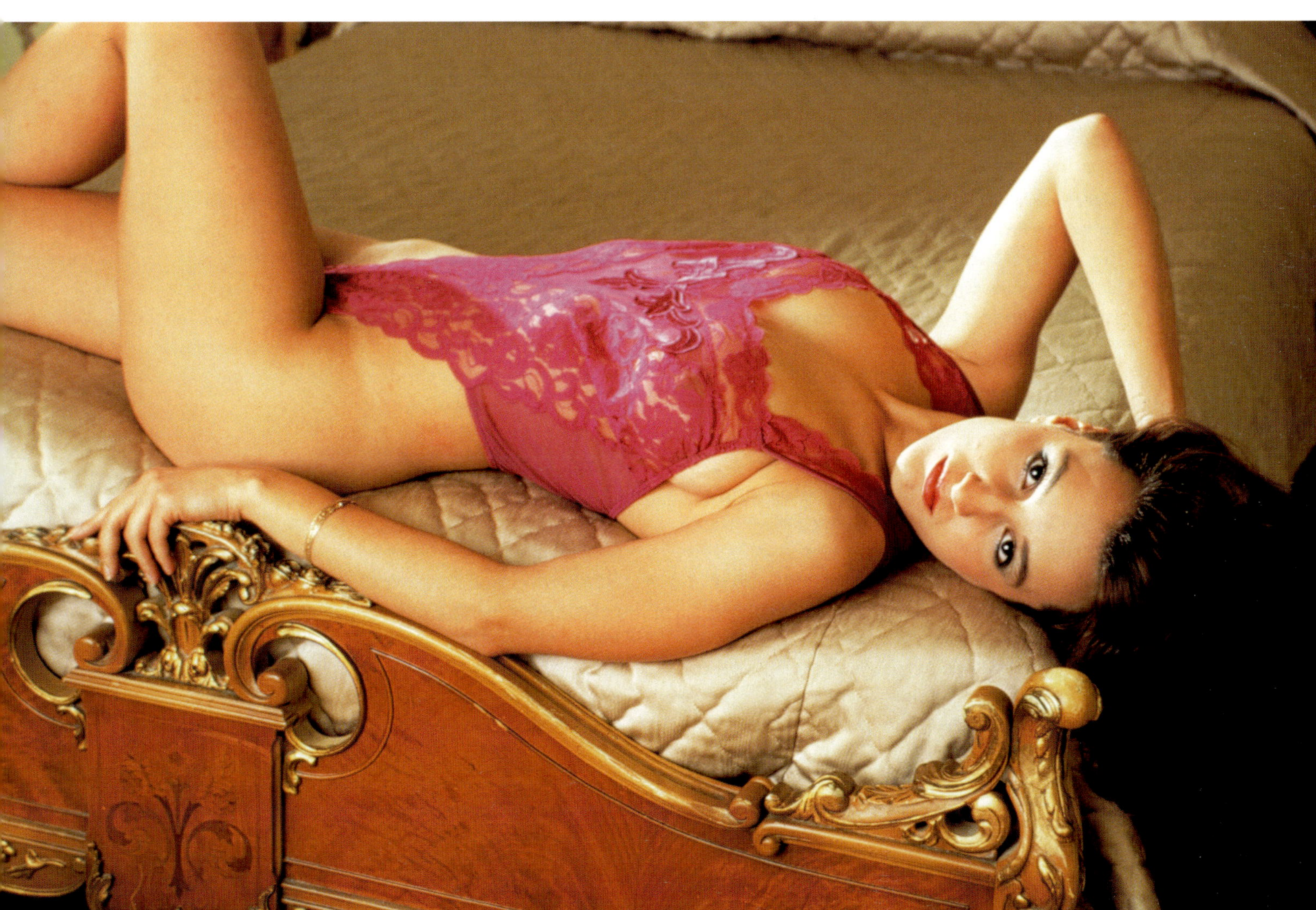

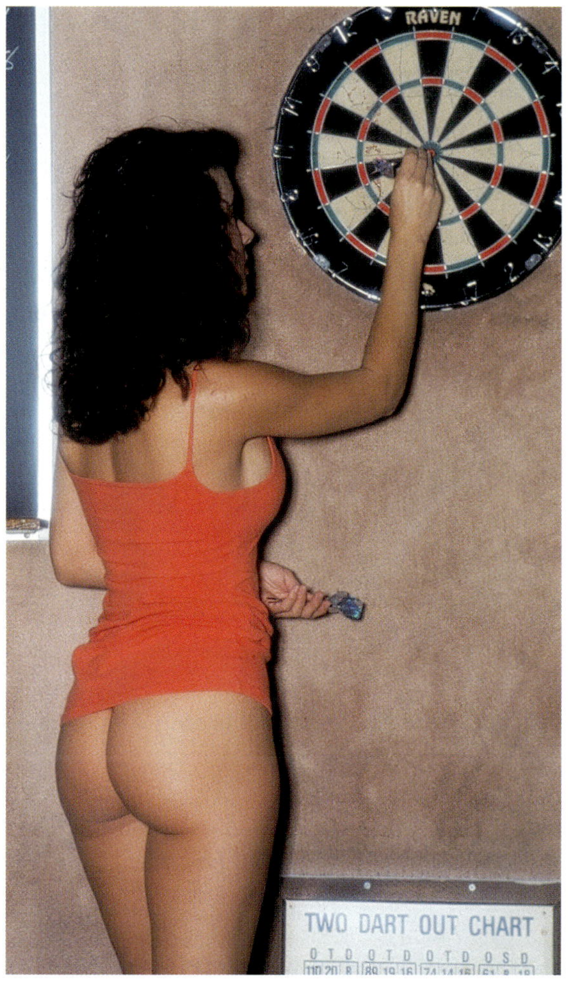

Here's a simple yet sexy glamour shot taken in a local bar. Props can give you ideas and opportunities for creative photographs. The photographer used minimal lighting equipment—just a shoe-mount flash unit. ©Glamour Portfolios

Some locations require that you be insured before you can shoot there. While working on location, it's important you have some form of business liability insurance. A typical minimum liability policy is available from most insurance companies for about $600 a year. This may seem high at the time, but keep in mind that the cost is a business deduction. The management at some locations may even ask you to provide proof of insurance before you are allowed to shoot. You can turn this situation into a marketing advantage when approaching a homeowner or hotel manager by telling them that you are fully insured. Having liability insurance shows them that you are a credible professional. Offering to provide a certificate of insurance—your insurance company should send one at no additional cost—may tip the scales when negotiating to rent or borrow a location to photograph models for your next glamour shoot.

The advantages of shooting in a home are similar to those of shooting in a studio. You have privacy and complete control over lighting and environmental factors. Another benefit of shooting in a home or hotel suite is that you can go from room to room and take advantage of attractive furniture and props with minimal cost and effort. If you happen to rent a house with an attractive backyard and a pool, you can shoot all day and change your background many times. While shooting at a house or hotel can be expensive, if you shoot all day and produce a large number of photographs in a wide range of locations, in the long run it could turn out to be a bargain.

When shooting in an occupied house, you must be firm with the owner regarding your need for privacy, especially if a homeowner gets a little too friendly with your models. You can usually avoid this problem by explaining to the homeowner that privacy is expected as part of the house rental and that you would prefer no one be in the same room when you are shooting. Most homeowners will, however, insist that someone they know be in the house at all times during the shoot to make sure that nothing is misused or broken.

Nightclubs and bars often provide good backgrounds for your glamour photographs. For this image, the photographer used a pool table as a prop. For other images in this series, he took advantage of a mirrored dance floor and an attractive bar area. ©Glamour Portfolios

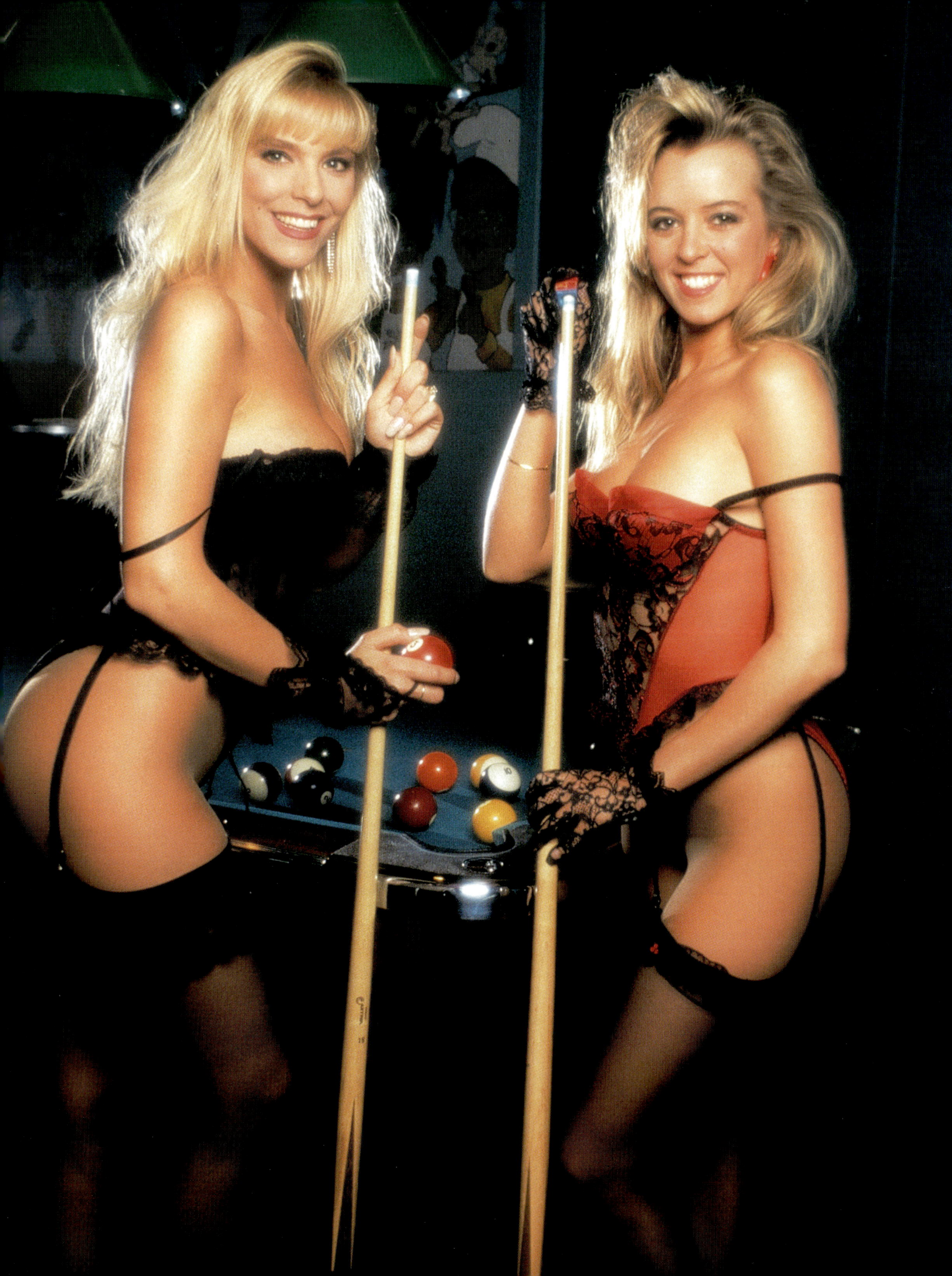

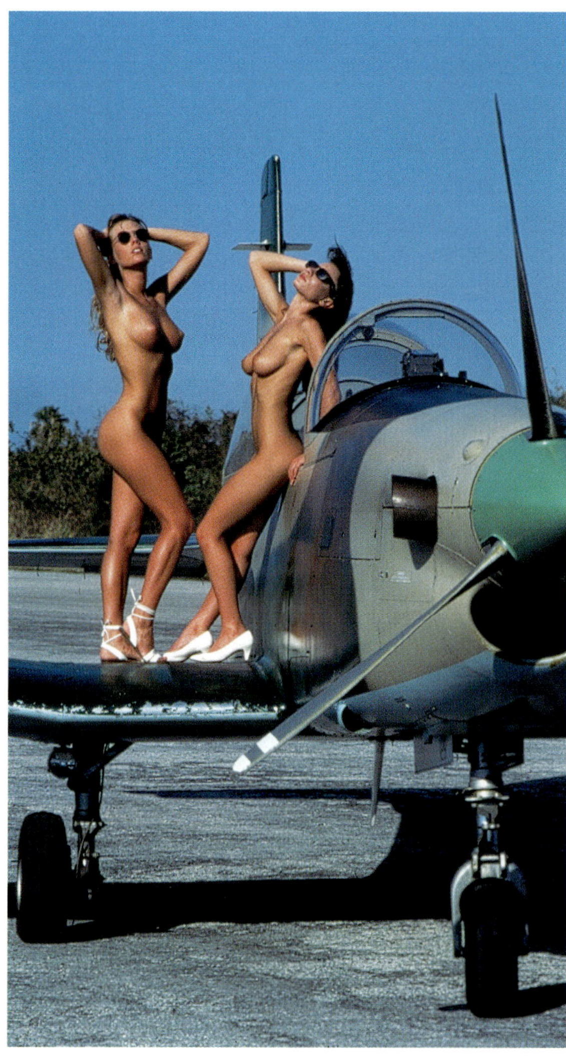

When looking for a location, it helps to have a friend who is well connected to personnel at a local Air Force base. (The location is a secret so no one gets in trouble.) A few airmen moved the plane around and enjoyed watching the photographer and models at work. ©Glamour Portfolios

TRIPS TO EXOTIC LOCATIONS

How many times have you seen a documentary about the making of a calendar or the *Sports Illustrated* swimsuit issue and said to yourself, "I wish that were me doing the shooting." It really does not take much work to turn this fantasy into a reality. Perhaps you won't have a famous client or any client at all. You will probably not have two assistants, a hair and makeup artist, and a stylist, but it's neither difficult nor prohibitively expensive to produce your own location shoot. See the next chapter for an interesting strategy for location shooting, but first here are the benefits and drawbacks of taking a trip with your models.

The most obvious advantage to location shooting is the scenery. Whether you travel to a Caribbean island or to a mountain range in Alaska, few things are more enjoyable or exciting than photographing a model in a beautiful natural setting. Along with the scenery, you can often take advantage of weather and lighting. Sometimes you can even get models to waive their modeling fees. You can offer to barter their airfare as well as hotel room and board in exchange for their modeling time. You would be surprised how many models will exchange their time for a nice trip. If you are in a part of the country that gets cold during winter, put the word out that you are looking for models for a trip to the Caribbean, and they will be standing in line.

Shooting in dramatic locations also offers you a chance to produce exceptional portfolio photographs. Whether you are showing your samples to models or art directors, people are always impressed with photographs taken in exotic locations. There is something about a natural setting that complements glamour and centerfold photography. If you have spent any time studying the work of well-known figure photographers, think about how many of the photographs that remain in your mind were nudes taken in outdoor locations.

Beyond the wonderful photographs you take when you travel, location shooting can be a great social and educational experience. If you enjoy traveling, you know the excitement of waking up in a new place far from home. Perhaps your spouse or significant other can accompany you and turn your shooting into part work and part vacation. Although your primary objective in taking a trip is to produce photographs, you will find many other good reasons for traveling.

Of course, there can be drawbacks to traveling. Depending on the airfares and hotel rates, your trip can quickly get expensive—particularly if you plan on taking more than one or two models with you. (Typical expenses for these kinds of shoots are discussed in the next chapter.) Remember, too, there are other considerations that can become much more serious than just the bottom line, such as weather extremes. It's just common sense to keep yourself and your models out of danger (as well as protect your valuable camera equipment).

If you have never traveled out of the country, you might want to first take a vacation to an "easy" location, such as Cancun, before traveling to other places with your models. Some locations are simply more "tourist-friendly" than others, and this is something you should consider before planning your trips. Learning to work effectively while traveling out of the country is a skill that takes time to learn. You need to be patient and understanding when dealing with people to avoid any problems.

Whenever you plan a trip, it is important that you consider how you will handle the inevitable last-minute cancellations, changes, and problems. It is especially important to have backup models. Knowing local weather conditions is important, too. For example, much of the Caribbean is rainy during the months of September, October, and November. If you plan on spending sunny afternoons on the beach with your models, you are better off planning a trip in January or February when rainy weather is rare.

As you can see from these examples, there is no shortage of potential locations for your glamour photographs, each with its own advantages and drawbacks. Undoubtedly you can come up with many more that will work for you. Regardless of where you shoot, try to make your choice of location part of the creative process as you plan your next glamour photography shoot.

It's almost impossible to take a bad photograph when you combine a good model and a beautiful beach. Here Rochelle relaxes as the sun sets on the coastline of Cozumel, Mexico. ©Glamour Portfolios

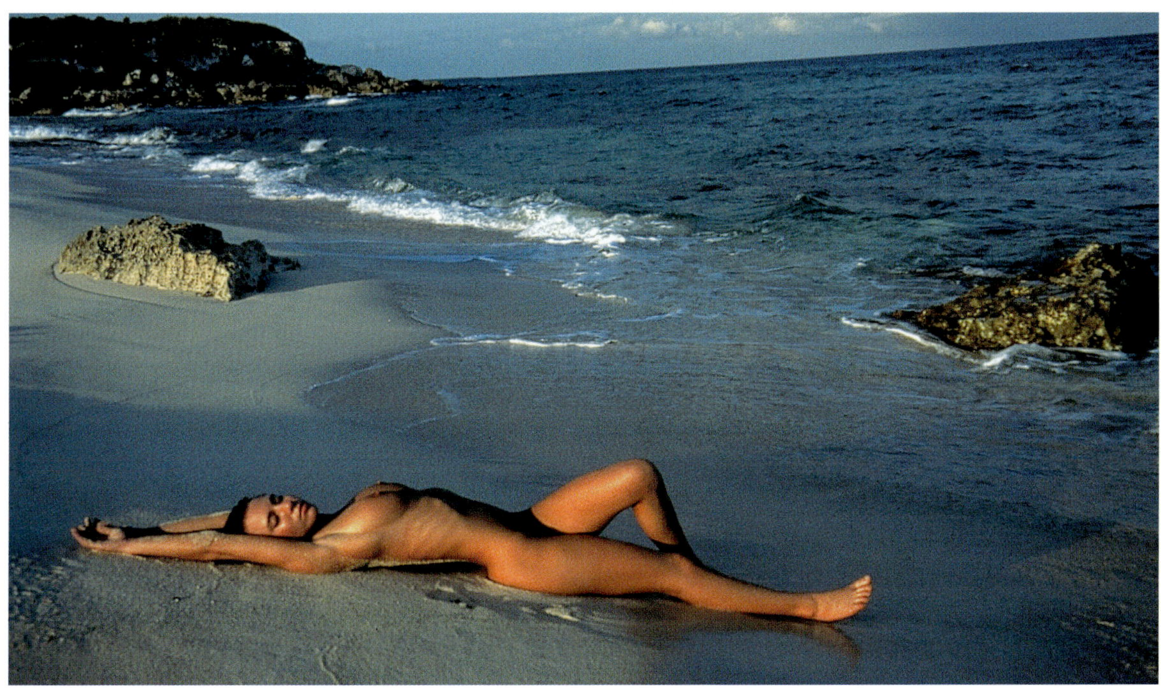

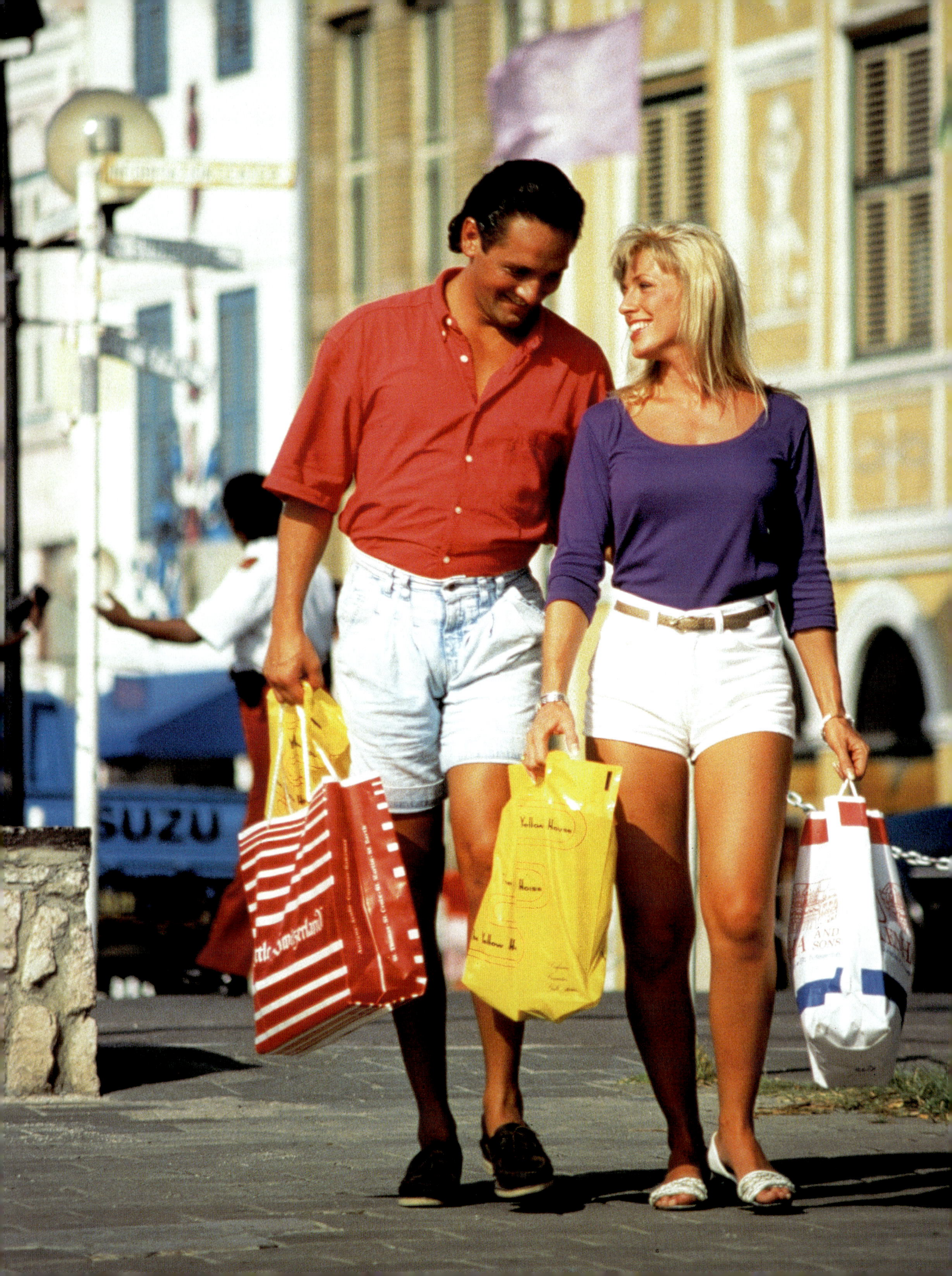
SUZU
Yellow House

6

The Free On-Location Shoot

How to barter your way to a Caribbean photo shoot

While photographers working on assignments usually have all of their expenses paid for by the client, stock and glamour photographers shooting for their files have to find creative ways to pay for their trips. If you're already an established professional, you may be able to afford a stock photography production trip. As you no doubt realize, traveling with models to the Caribbean or any other tropical location for a glamour shoot can be expensive. Even a trip to a relatively economical location, such as Mexico, can easily run to $5000 when you add up the costs of airfare, hotel, food, rental car, film and processing, and all of the other basic on-location expenses. Most part-time photographers or semiprofessionals will be hard pressed to comfortably meet all of the costs associated with this kind of shoot.

LOCATION SHOOTING CAN BE EXPENSIVE

We all agree: On-location glamour shoots can be expensive. How much? Let's begin by examining all of the typical costs involved in a modest trip for one photographer and four models traveling from the U.S. Midwest to Cozumel, Mexico, for a one-week glamour shoot:

Round-trip airfare for five @ $550 each	$2750
Three budget hotel rooms @ $60/night	1260
Rental car @ $300/week	300
Food @ $25/day per person	875
Film and processing: 100 rolls @ $14.25 each	1425
Miscellaneous expenses, tips, location fees, props	300
Total	**$6910**

Film and processing costs were based on current prices at the time this book was being completed. Any and all of these costs will vary widely depending on many factors. For example, the cost of traveling from Denver to Mexico is lower than it might be from other parts of the country, so airfare expense is a big variable. Also notice that the list does not include model fees. That's because this cost estimate is based on the assumption that the models will waive their normal fees in exchange for a free trip and portfolio photographs.

If the scenario I've described seems out of line to you, use your calculator or favorite spreadsheet program to determine a typical travel expense scenario that works for you and your style of photography. For example, you might choose to take only two models and rent a small house instead of staying in a hotel. Perhaps you feel it's important to bring along an assistant or a stylist. If shooting 100 rolls of film sounds like a lot, you can save some money by shooting less—although I feel this would be a false economy in light of the other expenses involved in such a trip. No matter what combination of factors you choose to manipulate, it is unlikely that you will be traveling with models to a Caribbean or Mexican locale for a week for less than $2000 to $4000.

Shopping is a major tourist attraction, and you'll want to cover it well. Even small islands will have at least one busy shopping district or street. Try to shoot specific locations for the tourism board and generic situations for your stock file. ©Glamour Portfolios

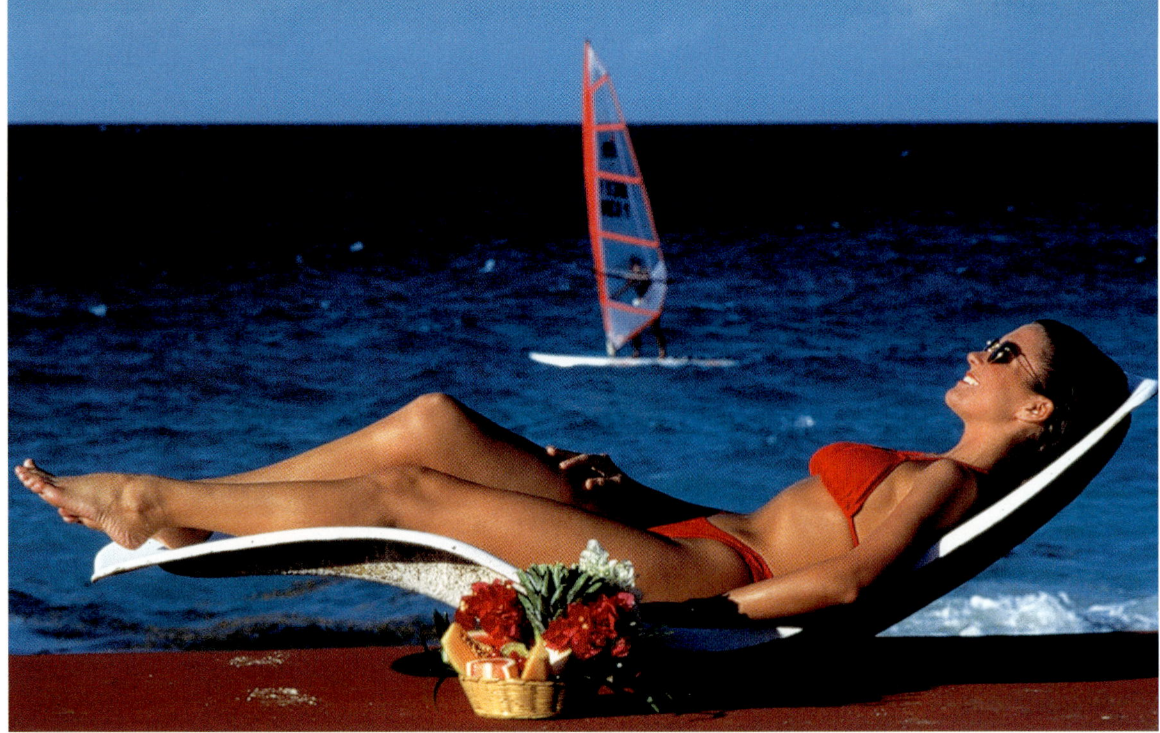

Here's a shot that has all the elements of a successful stock photo. An attractive model, a beautiful location, good color, and a universally understood concept. ©Glamour Portfolios

LET'S MAKE A DEAL!

One way to dramatically reduce your expenses is to find one or more barter partners who can pay for most, if not all, of your expenses in exchange for your providing a selection of photographs from your trip. Potential barter partners include tourism boards, airlines, hotels, and cruise lines. What this diverse group has in common is an ongoing need for up-to-date photographs to use for advertising and promotion. What makes this barter arrangement convenient is that that is exactly what you have to offer.

Here is how a typical barter arrangement might develop. You need to start by doing some research. Go to the neighborhood newsstand, pick up a few travel magazines, and look for ads for some of the less-traveled countries or islands. You can forget about locations such as Jamaica, Mexico, Aruba, and the U.S. Virgin Islands. Instead, you should specifically look for countries, islands, or hotels that have small ads with photos that look as if they could use some updating. Many smaller countries don't even have a government tourism agency. Instead, the address they have listed in their ad in many cases will be that of an advertising agency, often located in New York, that specializes in the travel industry.

Spend your research time looking for islands or countries that have limited tourism budgets. Select a dozen or so potential destinations, and call them to request a package of travel information. At this point, you should not discuss any potential business arrangement; get the information packets first. When the packages arrive, review them, and try to get a feeling for which locations could use some new photographs in their promotional material. A typical travel packet includes a few brochures from the tourism board as well as several from the local hotels and tourist attractions. If you open your package and the material looks as if it was printed 20 years ago (check hair and bathing suit styles), you may have found a barter partner! Even if some of the brochures look up-to-date but the main brochure looks shabby, perhaps the tourism board might like to update that one brochure.

After you've searched through a few magazines and have several possible locations, you might want to pick up a travel directory that lists tourism boards, hotels, and other similar contacts. You will find such guides in large bookstores and libraries. If your potential barter partner is a hotel, you can offer your services and photographs in exchange for room and

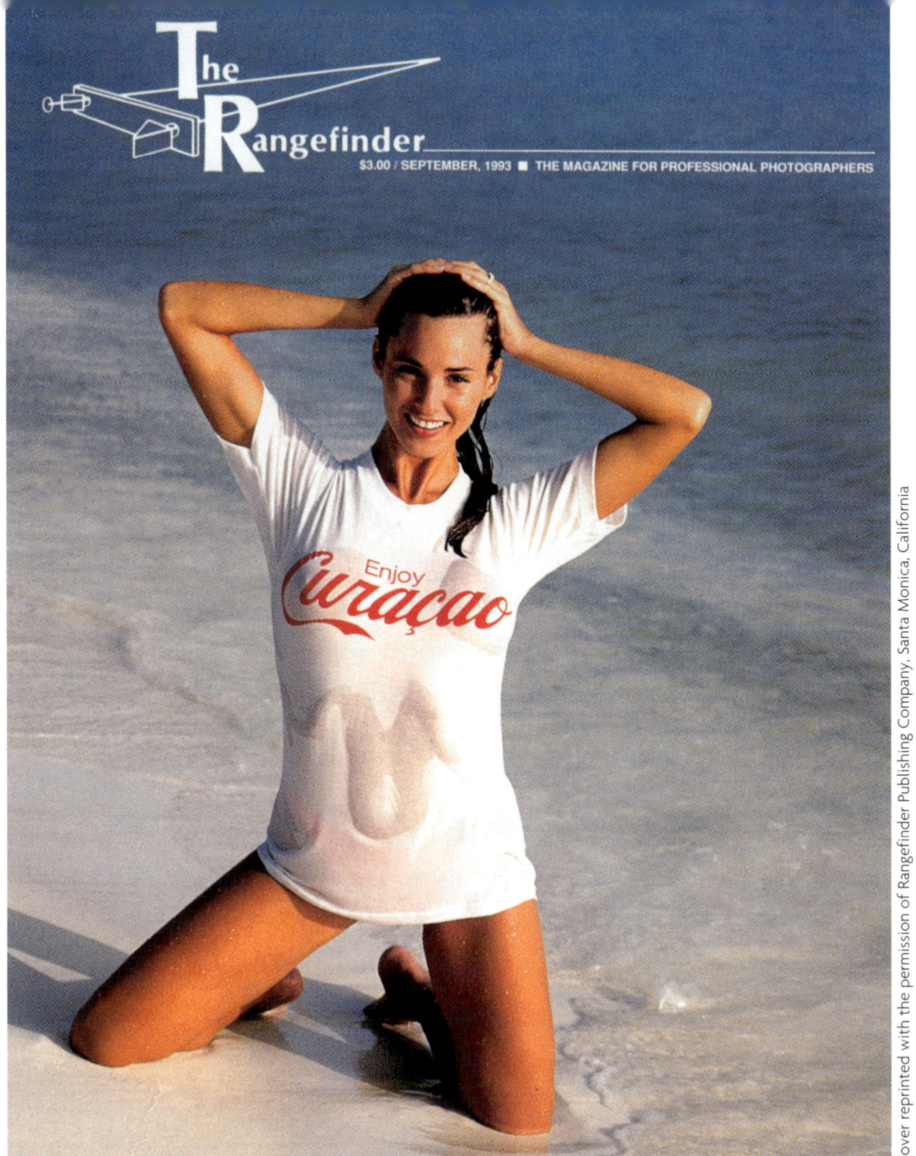

Although taken for the Curacao Tourism Board, this photo was sold several times and appeared on the cover of *The Rangefinder* magazine. Photo ©Glamour Portfolios

board. You will probably still have to pay for airfare, film, and processing. However, if you can arrange a barter deal with a tourism board, they may be able to supply you with a hotel room, food, airfare, and even a rental car. While it may take some time to sell your concept and negotiate the final deal, it is worth the effort.

To make a deal with a hotel or tourism board, first make sure you have an impressive portfolio and samples. Although your goal on location might be to shoot both stock and glamour photographs, your potential partner will only be interested in tourism-oriented images. Tourism boards have little or no interest in nudes or photographs of models in lingerie. Look through the pages of travel magazines, and you'll see photographs of couples on vacation, honeymooners, and people dining, gambling, swimming, playing tennis, and enjoying other vacation activities. If you don't already have similar photographs in your portfolio, clinching a deal may prove difficult, but don't give up! Since glamour photographers work with young, attractive women, start building your portfolio to include photographs of a model in a tennis outfit, sitting by a pool, or relaxing on the beach. If you do, your glamour portfolio will start looking more like a tourism portfolio! If you have any tear sheets or photographs made for a hotel, motel, or other tourism industry client, make sure these photographs are prominently displayed in your portfolio to show your potential partners.

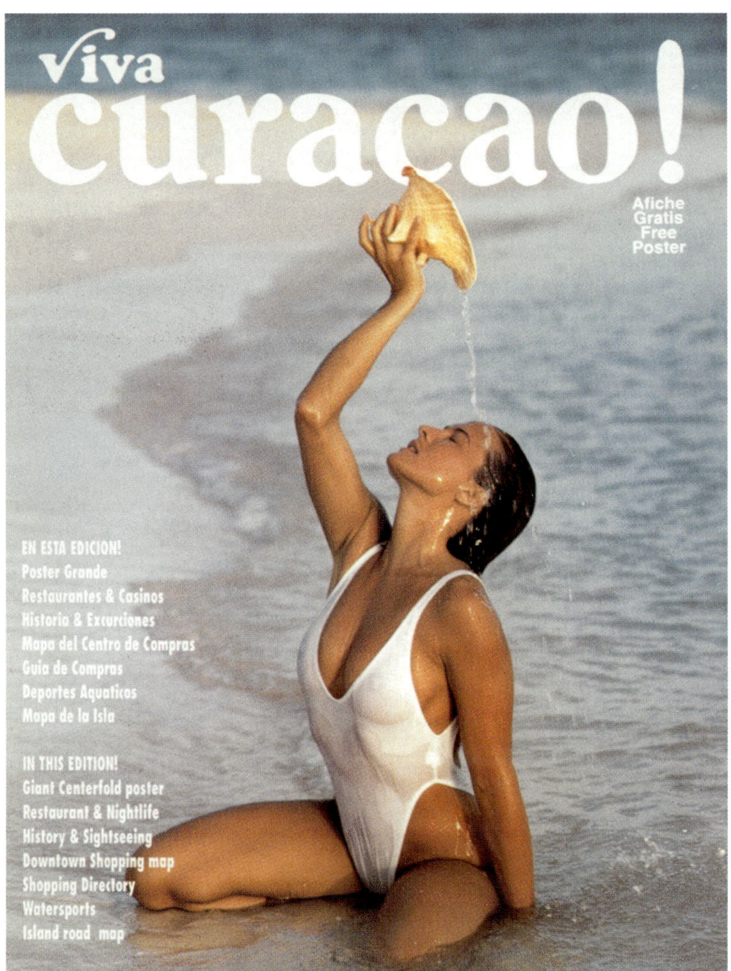

This photo was used as a cover for Curacao's local tourism magazine *Viva Curacao!* and makes a nice portfolio piece for both the photographer and his model. It's also generic enough to be sold many times for a variety of tourism-oriented clients. ©Glamour Portfolios

The next step is to prepare a cover letter. Although you may be primarily a glamour photographer, you want to show your strength as a stock or travel photographer. Make sure that your business cards and letterhead reflect these specialties. If you have a computer with a laser printer or high-quality ink-jet printer, you can make enough letterhead to cover your barter needs. If not, it would be a small but worthwhile investment to have letterhead and business cards professionally printed for this purpose. The design of your cards and letterhead does not have to be complex; they just need to contain your name displayed in a nice typeface, along with your address and phone number. You might want to place the tag line "Travel and Tourism Photography" under your name in smaller letters. Your goal is simply to make a good first impression.

Sample Cover Letter

Here's a sample cover letter showing the kind of information you might want to include in your first barter contact letter. The name and address shown are, of course, fictitious and included for formatting purposes only.

Mr. Stuart Jones
Director of Tourism, Barbados Tourism Board
100 Fifth Avenue
New York, NY 10010

Dear Mr. Jones,

My name is ‹your name›, a travel and tourism photographer located in‹your town›. During the past few years, I have enjoyed working with several tourism boards and hotels throughout the Caribbean.

Although I generally work on an assignment basis, I have also found that a barter agreement can be beneficial to all parties involved. The reason is simple: Many tourism boards and hotels need new photographs to update promotional material but don't always have the budgets required to fund a professional photo shoot.

A barter arrangement is simple, and no payment is exchanged. Usually the tourism board or hotel supplies transportation and room and board. In exchange, I will provide two to four professional models and photography services for a week, along with film and processing. We will travel throughout the island as required and produce a wide variety of photos from a preapproved list supplied by the tourism board. Typical photographs include shopping, sightseeing, hotel photographs, local attractions, beach scenes, gambling, water sports, tennis, and other common tourism situations.

At the end of the trip, all of the photographs will be processed and edited, and the tourism board will receive hundreds of original images for use in brochures, advertisements, posters, magazines—however you see fit. I will also add some of the photographs to my file of stock images and earn income from future sales through my own stock photo agency. It is an elegant "win-win" situation.

Enclosed are some samples for you to review from a recent tourism shoot that was produced on a barter basis.

If it's time to update the photographs in your advertising and promotion files, and you would like to save perhaps thousands of dollars producing them, I look forward to discussing a barter arrangement with you. There is no risk, and the benefits are many.

I will follow up with a phone call. In the meantime, if you have any questions or comments, please don't hesitate to contact me at your earliest convenience.

Sincerely,

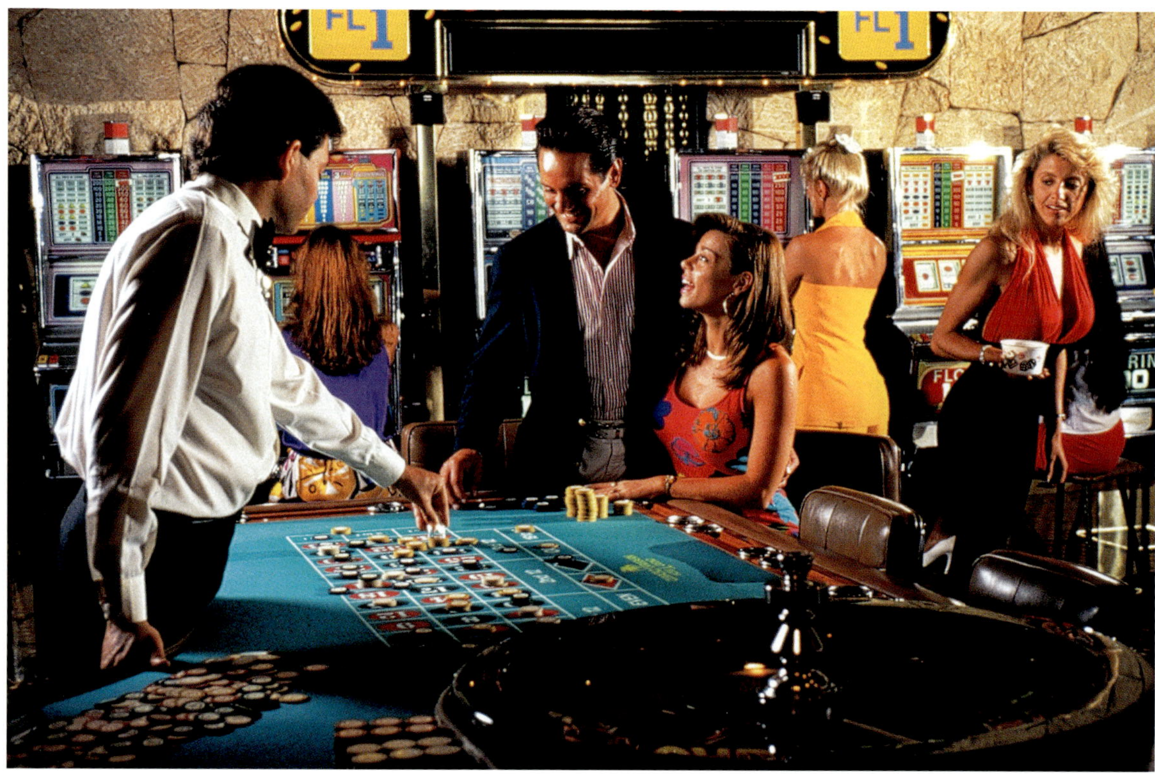

Gambling is another subject that is in demand by stock photo agencies. The tourism board made arrangements with the casino owner to allow us to shoot while the casino was closed. ©Glamour Portfolios

Barter Better

You may wish to begin the process of canvassing for potential barter partners over the phone. The advantage of using a telephone is that instead of waiting weeks for a response to a letter (if you get any response at all), you will get immediate feedback. Start by calling each one of your prospects to find out the name of the person responsible for producing the tourism board's advertising and promotional literature. Often that person will be the director of marketing or public relations, or a similar title.

Try to avoid calling on Monday or Friday. That is the worst time to call anyone with whom you are not already acquainted. On Monday, almost everyone is thinking about the work they have to get done that week. On Friday, they are thinking about their weekend activities. Stick to Tuesday through Thursday. Once you do get through to the right person, then you can begin your sales pitch, but getting past a protective secretary may prove to be a real challenge.

Let's say you are calling Mr. Thompson, the public relations director for the beautiful country of Grenada. Be prepared for some quick thinking when his secretary asks, "May I ask the purpose of this call?" At that point it is sink or swim for you, so take a deep breath, remain calm, and say something like:

> *My name is ‹your name here›, and I'm planning a photography shoot with several models in Grenada this spring. I thought Mr. Thompson might be able to use some of my photographs in the island's ads and brochures, at no charge, and I wanted to discuss this with him. Is he in, or when is a better time for me to call?*

You will probably be put on hold for a moment, and then you may hear, "Bill Thompson here, how can I help you?" Now that you have your foot in the door, this is the time to give your proposal its best shot. Here are some of the important points you should cover during that first conversation:

Point 1. You are planning a photo shoot and will be taking typical tourism-oriented photographs.

Point 2. Offer to make a large selection of photographs available for use by the tourism board in exchange for airfare, room and board, and production assistance.

Point 3. Explain that you and the models are not asking to be paid; you simply want to minimize your expenses and are looking for a barter partner who can use your photographs.

Point 4. Mention you have experience shooting tourism photographs and would be glad to work from a list of photographs needed by the tourism board.

Point 5. Offer to send samples of your photographs for their review. If you have worked for any other tourism clients, now's the time to mention them.

Once you get through this initial discussion, Mr. Thompson will either tell you that he has little interest or that your idea has potential and he would like to discuss it further. At this time, he might request a proposal in writing.

A successful barter arrangement must be a "win-win" arrangement. Your barter partner will want a large number of professionally created photographs of specific situations, detailed in a photo list given to you. These photographs will, no doubt, include your models being shown at many different tourist attractions, beaches, restaurants, shops, and museums. If free room and board are arranged for you, the hotel that is supplying those benefits will expect excellent coverage of the hotel's facilities. Even the rental car agency will expect a photograph of your models at a well-known tourist site standing and smiling by the agency's beautiful car. You get the idea: If a business is helping the tourism agency fill its end of the barter arrangement, that business will expect photographs in return. You expect airfare, a hotel room, food, a rental car, and an assistant to make all the arrangements necessary to fulfill the requirements of the photo list.

Be sure to schedule time for shooting glamour photographs, too. The tourism board probably won't need any photographs of your models in lingerie or less. So if you want time to shoot glamour and centerfold photographs and plan on spending a week on the island, offer to shoot for the tourism board for five days and explain that on the other two days you will be shooting for yourself.

If you are currently selling your images through a stock photo agency, you will no doubt notice another benefit of bartering with a tourism board or hotel. The shot list that your barter partner gave you will be similar to the "want list" the stock photo agency will periodically send you. That's why it's a good idea to think of your barter partner as part of your stock photo production staff. When you do, you will quickly see why this type of arrangement can help you build a stock file of tourism-oriented photographs at minimal cost.

Usually the tourism board can help get you whatever it is you need to shoot top-quality photographs. For example, if you want to shoot in an upscale restaurant, they can try to arrange it. If you think a 60-foot sailboat docked in the harbor would make a nice shooting location, they can try to contact the owner to make the necessary arrangements. Don't just look at your barter partner as a means to lower your overhead, but also as your local production partner, making all the necessary arrangements by supplying you with local know-how and contacts needed to produce a first-class shoot.

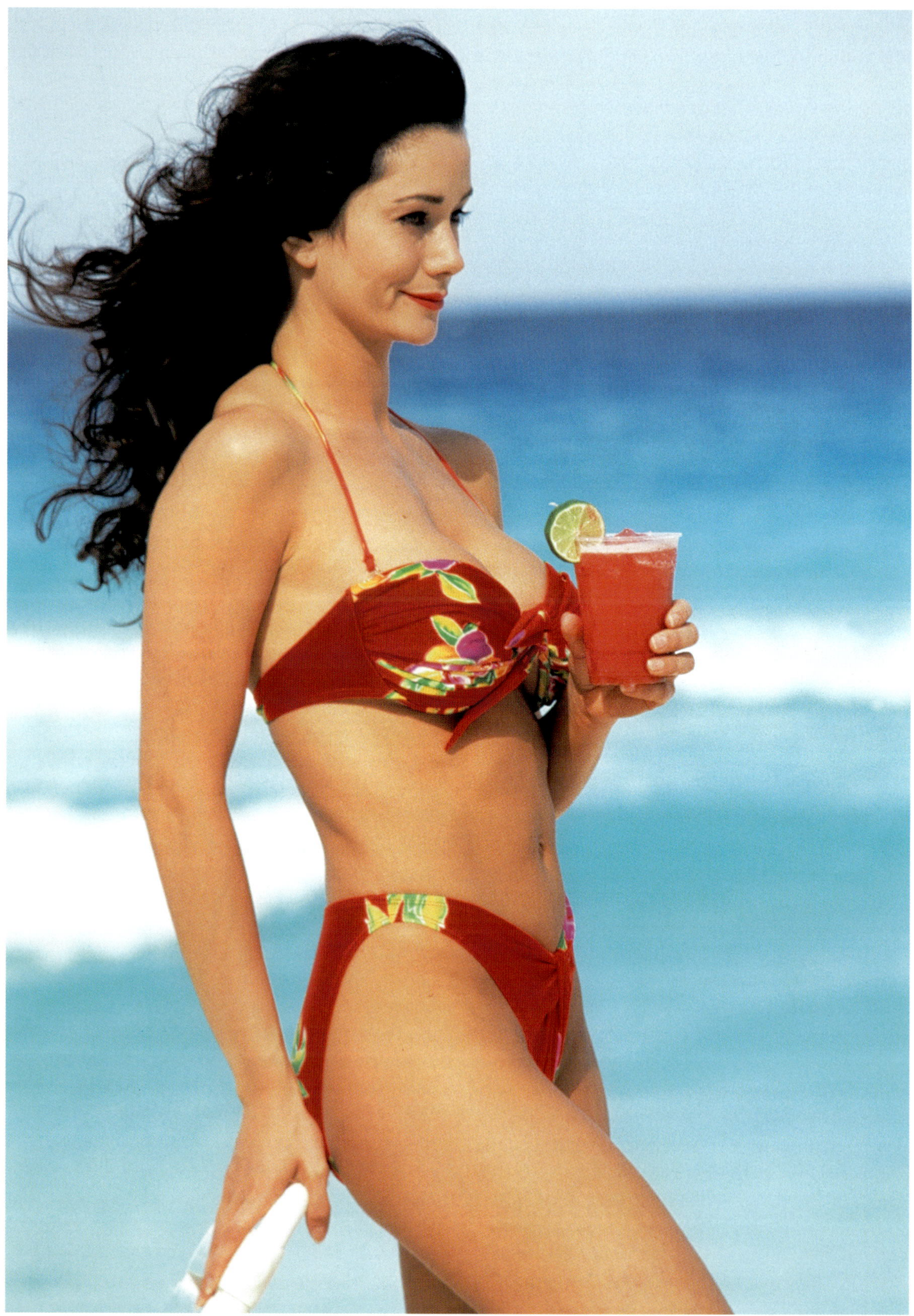

If a hotel is supplying you with room and board, the hotel management will expect photographs in return. Here is an example of one of the numerous images that the Glamour Portfolios' photographer gave to the hotel he stayed in for use in the hotel's ads and brochures. ©Glamour Portfolios

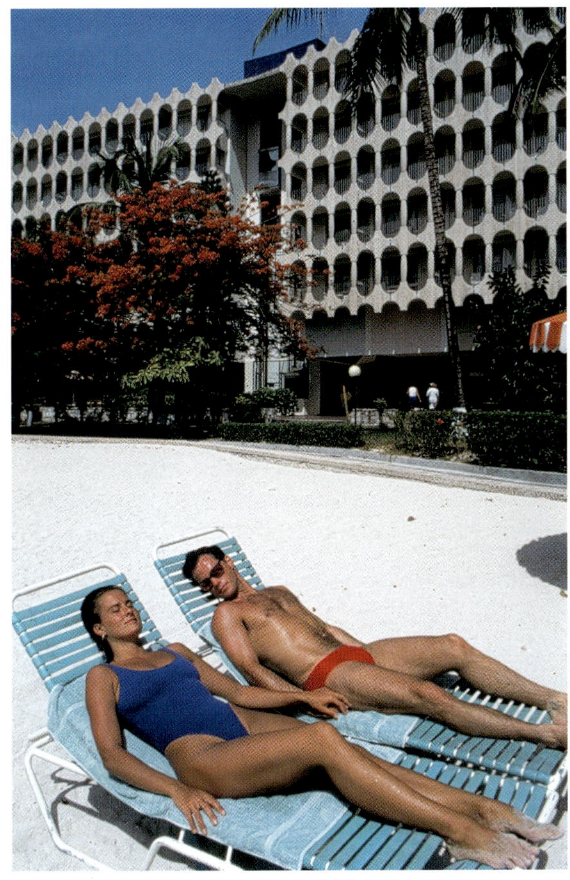

Pros and Cons

There are, of course, some potential disadvantages to any barter arrangement. This arrangement might not work if you are not interested in shooting travel-oriented stock photographs and prefer to shoot nudes all week. To fulfill your part of the bargain, you will have to spend a lot of time shooting the photographs needed by the tourism board, and, unless the hotel you are shooting at is a nudist resort, you had better keep clothes on your models most of the time!

Another point to consider is that the shot list handed to you by the agency will be long and filled with many specific photographs. Even if you are shooting for stock, some of those images will be of little use to you or your agency. However, if you are a skilled stock photographer, you will probably be able to turn most of the situations into saleable photographs.

The overall benefits and savings earned by working out a good barter arrangement can be impressive and help the part-time or semi-professional create a large, marketable file of tourism and glamour photographs at minimal cost. It will take a lot of time and persistence to find a barter partner and put together a workable deal, but you will be rewarded for your efforts. Remember that you won't be paid in cash—this is a barter deal. However, a few weeks after you return from your trip, you will have hundreds of new photographs for your stock files and a great selection of glamour and centerfold photographs to sell.

A stock photograph of a beautiful woman holding a colorful drink can be sold over and over again anywhere in the world. ©Glamour Portfolios

LETTER OF AGREEMENT

After you have made your verbal agreement with your barter partner or partners, it is a good idea to put the whole arrangement in writing. In order to avoid any possible misunderstanding between the tourism board, their agency, and you, it is prudent to clearly define the arrangement in a letter of agreement. A sample letter follows:

LETTER OF AGREEMENT

The following will be the basis for the arrangement between the photographer and all of the parties involved:

The photographer, his assistant, and five professional models will be visiting ‹destination› for a weeklong stock photography shoot beginning ‹date›. To facilitate the trip and to make photographs available to the Tourism Development Board and the advertising agency, the following terms have been agreed to by all parties:

1. The photographer, assistant, and models will waive all photography and modeling fees, and will provide model releases for all of the photographs taken during this shoot.
2. The photographer will take a reasonable number of photographs of specific locations, tourist attractions, restaurants, hotels, casinos, government buildings, etc., as requested by the Tourism Development Board and their advertising agency. If required, the photographer will also take specific photographs for the hotel in which the group is staying.
3. The photographer will pay for all film and processing, and will provide the advertising agency and Tourism Development Board with a selection of original 35mm transparencies.
4. The Tourism Development Board will provide the photographer and members of his group with the following:

1. Round-trip airfare from ‹departure city›
2. Hotel rooms and all meals while on the island
3. Ground transportation to and from all photo locations
4. Assistance with obtaining permission for use of locations such as stores, casinos, hotels, etc.

5. The photographer, his assistant, and models will be responsible for any incidental costs, such as telephone calls, laundry, etc., while staying at the hotel.
6. The Tourism Development Board and advertising agency will receive unlimited use of the photographs for advertising and promotional purposes. Whenever photographs are used, the photographer will receive a photo credit.

Please contact me if you require any modifications of the above terms and conditions, otherwise this letter will serve as the basis for our agreement and understanding.

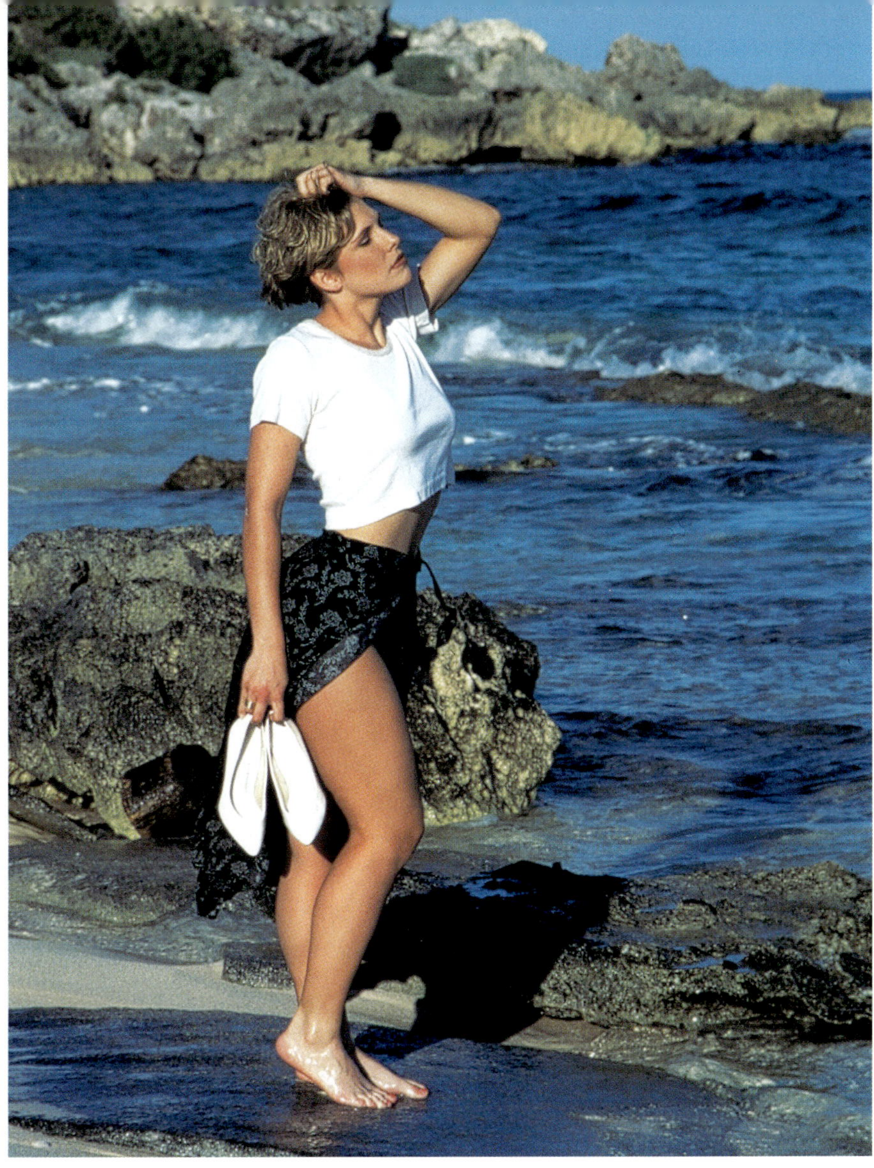

When shooting models at a beach location, try to use a variety of outfits, including swimsuits and, as shown here, casual sportswear. Different types of clothing will permit a wider variety of stock sales. ©Glamour Portfolios

How Many Images Are Enough?

While most of the terms of the letter of agreement are clear, you may be asking how many photographs constitute a "reasonable selection" of images that the photographer will be required to provide to his or her barter partners. There is no set rule as to how many free photographs you need to provide; this is a very important topic that needs to be discussed with your partners during the original negotiations, and you should make a minimum number of images a part of the letter of agreement.

The decision on what the final number will be is more a factor of how many subjects your partners request from their shot list, how detailed the coverage they require is, and how much time and film you are willing to trade in exchange for all expenses being covered. You need to be fair, and your barter partners need to be reasonable.

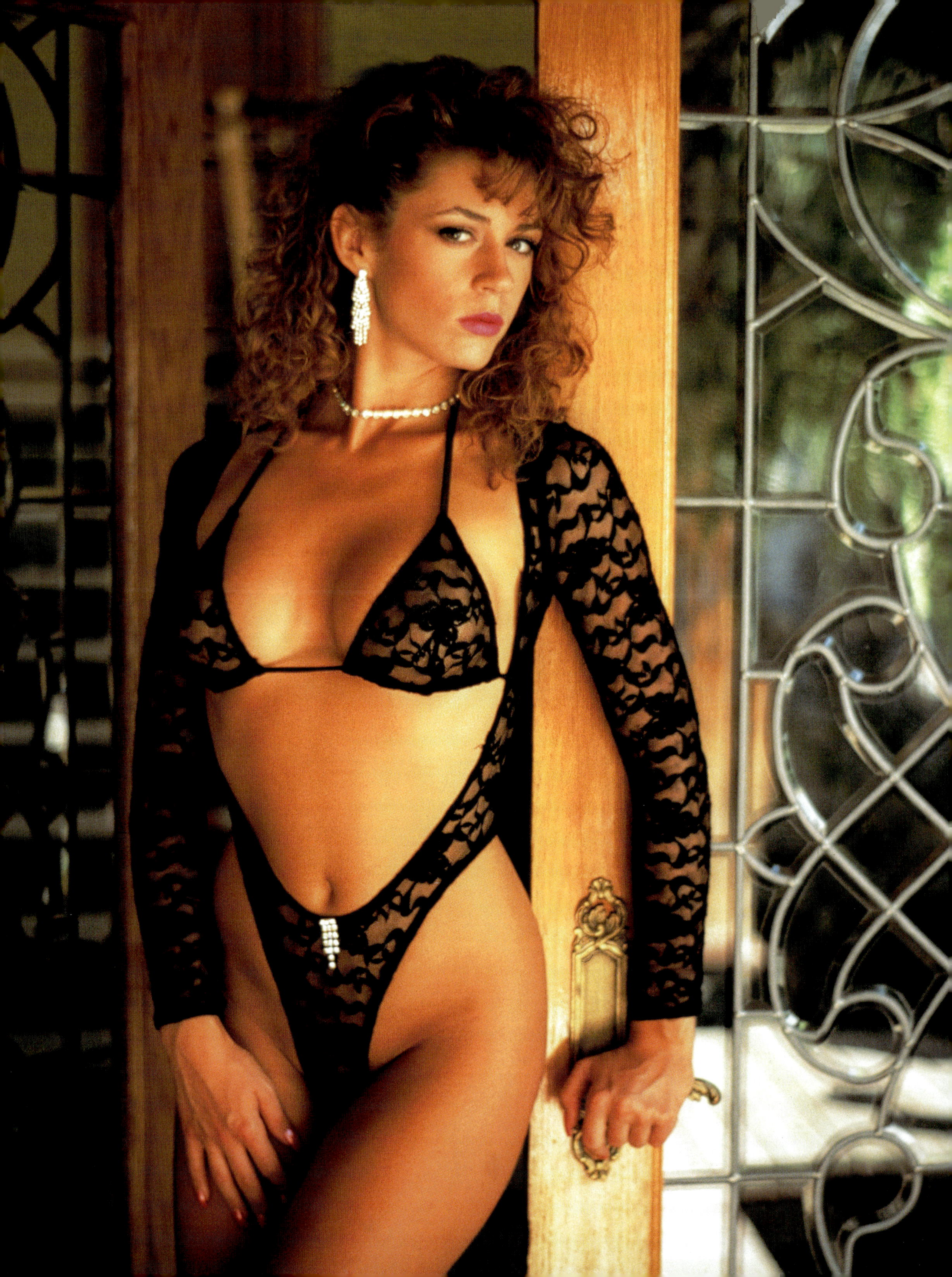

7

How to Pose Your Models

How to pose models in tasteful but sexy ways

When creating saleable photographs, one of the most important skills a glamour photographer can develop is knowing how to pose models. Anybody can make a photograph of a beautiful model, but if her pose is awkward, clumsy, or unattractive, it will reduce your ability to sell those photographs. Since you will often be working with beginning models, it's important that the part-time glamour photographer develop a basic understanding of posing techniques that will assist your model as she moves in front of your camera.

POSING TIPS

One of the easiest ways to learn about posing models is to look through magazines. You will quickly notice how the poses used in a typical fashion magazine like *Vogue* are different from those that you'll see in a men's magazine like *Playboy*. While models in both magazines are beautiful and sexy, the poses found in a fashion magazine are usually less suggestive or sexual in nature.

Sometimes you might want to pose your nude model in a non-suggestive manner. Can't be done, you say? All you have to do is look at classic figure studies produced by painters. Examine the nude images produced by photographers such as Edward Weston. Even though the model is often totally nude in this kind of classic photograph, she is portrayed in an almost asexual manner and rarely has eye contact with the camera.

The markets you will be targeting to sell your photographs will help determine what poses you will choose. Any pose that is too suggestive or sexual in nature will probably not sell in many traditional glamour markets. If you are interested in selling photographs for adult-oriented uses, then your photographs must not be too conservative. Before starting to pose your model, give some thought to how and where your photographs are going to be marketed.

A FEW POSING GUIDELINES

A model's pose is really a form of body language. It can determine as much of the style and character of your final photograph as the expression on her face. Regardless of the final usage of your images, here are a few suggestions that will help you create glamour poses that work:

1. Keep your poses elegant and natural. If your model can't easily put her body into the pose you are suggesting, it's probably not a good pose.

2. Poses should flow naturally. When a model is in a good pose, it shouldn't look like a pose at all. She should appear natural, at ease, and comfortable. That's not to say that a pose can't be dramatic or exciting, but if your audience is thinking more about the pose than the model, it's probably not a great pose.

Here a doorway is used not only as a compositional element, but also to assist the model with her posing. Just the simple act of holding onto the doorknob is enough to place the model in a natural and comfortable pose. ©Glamour Portfolios

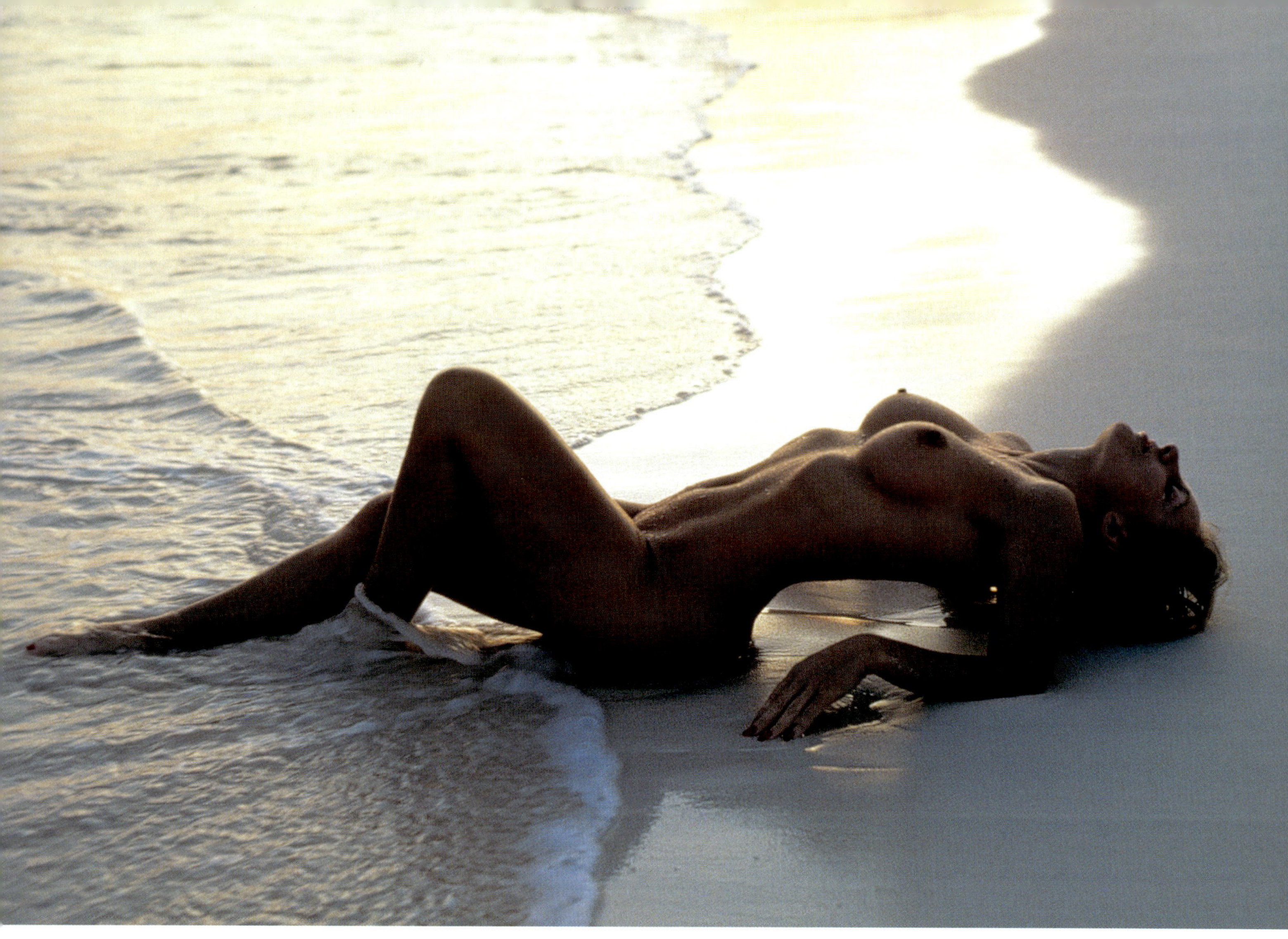

Since there are no clothes or props to date the photograph, the elegant and timeless pose used in a classic full-length figure study can help an image sell for years to come. ©Glamour Portfolios

3. Avoid tacky or dated poses. Just as lighting techniques change over time, so do poses. If you take a look at some of the magazines from the '50s or '60s, you'll see what I mean. Not only do the lighting, hairstyles, makeup, and props have a dated look, but many poses, particularly in men's magazines of the day, have a "cheesecake" or "pinup" style that is clearly no longer in vogue. Current glamour photography styles are more sensual, provocative, and, above all, natural.

4. Avoid pornographic-looking poses. For beginning glamour shooters, it's often difficult to decide where centerfold photography ends and pornography begins. Go to a newsstand and review some current magazines to see poses that demonstrate the difference. A quick comparison of the photographs seen in *Playboy* and *Hustler* should be all the education you need on this subject.
A Supreme Court Justice once remarked about pornography, "I know it when I see it," and it's important that you be able to tell the difference, too. Nothing will turn a beautiful glamour photograph into pornography faster than a sexually explicit or tasteless pose. A photographer I know uses the following rule to determine when he has crossed that line: "If I feel comfortable showing the photo to my wife, it's a glamour shot. If not, it's probably porn."

5. It's a good idea to let your model sit or lean on a prop. Nothing is harder for a beginning model than standing in one place and trying to strike a variety of different poses. Look around your location to see if your model has something to lean or sit on. If you're shooting outdoors, let her lean against a rock, tree, car, or bench—anything! If you're shooting indoors, a big, comfortable armchair, couch, or bed will bring out natural and often sexy poses. You will be surprised to see how quickly a beginning model who looks and feels awkward while standing becomes elegant and natural when she's given a comfortable prop to work with.

Don't make beginning models stand to strike a pose. Most inexperienced models feel more comfortable when seated or leaning against something. The more relaxed they are, the better their poses and expressions will be. ©Glamour Portfolios

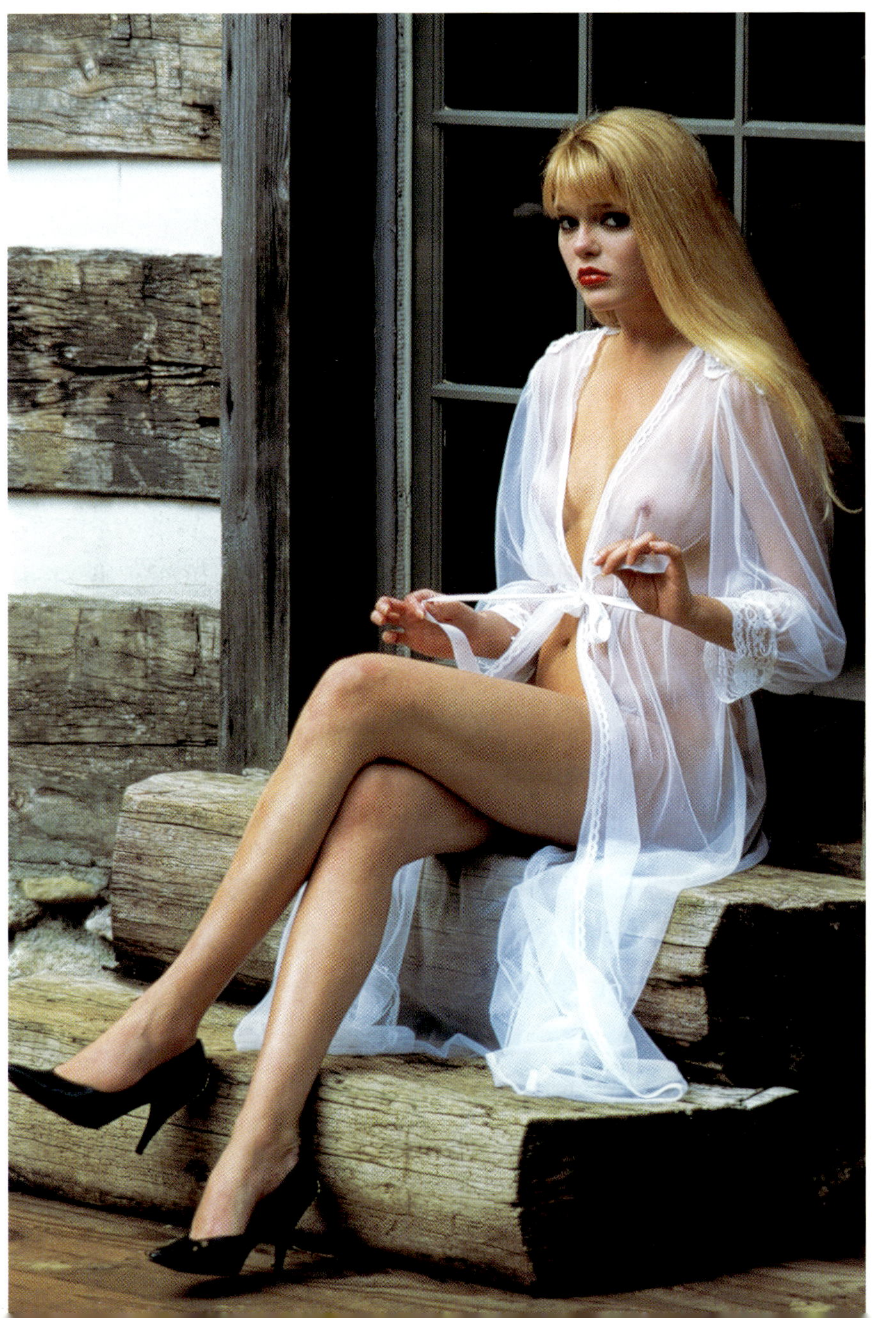

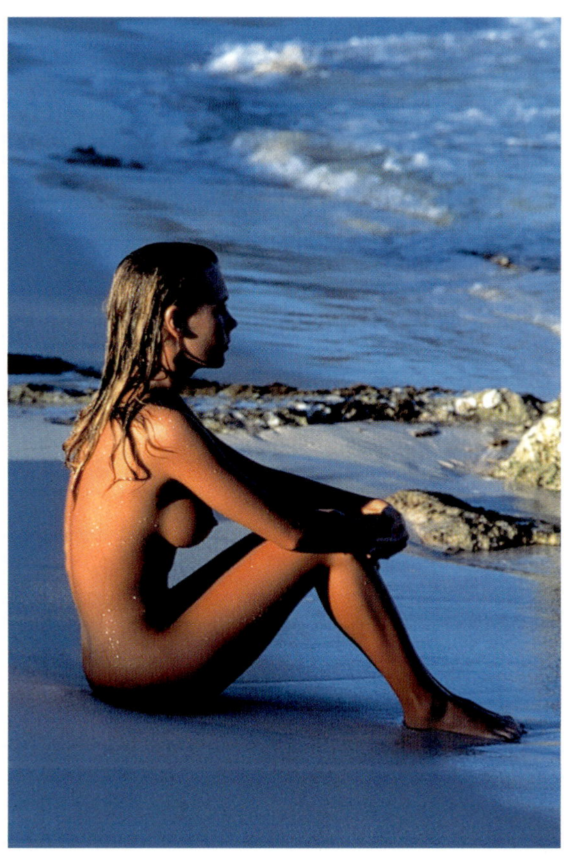

Sometimes good poses happen by accident. After an extended shoot on the beach, the model sat down to rest. The photographer liked what he saw and took a few photos. The resulting photo worked better than other photographs from the same session. ©Glamour Portfolios

A POSING SEQUENCE

It is a good idea to develop a standard sequence of poses that you can use with every new model. One technique that is successfully used by Glamour Portfolios' photographers is to guide their models through a simple yet elegant striptease. This method works well, because the goal is to create a variety of photographs during each session. When the session is finished, there will be some photographs with the model fully clothed, a few topless photographs, and several nude images. Once your model is familiar with this technique, you will find that it is an efficient and easy way to shoot.

Here's how this method works:

Start with the model fully clothed. Shoot a few head shots, some mid-length photos, and then several full-length shots. Besides being useful for traditional glamour sales, the model will probably want some of these photographs from the shoot for herself.

Once these shots are made, have the model begin removing her clothing. Shoot some photographs with her blouse off, then have her remove her bra while you continue shooting. Be sure to take photographs from a variety of angles and with different facial expressions.

If your model is agreeable to doing nudes, continue the sequence by having her remove her panties. Again, shoot from a variety of angles. Try to shoot some nudes without showing pubic hair. In some Asian countries, such as Japan, showing pubic hair is banned, even in adult magazines.

Shooting a 36-exposure roll of film during this sequence is a simple way to get many marketable photographs of a single model wearing one outfit. After your sequence of photographs is completed, have the model change her outfit, and go through the sequence again in the same or at a new location.

Photographing your model in a step-by-step sequence is an efficient and creative way to maximize the number of saleable photographs from each session. In this sequence, the model starts off completely clothed then removes one element of her outfit at a time. By changing the focal length of a zoom lens, you can quickly vary the framing from a head shot to a full-length shot for each pose in the series. ©Glamour Portfolios

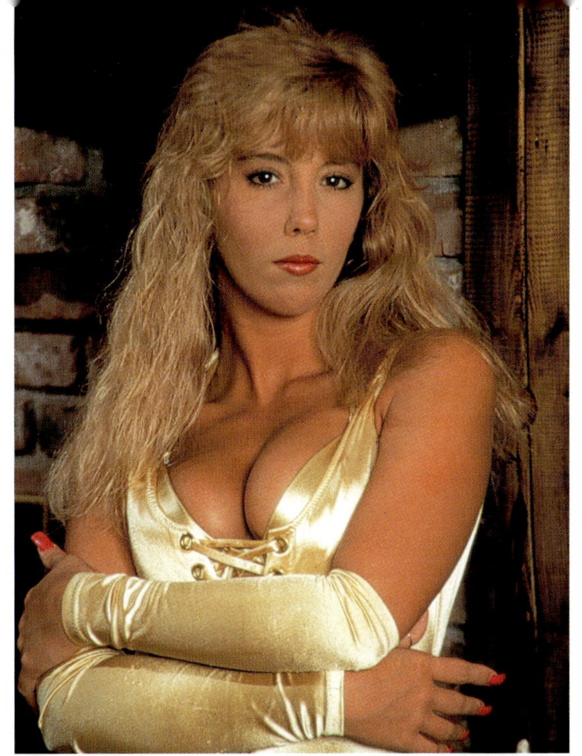

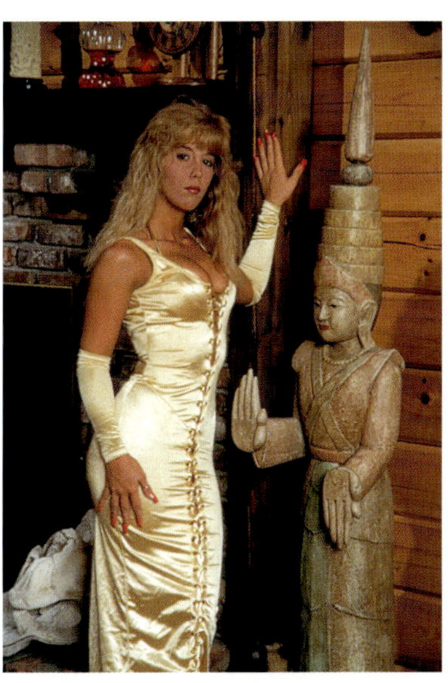

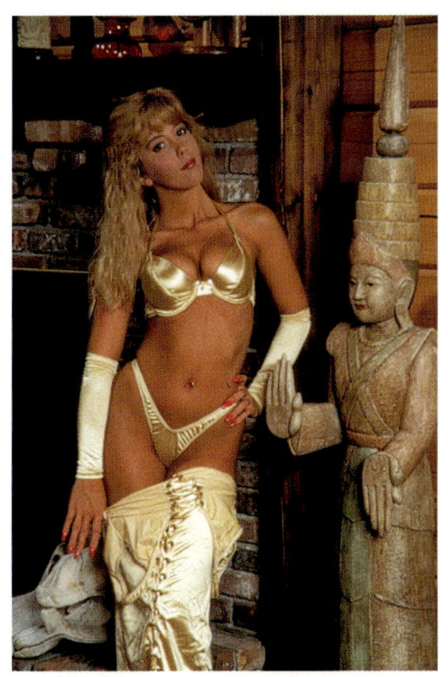

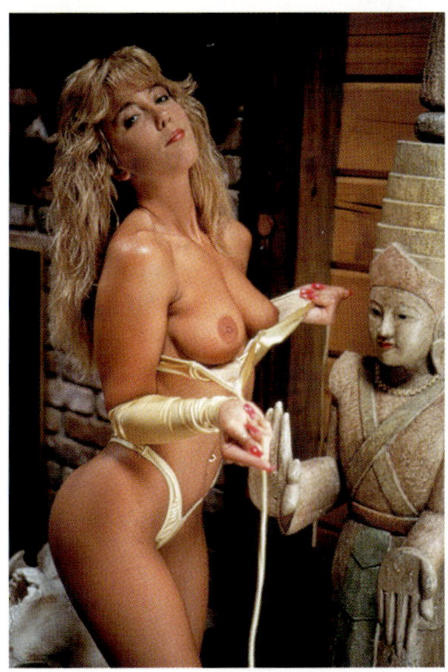

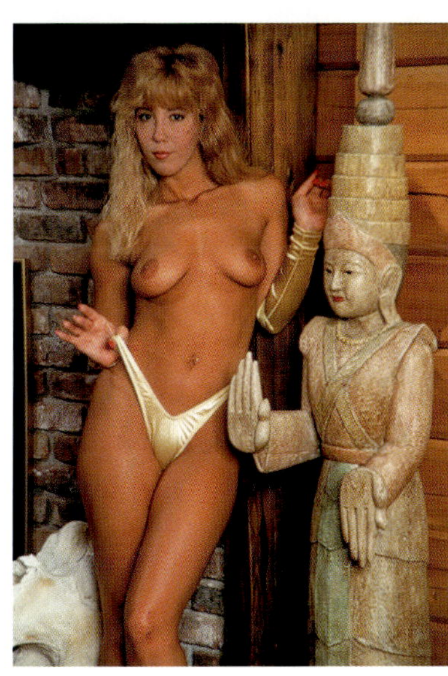

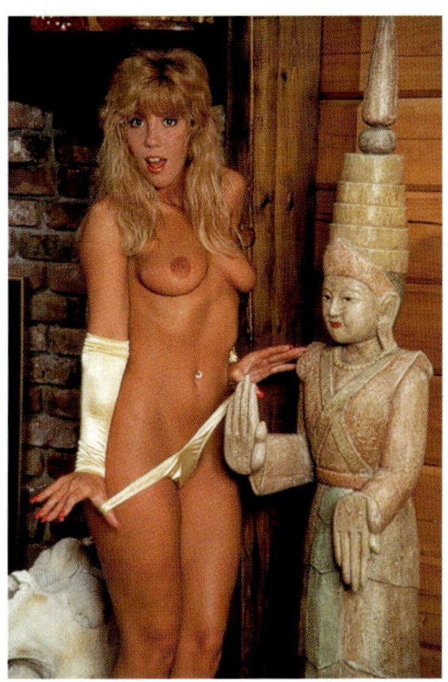

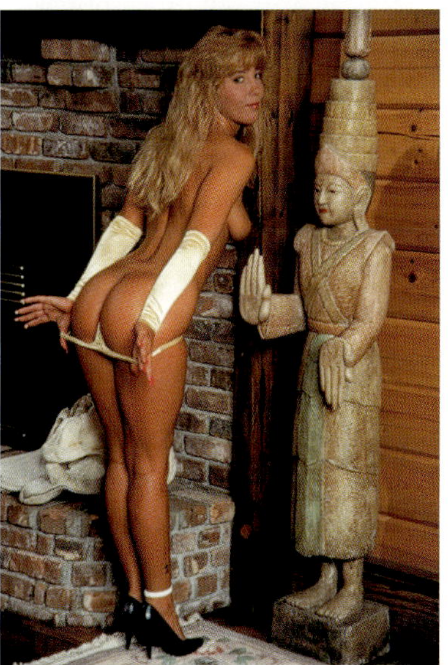

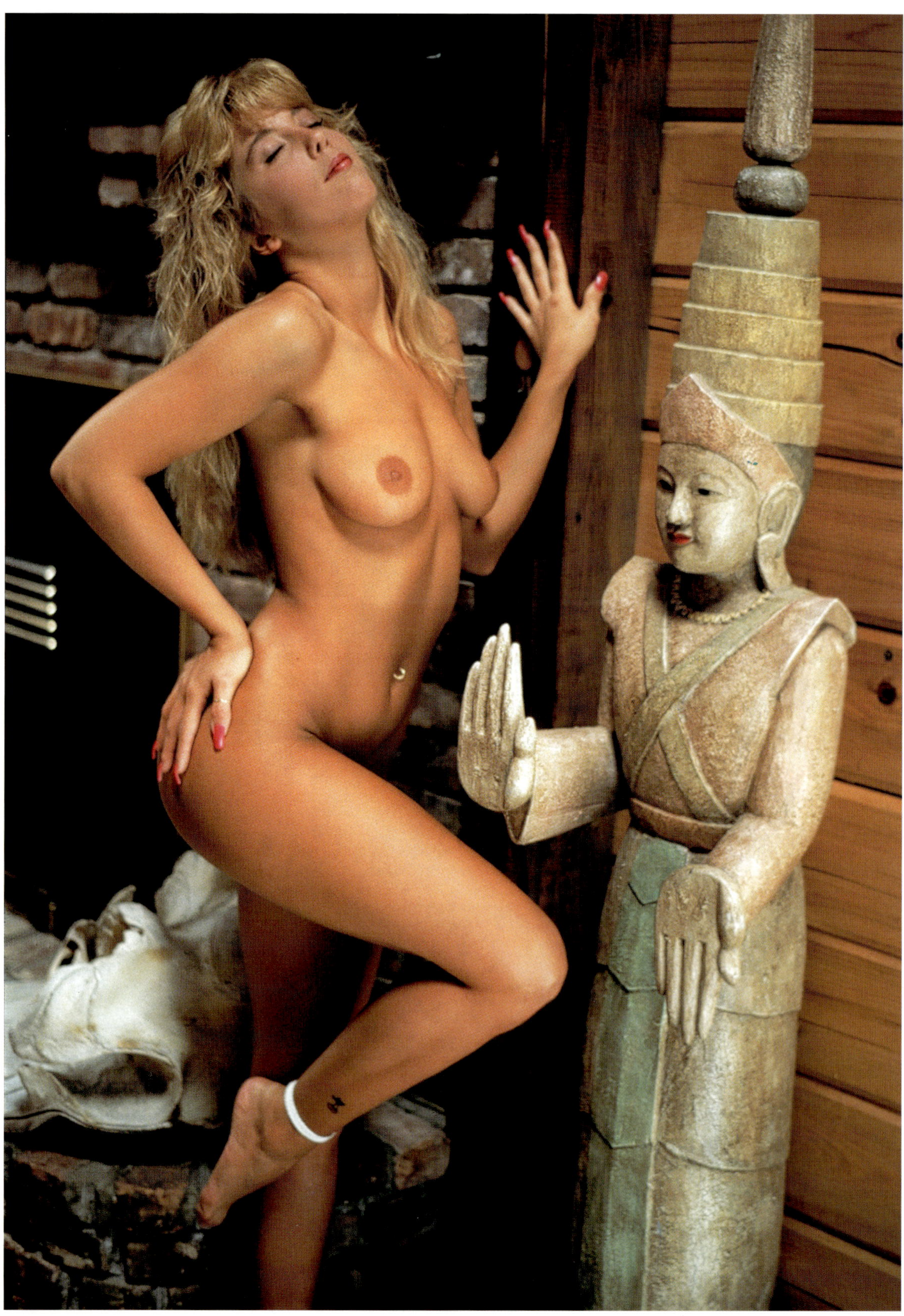

Improving on Mother Nature

Few models are perfect. Even many top models have some minor imperfections from gaps in their teeth to tattoos. If you asked your model to appear nude during your initial casting session, you shouldn't have any surprises when she undresses during an actual photo session. The secret to getting the most useful images from each session is keep your model's flaws in mind as you have her pose. Tattoos, as long as they are small, are easy to work with. Just turn your model so they don't show, or have her cover them with a piece of clothing or a hand. If the design is attractive, you can include tattoos in some of your shots, but keep in mind they can limit sales. A small flower is one thing—a skull and crossbones quite another.

You should also be aware of the possibility of scars from breast augmentations. Usually these will be found under the breasts or sometimes near the armpit or nipple. In addition to scars, breast augmentations don't always look natural. It's important to be aware of this fact before you start shooting, and it's another reason for getting a good look at your model during your initial casting session. One way to improve the appearance of less-than-perfect breasts is to have your model cross her arms, squeezing the breasts together. This pose will make her breasts appear larger, and any gaps in her cleavage will be minimized. Scars underneath her breasts can also be hidden by having her hold her breasts in her hands or by creatively draping garments to hide imperfections.

Here's an image of a model who looks playful and at ease. The photographer took advantage of simple props that aided the model in her pose. ©Glamour Portfolios

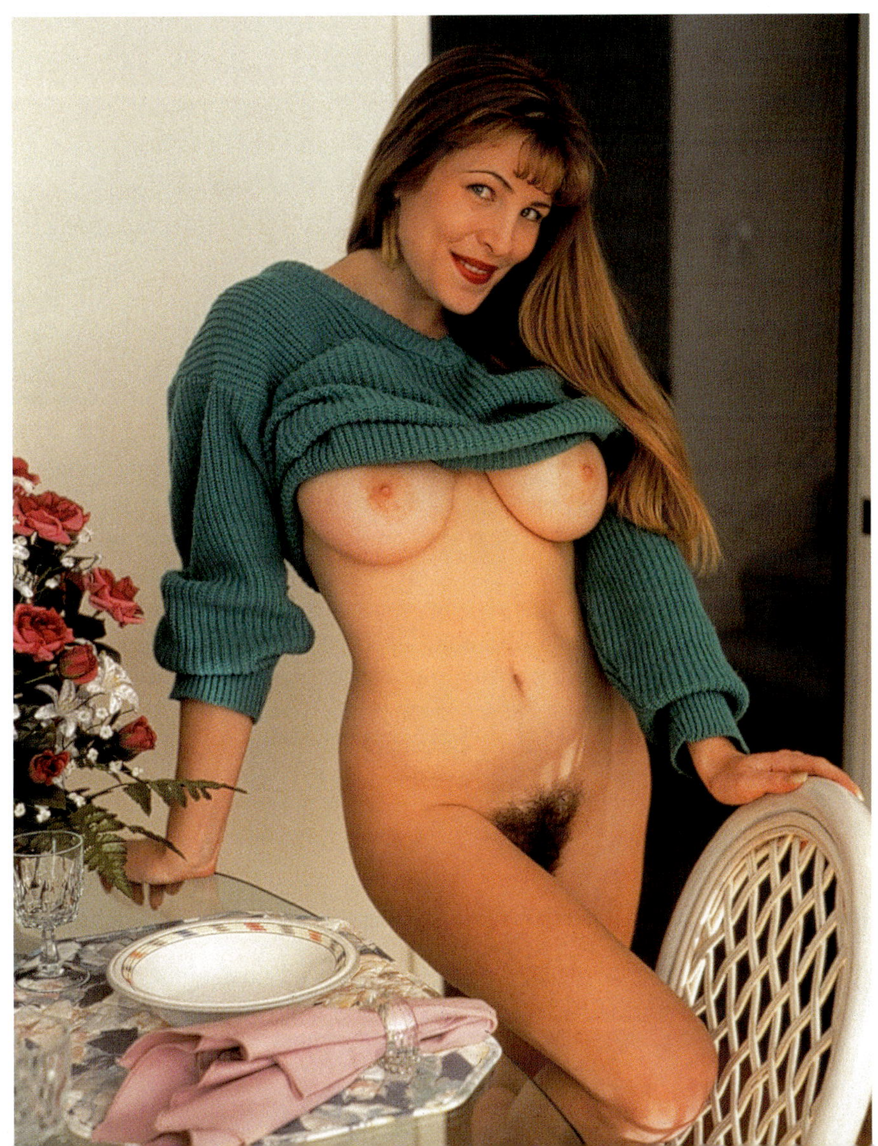

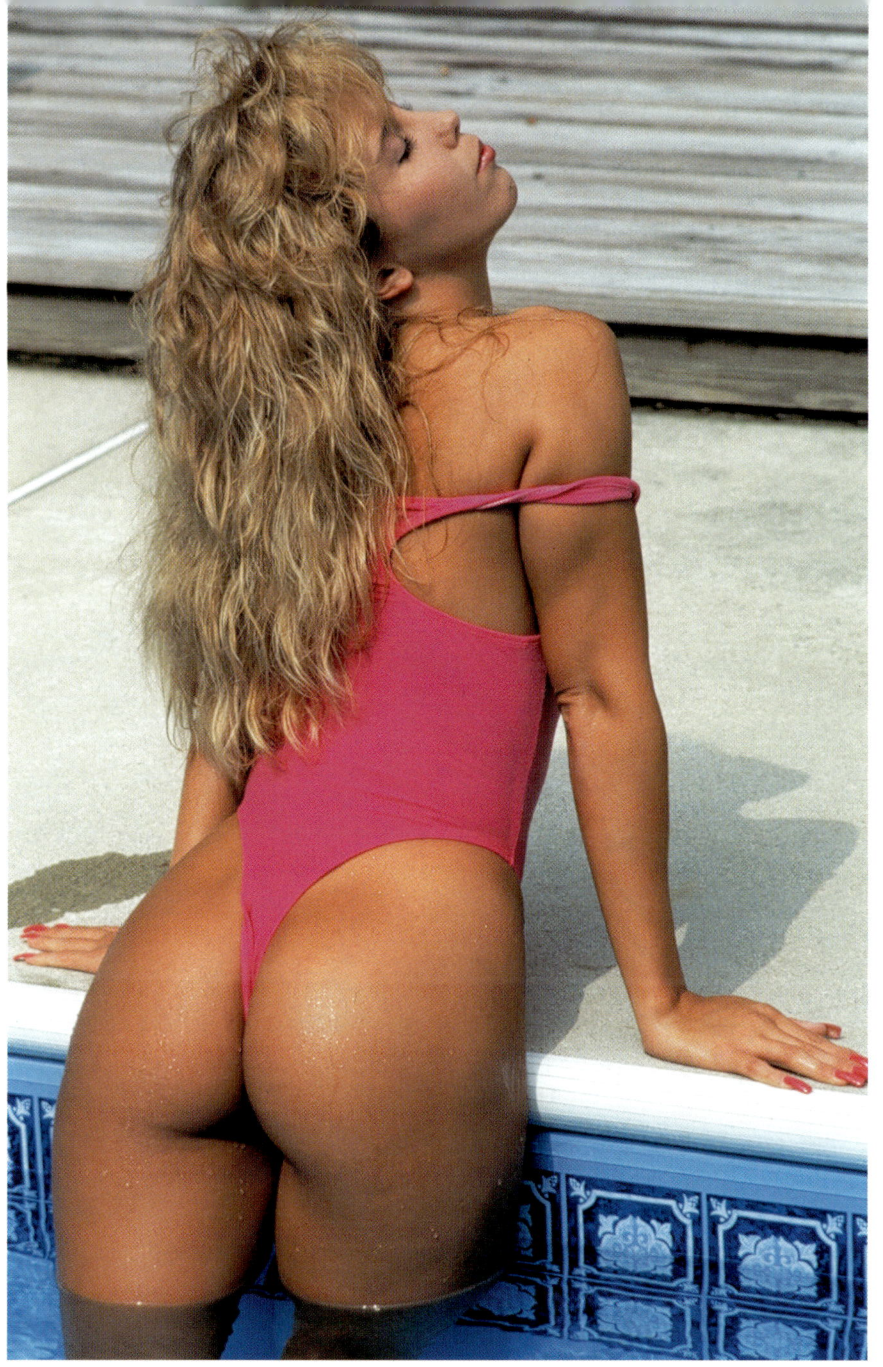

When posing models, don't forget to have them turn their backs to the camera for some shots. Often models look as sexy from the back as they do from the front. ©Glamour Portfolios

Just as it's important to minimize any flaws your model might have, it's equally important to look for her strong points and accent those features. Are her eyes particularly beautiful? Get in close. Does she have long, shapely legs? Shoot several images from a low angle. Are her breasts large and attractive? Avoid poses where she might be lying on her back. Does she have long, flowing hair? Here the reverse may be best—pose her lying on a bed or the floor with her hair arranged behind her. All of these positive features led you to hire her in the first place, and making them part of your posing sequences will help increase sales of your photographs.

This pose accentuates the model's slim waist and hips as well as her long, beautiful hair. ©Glamour Portfolios

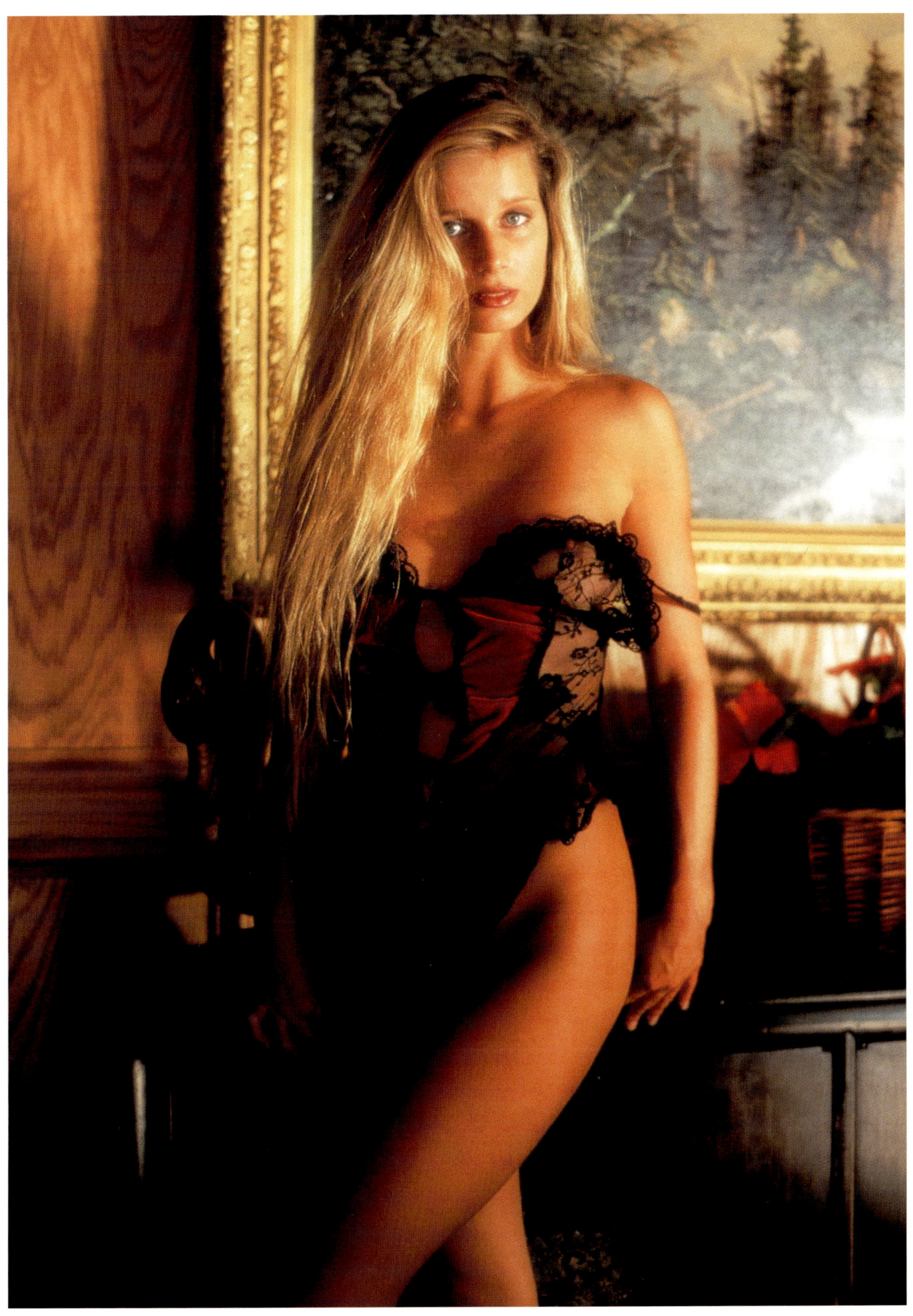

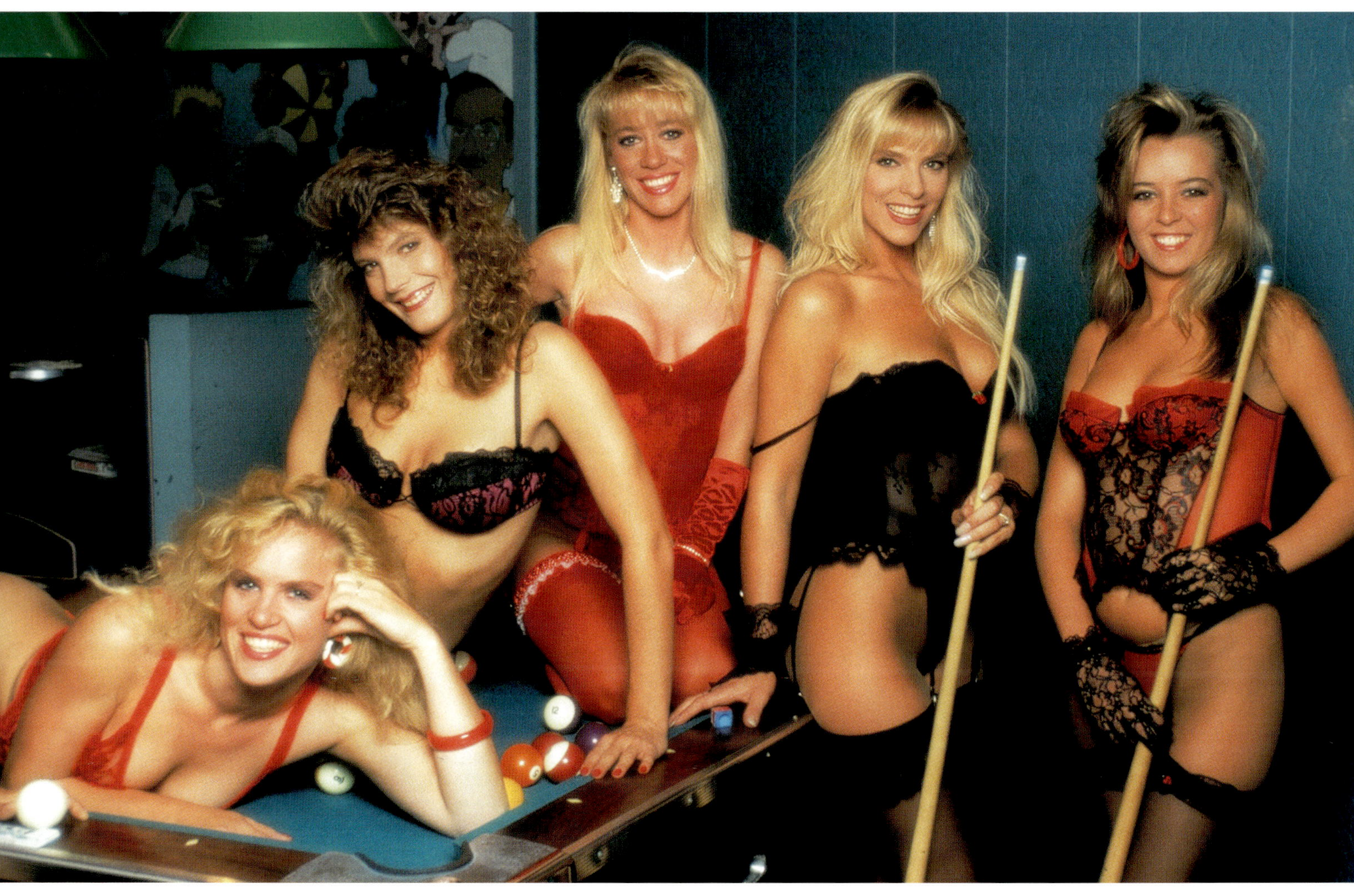

Posing several models at once takes patience and a watchful eye. Pose each model one at a time, and take a few shots. Then switch poses. Allow the composition to flow and not look too cluttered. ©Glamour Portfolios

Hair and Makeup

One important aspect of your shooting often overlooked by beginning glamour photographers is the importance of having good hair styling and makeup. Depending on your budget and the style in which you like to shoot, you have two choices: You can hire a professional hair and makeup artist or have the model do them herself. There are benefits and drawbacks to both options.

For many shoots, particularly when you do not plan to shoot tight head shots, the model might be perfectly capable of doing her own hair and makeup. If this is the case, be sure to go over the style of makeup you want to see for the session before the model starts applying it. Just to be safe, keep an eye on her face while she applies her makeup. Unless you are looking for a dramatic effect, it's important that you keep the makeup clean and simple. Makeup that is too stylish might look dated a few years from now and can have a negative impact on your sales. Similarly, hairstyles should be simple and classic. Avoid any hairstyle that detracts from the overall shot so that you can maximize image sales.

If you feel your model is not capable of doing a good job with her own hair and makeup, or if you're looking for a particular style, you might want to hire a professional hair and makeup artist. If you are located in a large city, it isn't difficult to find hair and makeup artists through a talent directory or references from other photographers. However, if you're in a smaller city or town, it might not be as easy. Consider approaching an upscale salon to see if staff members would freelance for photo shoots. Often you can get someone to do hair and makeup in exchange for photographs of themselves. If a barter arrangement isn't possible, expect to pay at least $50 - $100 per hour or per head.

One thing to keep in mind—particularly when working with beginning hair and makeup artists—is that they often try to create dramatic styles. They want their work to be noticed, and it takes an experienced hair and makeup artist to do a truly natural look. Just as when working with a model, good communication is important when working with a makeup artist. Describe the look you want, and keep an eye on your model as her makeup is being applied and her hair styled. The last thing you want is to frustrate the model and makeup artist by having them work for an hour or more just to have the final results unsuitable for your photographs.

Lights, Camera, Action

Once her hair and makeup are done, it's time to begin shooting. Remember to give your model time to warm up. When working with beginning models, don't expect them to walk in front of your camera and move effortlessly from pose to pose. Give instructions clearly, and stay calm and relaxed if the model is having any difficulty following them. The better you are at expressing your ideas and making your model feel at ease, the better your photographs will turn out.

Some photographers bring sample photographs to a session in order to help the model visualize their poses more easily. If you're doing a full glamour shoot, there is nothing wrong with bringing a copy of *Playboy* magazine and showing your model the type of poses and attitude you are looking for.

Whether you are shooting a model in a dress, swimsuit, or totally nude, keep in mind that a model's pose is among the most important elements of your finished photograph. A great pose can turn an otherwise average shot into one that can be sold again and again. Look beyond the model's eyes, expression, garments, and your location and props. Those are important, but don't forget that the pose can help pull all the elements together into a visually exciting, creative, and marketable photo.

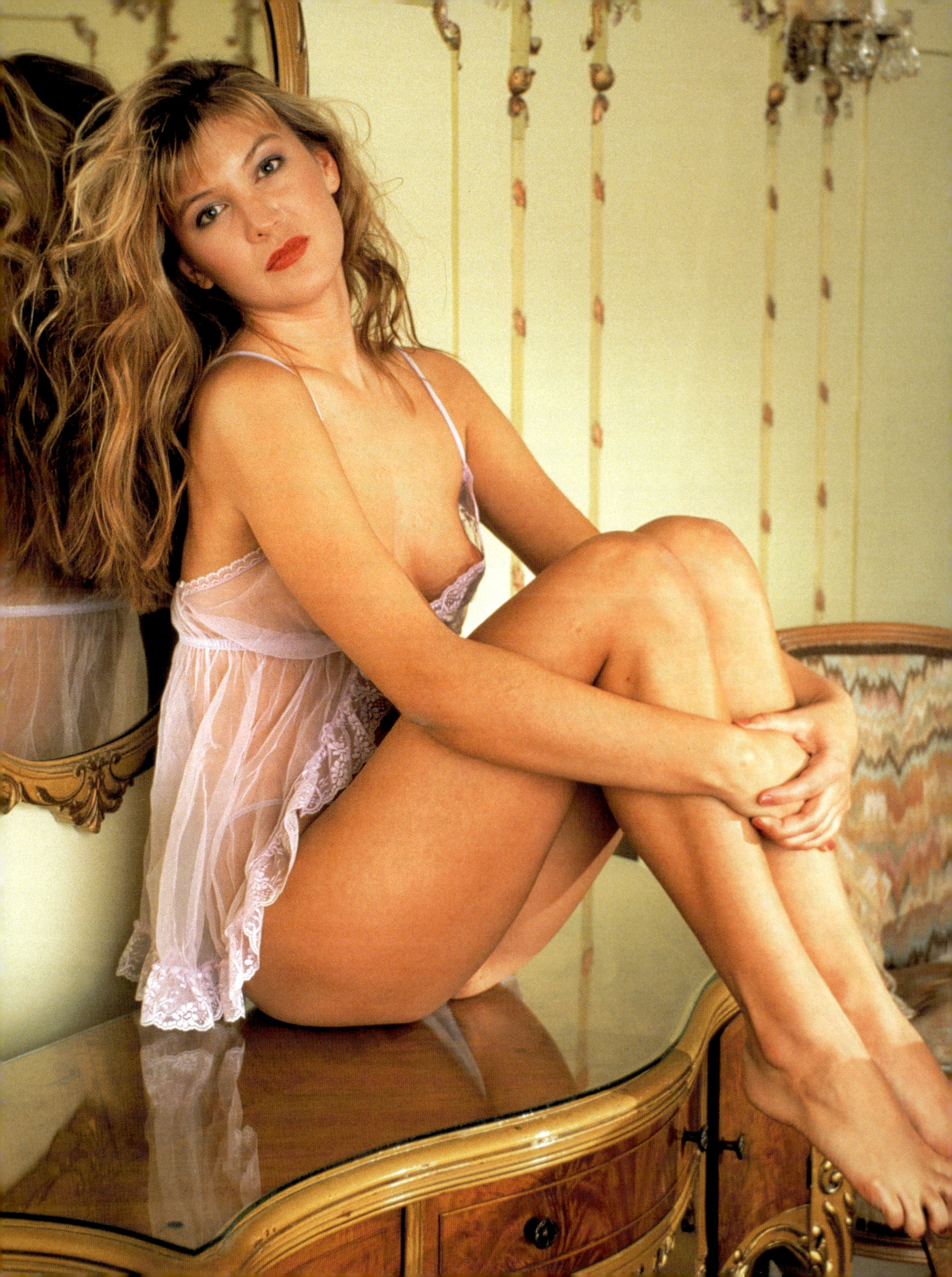

8
Working From Home

How to create a successful workplace at home

As a part-time glamour photographer, it is likely that you will be working out of your home. Working at home is the dream of many, but not everyone is suited to having a home office. Some find there are just too many distractions—lawns to cut, cleaning to do, and errands to run. On the other hand, for those who revel in sorting slides in sweats, e-mailing in pajamas, and setting you own schedule, there is no better life.

Perhaps your home office will be nothing more than a desk in the corner of your den or basement—a place where you can keep business papers. As your part-time photography business starts to grow, you will soon find that you need more room to store your photographic equipment, accessories, lights, slides, prints, and all of the paperwork that goes with running a well-organized business. Don't be surprised when you quickly outgrow that corner desk and start thinking about spreading out a bit.

IT'S A SMALL WORLD

Each year, an increasing number of people work from their homes, taking advantage of e-mail, fax, overnight delivery services, and the Internet. Some work full-time doing the same job they might be doing at an office, while others work part-time, perhaps making some extra income from their hobbies.

As a part-time glamour photographer, you can start your business small—working just a few hours each week or even each month. If things go well and your income starts to grow, you will need to expand the space dedicated to your business. There are many successful companies that started in the homes of entrepreneurs with just a good idea, a bit of luck, and a healthy dose of determination. Apple Computer, for example, was founded by two guys working out of a garage. While that particular instance might be a bit extreme, there are many examples of business novices coming up with good ideas and building their hobbies into large, successful businesses. With the Internet available as a powerful marketing and research tool, it's never been easier to start a business and have instant, worldwide access to new customers.

One of the biggest battles you will wage in setting up your home office is finding enough space to get started. No matter how large your home office may measure in square feet, it just never seems big enough for the project you are currently working on. While space may always be at a premium, there are ways to maximize your utilization of that space. You just have to learn to be creative. Most home offices are in basements or, like mine, in spare bedrooms. Of course, you can also make use of attics, lofts, and garages. Be sure to consider the design, aesthetics, and style aspects of creating a functional home office. There are books available on this subject that can help you make the most of your home space.

If you happen to have attractive rooms in your house, take advantage of them, and use them as backgrounds. If not, rent a hotel room or fantasy suite, available in most cities. ©Glamour Portfolios

Setting Up Your Office

Just as each photographer's visual style differs, so will his or her work habits. Here are some basic concepts you should keep in mind when setting up a home office.

Keep your work space separate from other rooms regularly used by family members. Rather than setting up your desk or office in your family room, living room, or bedroom, seek out a quiet corner of your home where you can work undisturbed. Although one of the biggest benefits of working at home is being near your family, this doesn't mean your children can be running around playing hide-and-seek while you're on the phone speaking with models or clients. A good location for your office might be an unused bedroom or an empty corner of your basement. If you live in an apartment or condominium and don't have any extra room, consider purchasing a computer armoire for your bedroom that opens up into a small office workspace. This way when your work is done, you can close the doors and your mini-office disappears. These kinds of armoires are available in many furniture stores.

Set up specific home office hours. Even if you work only a few hours a week, it's a good idea to schedule those hours and stick to the schedule. That way, your family will know when you are working and will (hopefully) respect those hours as your "private time." If you are constantly running up and down to your office when your spouse or children want you to spend time with them, you'll quickly find that your family will begin to resent your part-time business. Working from home is a balancing act that requires thought and understanding; having scheduled hours is the best first step to balancing your glamour photography business with your family life.

Don't go overboard buying expensive office equipment. The whole idea of working from home is to be productive and efficient in a home setting, and there is really no need to fill your office with oak filing cabinets, Formica worktables, or other paraphernalia to mimick a traditional office. Your home office can be casual and homey; it doesn't have to look like an office at all, mine certainly doesn't. Your desk can be a secondhand dining room table; your filing cabinets can be a series of wicker baskets. Whatever design you choose, keep an eye on your bottom line. It is much better to invest your profits in model fees and photo shoots than on expensive office equipment.

If possible, your home office should have a window so you can see what's going on outside—if the sun is shining or if it's starting to snow. This feature is important to maintaining a healthy emotional outlook, but you may be limited to what space is available in your house. If you don't have any windows, pick up travel posters to create your own "window on the world." Why not decorate your office with a few 16x20-inch prints of your favorite travel photographs?

Get the best ergonomic chair you can afford. It may sound like a minor detail, but buying a chair that provides the best back support will keep you comfortable, healthy, and productive.

Listen to your favorite kind of music while working. Don't use a radio, because commercials will interrupt your concentration. Instead, use your computer's CD-ROM drive to play your favorite CDs. Connect a set of speakers to the computer for better sound.

A Computer, Too

The heart of any home office is the computer. Since it will probably be obsolete in about nine months, your computer should be the fastest one you can afford. If you don't, after it's obsolete, you will berate yourself for not buying the best you could have. Tip: Take advantage of the "same-as-cash" promotions offered by some computer superstores to buy your computer now but pay later without interest charges.

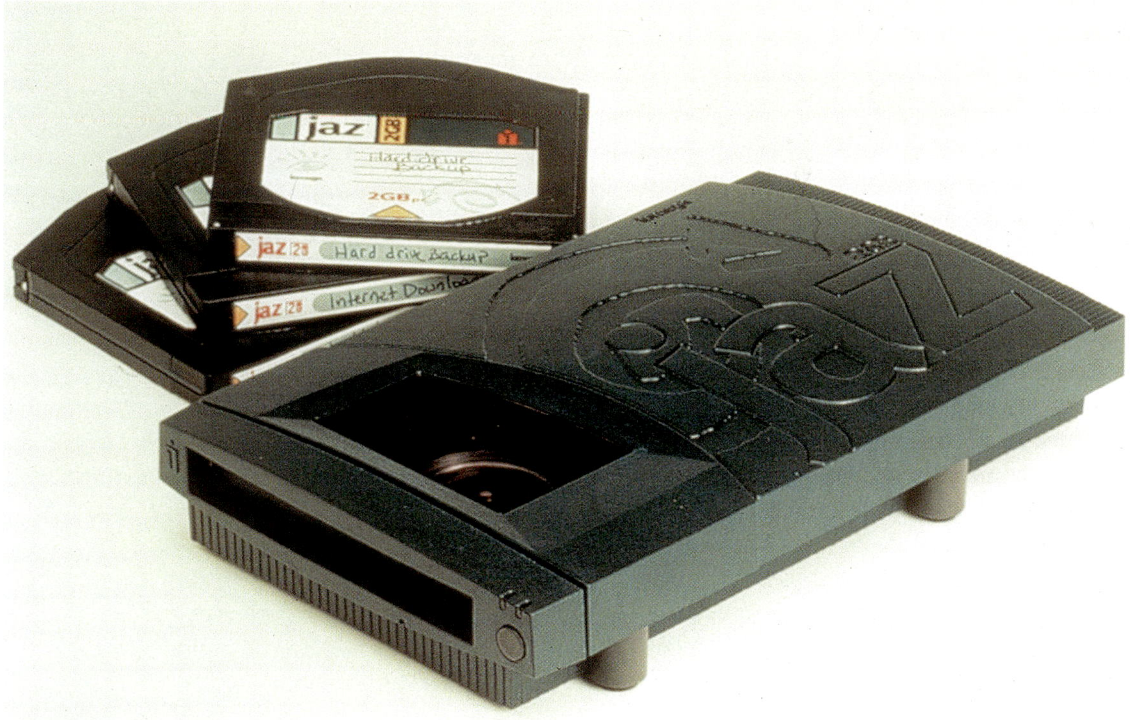

One home office essential is removable storage, such as the 2GB Jaz drive from Iomega. You can use the cartridges to store images for your Web site, your promotional material, or to back up your hard disk. Photograph courtesy of Iomega

You may even need to buy a backup computer. Assign the second computer duties such as e-mail, and use it to try installing programs that might crash your primary computer.

Mac OS users—I know this is heresy to some—should consider a Windows computer as a second machine. Having a Windows machine gives you access to programs not available for the Mac OS and provides the cross-platform flexibility at-home workers need. By the same token, Windows 98 users might consider a Mac OS machine as a second computer. To make interaction between the different operating systems easy, Mac OS users should install a copy of DataViz's MacOpener software on their Windows computer. This indispensable utility lets Windows users read and write Mac OS floppy disks. MacOpener supports SyQuest, Iomega, and Bernoulli removable media; CD-ROM and Sony MO drives; and Mac OS hard drives. When running MacOpener with Windows 95 or 98, the full file name is retained when moving files from a Macintosh disk onto the PC's hard disk. The program also lets you preview Mac text and graphics files before copying them.

You are going to need a modem for your e-mail and Internet access (more on that in the next chapter). You don't need to spend a lot of money; forget voice mail features and other bundled software. All this does is slow down your computer, so go for the hardware. The speed of transmission will, in most cases, be limited by the telephone network you are connected to, not the modem. With a "splitter" (you can purchase one at Radio Shack), you can plug your modem into the same line your fax machine is using.

Back up, back up, and back up—everyday. It is insanity not to do so. Get two Iomega Zip or Jaz drives—one for each machine. Get one internal and one external model to be able to swap back and forth or carry to a service bureau or client's location. Zip drives and disks are inexpensive, and both Mac OS and PC-compatible versions are bundled with backup software. Each week put a backup disk off-site in your safe deposit box. If you do not already have one, talk with your banker and get one. Some checking and savings plans offer a free safe deposit box. At-home workers need to take advantage of as many of these cost-saving options as they can.

Communication

One of the most important considerations when setting up your work-at-home environment is your communication system. Effective communication is your only link with other people and will have a major impact on your success. You need it all: voice, data, fax, and e-mail, but you do not have to go broke in the process.

Let's start with your telephone. Bite the bullet and have a second line—a business line—installed. By having a separate phone and answering machine, you can turn off the ringer on that phone in the evening so you won't disturb your family. A second line will add a listing in the phone book and keep your kids from tying up the line when they are home from school. Also, with a separate line, you can prevent your kids from taking any messages from your models. Imagine coming home from your day job to be greeted by your 12-year-old son with the following message: "Dad, a girl named Tammy called, and she wants to know if she should bring her red bra and panties to the shoot." Needless to say, it's better to have complete control over your phone messages.

Even if you don't have any children, having a dedicated business line provides additional flexibility for your communications system. You'll need an answering machine or voice mail from your local telephone company. A cordless phone is my recommendation, so if you briefly leave your home office for any reason, you can carry the phone and answer any important calls you are expecting. Don't get call-waiting. It says to your clients, "Excuse me, I have to take a call from someone who may be more important than you are." Do get caller ID. It allows you to screen calls and can be programmed to divert telemarketing calls that are common during the early months of any new at-home business.

Purchase a separate fax machine. Fax modems are too slow for incoming use and can tie up your computer. You can combine two functions and buy a fax/answering machine that will automatically recognize the difference between a voice or fax call. Have a jack for the home line installed in your office when your business line is installed. That way you can give your home

Indispensable Software

One of the best ways to make labels for your glamour slides to include your copyright and filing system information is with Perfect Niche's CRADOC Caption Writer software. For many years it has been the de facto standard in slide-captioning software. The current version supports Avery slide labels and lets you print up to five lines of text with approximately 28 characters per line. The program provides sequential numbering (alphanumeric or numeric), roll/frame numbering, and even bar codes. Its database capabilities automatically save label information and stores it for printing. A search function lets you find a label with any word or number, and you can export data into other programs, such as Microsoft Excel or Works, WordPerfect, dBase, and FoxPro. Perfect Niche can supply archival labels that have a pH between 7.5 and 8.0 and have been tested for photographic use.

number as a "dedicated" fax line. Even inexpensive fax/answering machines can be programmed not to ring so the noise won't interfere with the telephone conversation you might be having on your business line.

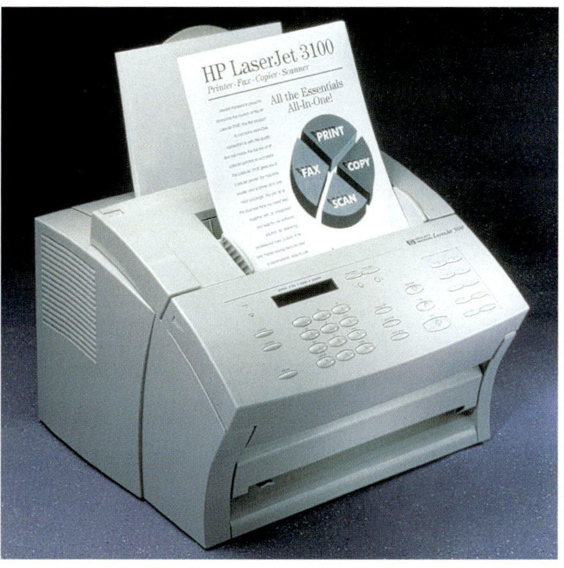

Multifunction peripherals, such as this HP LaserJet 3100, combine the functions of computer printer, fax machine, desktop copier, and scanner in one package—saving precious home office space. Photograph courtesy of Hewlett Packard

Because they share many of the same components, it was inevitable that the functions of a scanner, copier, fax, printer, and answering machine would be wrapped up into a single unit. There is even a buzzword for these devices—MFP for "multifunctional peripheral." MFPs are available from many companies, including Hewlett Packard and Brother, and models that print, fax, and copy in full color are becoming more common. Although you'll spend more for an MFP than for a fax machine or printer, it is less costly than purchasing a separate machine to perform each function. And if space is a consideration in your home office, there are also obvious benefits to having multifunctional peripherals.

The least expensive e-mail option is—free! Juno Online Services' software is free, and access is free—usually through a local telephone number. The software is currently designed for Windows-based computers, but Juno expects to have a Mac OS version available in the future. Juno's software displays commercial messages, but anyone who has surfed the Internet knows there's nothing unusual about seeing ads for everything from diet colas to sneakers to automobiles while on-line. You can get the free software by calling 800-654-JUNO. After running the setup program, it asks for basic information about your computer and telephone, then automatically configures itself. At that point you get to pick your e-mail address and a password. Next you see the member questionnaire. If you ever filled out a warranty card, you will recognize this as market research. After filling in this information, it's a matter of launching and using the service.

Home Office Benefits

One of the key benefits of working out of your home is that you get to spend more time with your family. Although it's usually a good idea to separate your family time from your work time, at least you can be close to them while you're working. You'll find that a commute to your basement is faster and more enjoyable than sitting in traffic. Another benefit is that you can give your business time to grow before investing in outside office or studio space, unless your photographic specialty requires the use of a studio. Many photojournalists, photo illustrators, and travel photographers don't need a studio on a full-time basis. If they do, there are rental studios available in most cities. You can do the same thing.

A great benefit to having a home office is that it is usually tax-deductible, along with other business-related expenses. The Federal government has recently relaxed the rules regarding deductions for home offices, but before you go overboard, seek the advice of an accountant, or you might find yourself in the middle of a tax audit.

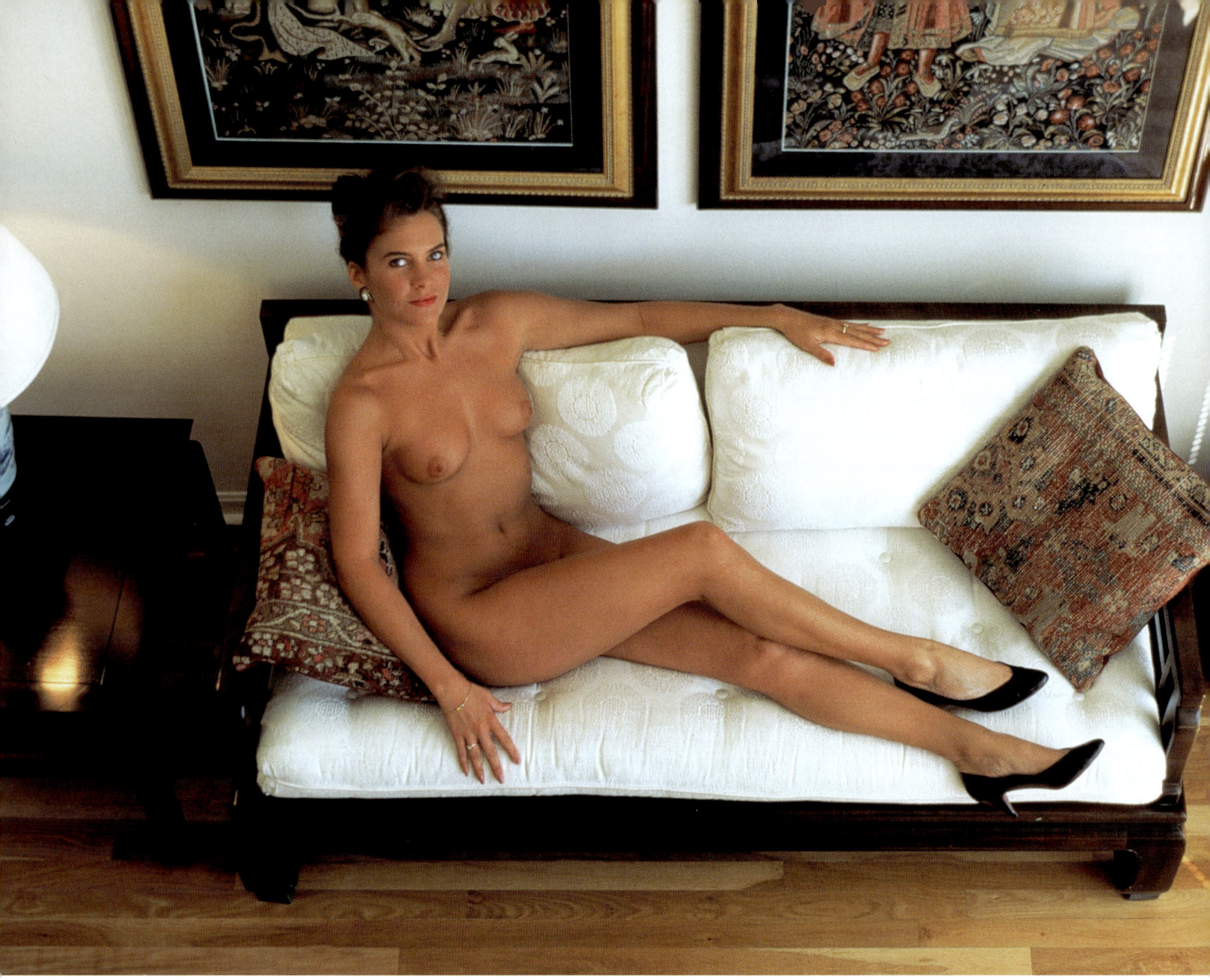

If you're running your glamour photography business from home and you have children, a lockable office or filing cabinet is a must. You don't want your images to be "show-and-tell" for the neighborhood kids. ©Glamour Portfolios

Taking advantage of a flexible work schedule is a great benefit of running a part-time, home-based business. While now you might have a 9-to-5 job, working part-time means you can create a schedule that works best for you. Perhaps to start, you'll only work on weekends. If you prefer, you can work evenings after your regular job. The point is it's not when you work but how productive you are in the time available. Because you are your own boss, you can work as many hours or as few hours as you choose.

There Are Drawbacks, Too

Although there are real benefits to working from home, there are drawbacks, too. If you work out of your home, some models or clients might not think of you as a "real" professional. They may be used to dealing with photographers who have studios. It is easy to overcome this attitude if your home is impressive-looking, or at least neat and clean with a separate office. If your house is a mess and your kids are running around while you try to have a meeting, you will not make a good first impression.

The same negative attitude may be true of some of your would-be peers. When I started my own business working out of my home, members of a local professional photographers' association almost wouldn't let me join, because they looked askance at photographers who had home offices. They even had a derogatory name for us—"bathtubbers," as if we would develop our prints in our bathtubs.

If you are regularly interviewing models for your glamour photography, you might want to give some consideration to the flow of sexy, young women coming in and out of your front door. Although totally innocent and professional, it might cause your neighbors to wonder what you are up to. Keep in mind that some of the models you may be interviewing might dress in a sexy or provocative manner. One photographer I know went so far as to have a separate driveway constructed, along with a separate entrance for clients and models.

Just as you will want to keep your family members away from your phone messages, it's important to have enough privacy in your office area for meetings and to make sure that young, wandering hands and eyes don't wreak havoc on your photographic files, negatives, slides, camera equipment, and computer. Obviously if you have young children, you should consider setting up your office, home studio, or storage area in a part of the house that can be locked when not in use. If that's not possible, it is important you discuss the need for privacy with your family.

The most important drawback of working at home is that it can become a distraction and take time away from your family. It's human nature to be so involved in a project that interests you that you may wander off to your office when your family members thought you would be spending time with them. Don't give in to temptation; make sure you give your spouse and children all the time they deserve.

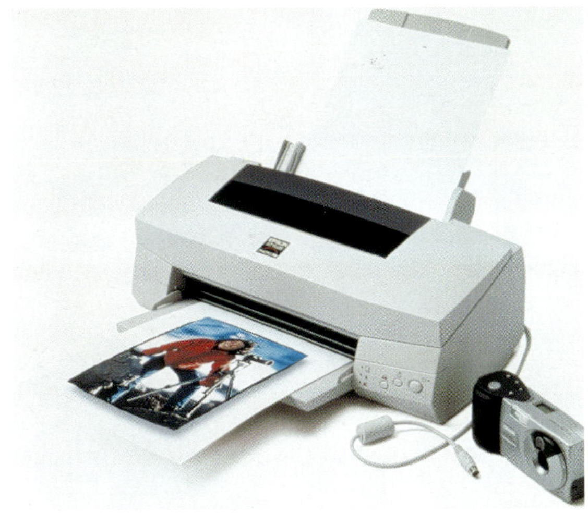

One indispensable home office computer peripheral for glamour photographers is a photo-quality ink-jet printer, like the Epson Stylus Photo 700. These inexpensive printers can produce photo-realistic output that can be used for promotional and marketing purposes. Photograph courtesy of Epson

THE PERFECT HOME OFFICE?

Make sure to fill your home office with items from your hobbies and collections so that it's a fun place to spend your time. Hang pictures on the wall, and display memorabilia that reflect your other interests, not just your job. In my case, this includes photography and Porsche automobiles. As I sit in my office chair, I look up to see a die-cast model of the latest Porsche race car placed in the hutch area of my computer workstation. To my right sits my other Windows NT computer, topped by a framed color image made by legendary photographer Edward L. Bafford. In short, I've designed my home office to be aesthetically, as well as physically, comfortable.

If you give careful consideration to the benefits and drawbacks, and respect the wishes and needs of your family, there's no reason that working from home should in any way hinder your creativity and success as a photographer.

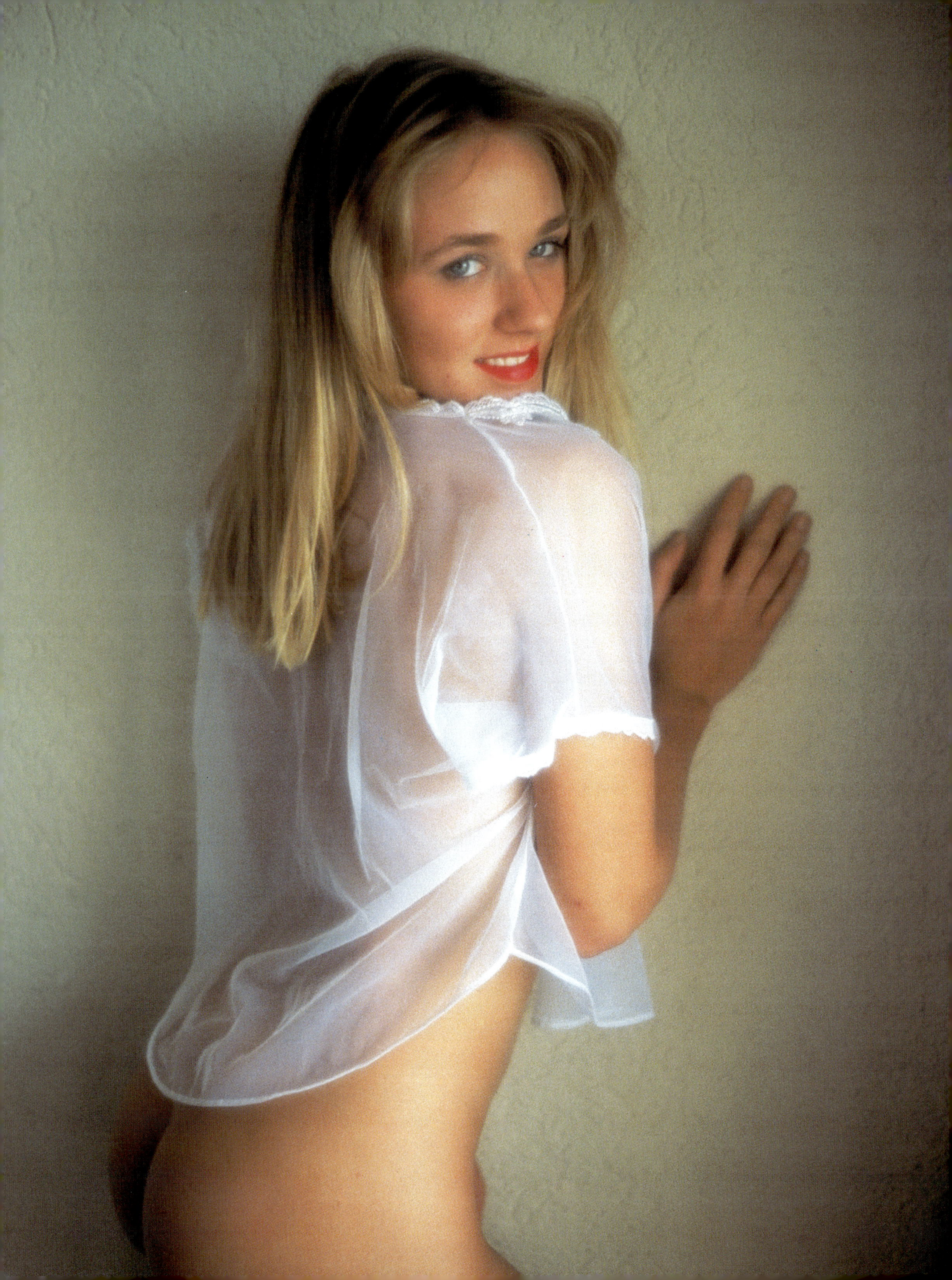

9

Selling Your Photographs

How to market your glamour images

If you want to be a successful glamour photographer, it's important that you put as much creative energy into marketing your images as you do in creating them. Many photographers sell their images directly to clients, while others depend on representatives or stock photo agencies to do this for them.

Until recently, the vast majority of stock photographs sold were in traditional film formats, usually 35mm slides but sometimes 4x5-inch and 8x10-inch transparencies. Now an increasing number of photographers are taking advantage of digital imaging technology and the Internet, which offer many benefits for the part-time glamour photographer as well as new outlets for sales. Let's examine several methods that photographers can use to market their glamour photographs.

STOCK PHOTO AGENCIES

A stock photograph, by definition, is one that already exists and is ready to be used by a client. Stock images have been around almost since the invention of photography, and many of the images you will produce fall into this category. If you have created a photograph for a particular client, you might not be able to use it as a stock image, or if so, there may be some restrictions on how it may be used. On the other hand, if you've photographed models on your own and secured the proper releases, you probably already have a growing library of images ready to be licensed for use. Notice I've used the word "licensed" instead of "sold." By licensing photographs, you can profit from the multiple use of your images. For example, a photograph of a young woman in a bikini can be licensed many times for a calendar, magazine, postcard, or magazine ad, provided the buyer does not restrict other uses of that image. Selling only the rights to use your images for a specific purpose is far more advantageous and profitable to the photographer than selling the image outright and not benefiting from subsequent use.

Traditionally, stock images have been available directly from photographers, but more often than not are purchased from agencies that do the work of sorting and cataloging all of the images they have on file. These images may have come from a photographer's previous assignments or may have been shot specifically for stock use. The availability of stock photography gives advertising agencies, publishers, and independent designers the ability to integrate photographs into layouts without the inconvenience and cost of shooting an image when a similar one already exists.

There are pros and cons to having a stock agency market your photographs. You need to first determine if using an agency is the right business direction for you. Depending on any one of many factors, it may be more profitable to market your own photographs. Before making a decision, following are a few factors you should consider.

For this simple portrait, the photographer took advantage of diffused lighting from a nearby window and used a soft-focus filter. ©Glamour Portfolios

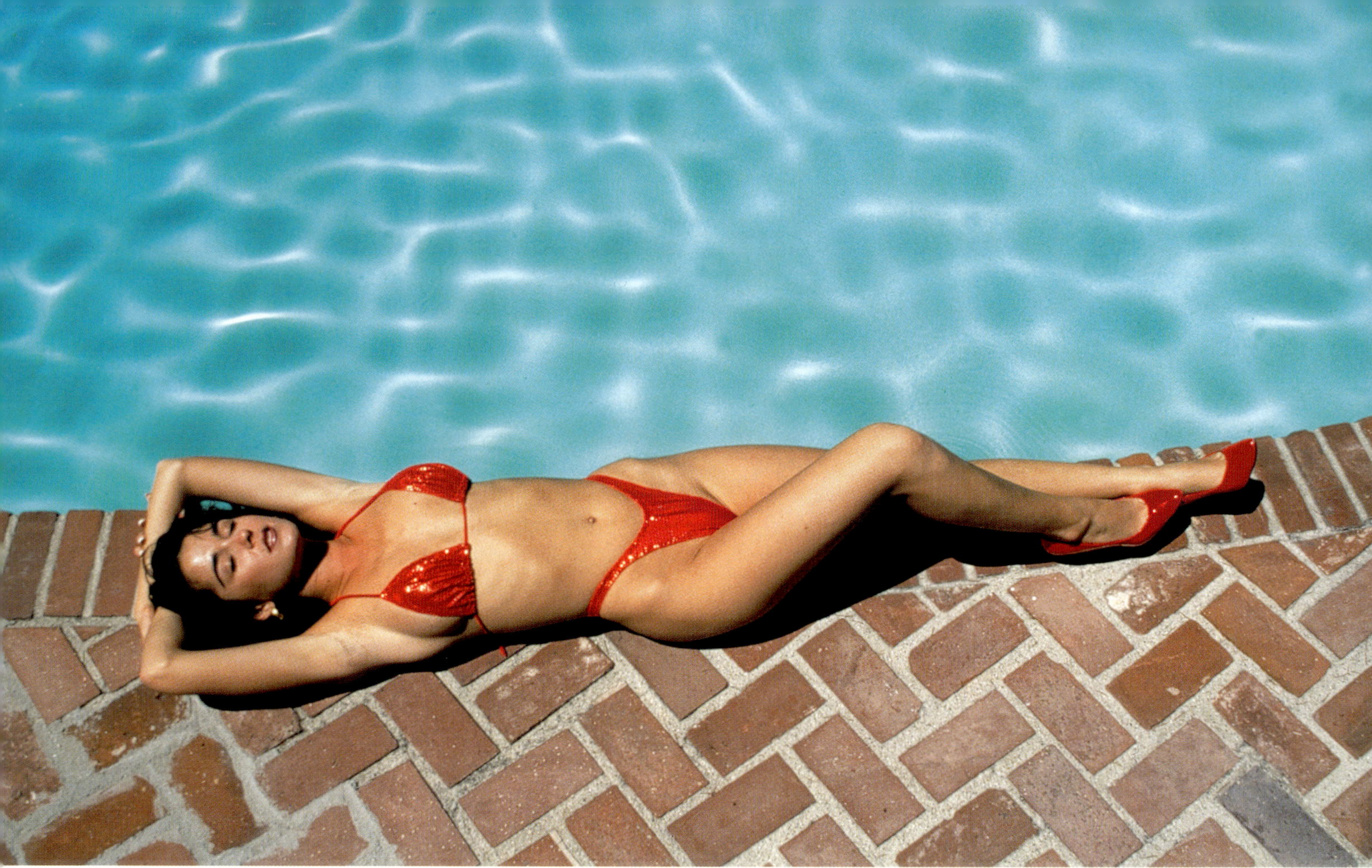

By leaving a lot of room for type and other graphics, you can increase the marketability of a photograph. You should think in terms of how your photo will be used in a layout, and make variations in the cropping that will allow it to be used as a background or main shot. ©Glamour Portfolios

Start by determining if your style of photography is actually marketable by an agency. No matter how great you consider your photographs to be, it doesn't mean they can be marketed by a stock photo agency. If your photographs are artistic in nature, they might not fill the needs of agencies looking for images that have direct commercial application. Many stock photo agencies believe that a really good stock photo can be easily described in a few words or in one sentence. For example, "blonde sitting on a deserted beach" or "nude brunette on a motorcycle" describe what these images might look like; only the particulars—which beach, what kind of bike—are lacking. It is those secondary factors that will ultimately make one image more saleable than another. If you can't simply and easily apply similar descriptions to your own photographs (although beautiful and artistic), they may not have any sales potential.

One way to find out what kind of photographs sell is to study the catalogs published by many stock photo agencies. If you don't have access to any of these catalogs, use the Internet. Some of the Image Bank's stock files can be seen at www.imagebank.com. You might also want to check Comstock's Web site at www.comstock.com to see the kinds of images they are currently selling. Each of these Web sites contains hundreds of images in a variety of categories. If you look through the "people" section, you'll get a good idea of what a traditional stock photo looks like. While your photographs don't have to be similar, you should be able to visualize some of your photographs appearing on these pages. If your style is too abstract or not easily described, it might be difficult to sell your photographs through an agency.

One problem you might encounter is that some agencies do not actively market centerfold-style photographs. Almost all stock photo agencies that have photographs of people in their files need photographs of attractive women in a variety of situations and settings for use in calendars, posters, and other glamour markets. However, only a small number of agencies will sell nude photographs, particularly those that may appear to be provocative.

Another consideration when considering representation through a stock agency is how many photographs you presently have and how many you plan to produce in the future. In opening discussions with stock photo agencies, the first thing you'll learn is that they expect regular submissions from you. If you have a few hundred or even several thousand photographs ready to submit, that's just the tip of the iceberg. For an agency to become interested in representing your work, they will expect you to submit new photographs every month—or at least several times a year—to update their files with fresh and marketable photos. If you can't commit to that kind of production, an agency might not be interested in your photographs, even if your initial submission is of high quality and easily marketable.

By taking advantage of a simple concept and dramatic lighting, the photographer created a timeless image that is both artistic and highly marketable. ©Glamour Portfolios

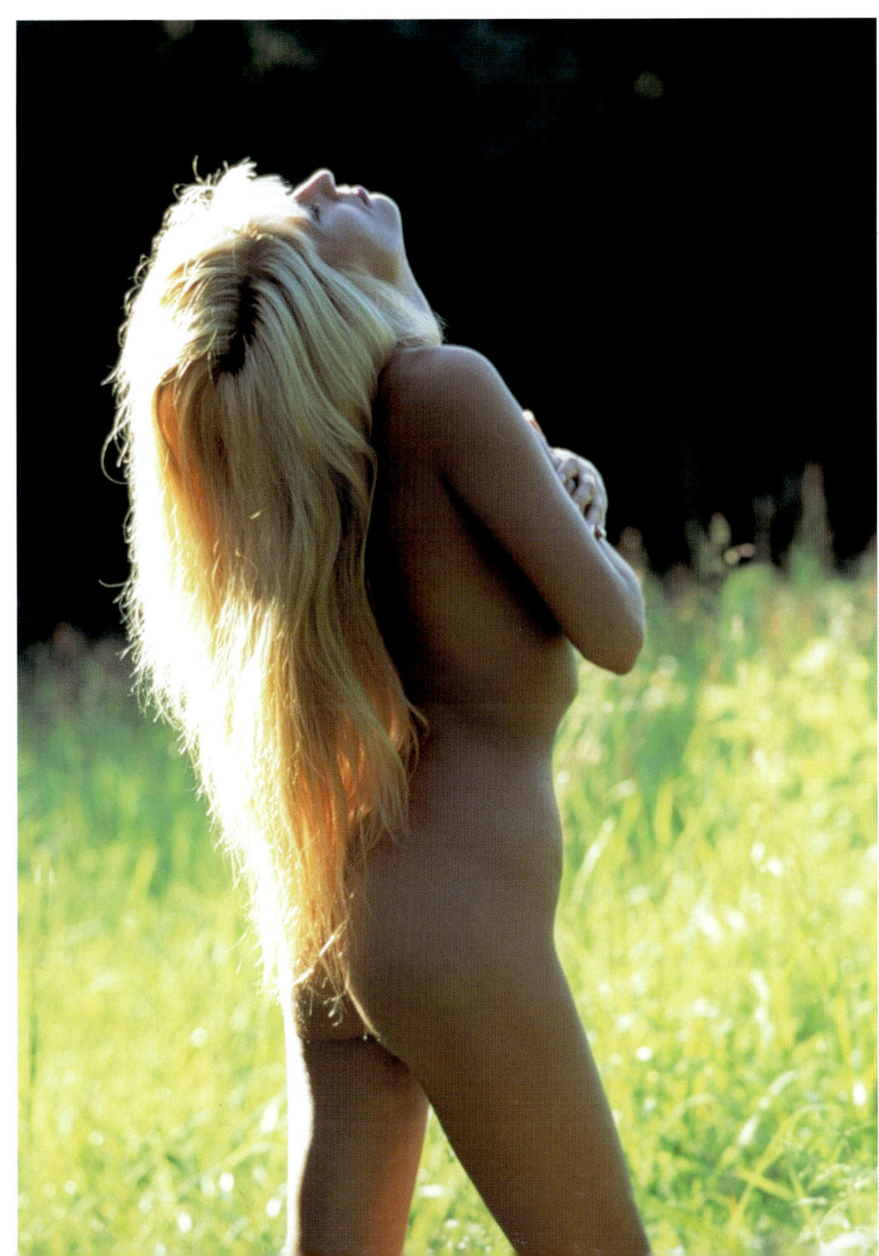

One subject that often surprises beginning stock photographers is the amount of commission taken by the agency when they license one of your photos. The vast majority of stock photo agencies charge a 50-percent commission, and before you consider having an agency market your work, you need to feel comfortable with that kind of figure. Of course, the whole purpose of an agency is to market your photos, so the actual amount you earn at the end of the year should be of greater concern to you than the percentage charged. It's better to earn 50 percent of $20,000 in licensing fees than 100 percent of $5000 in fees. Unless you are a marketing pro, it's more likely that an agency will do a better job of marketing your images than you, because that's all they do.

Which Agency Do You Want?

Once you've determined that you want to have a stock photo agency represent your work, the next step will be to find the right agency. Just as photographers tend to specialize, so do agencies. In your research on stock photo agencies, you will find, for example, that some agencies handle only nature photography, others represent the work of photojournalists, and some are only interested in scientific photographs.

The perfect match has the photographer regularly supplying photographs needed by the agency and not competing with other photographers with a similar style or subject matter. As a glamour or centerfold photographer, you will probably do best by having your work represented by a large agency that handles lifestyle or human-interest photographs. Better yet, try to find an agency that specializes in glamour photography.

As part of your research, obtain a nationwide list of agencies to see who is selling photographs of people, glamour images in particular. PACA, the Picture Agency Council of America, is a trade organization made up of dozens of stock photo agencies. PACA publishes a directory of members, which includes a description of each agency, the types of photographs in their files, and contact information. To obtain a copy of their directory, send $15 to:

> The Picture Agency Council of America
> P. O. Box 308, Northfield, MN 55057-0308

For more information, you might want to visit PACA's Web site at www.indexstock.com/pages/paca.htm. The site also has a copy of their code of ethics, which makes interesting and informative reading for the beginning stock photographer.

Once you've found several potential agencies, the next step is to contact them for a copy of their submission guidelines. The specifications include information about the type of images the agency is looking for and the preferred manner of sending images for consideration. Most agencies request an initial submission of a few hundred 35mm slides representative of the images in your files. You can send originals, but each slide should be clearly labeled with your name and copyright notice. Make sure the slides are carefully packaged and that you include a cover letter.

Since you are looking for a long-term relationship, there is some information you will want from them before making the decision to have them represent your work. One important factor to consider is the size of the agency. A small agency might represent the work of only a few dozen photographers, while large agencies represent hundreds or even thousands of shooters. A small agency might provide a more personal touch and get to know your work better, but a large agency may have more customers and a larger sales force. Be sure to ask how many photographers are represented, along with the number of glamour and centerfold photographers they represent.

When working with stock photo agencies who are unfamiliar with your photography style, correct captioning of your slides is especially important. Titling this image "woman at desk" would have different meanings for different kinds of photo buyers. ©Glamour Portfolios

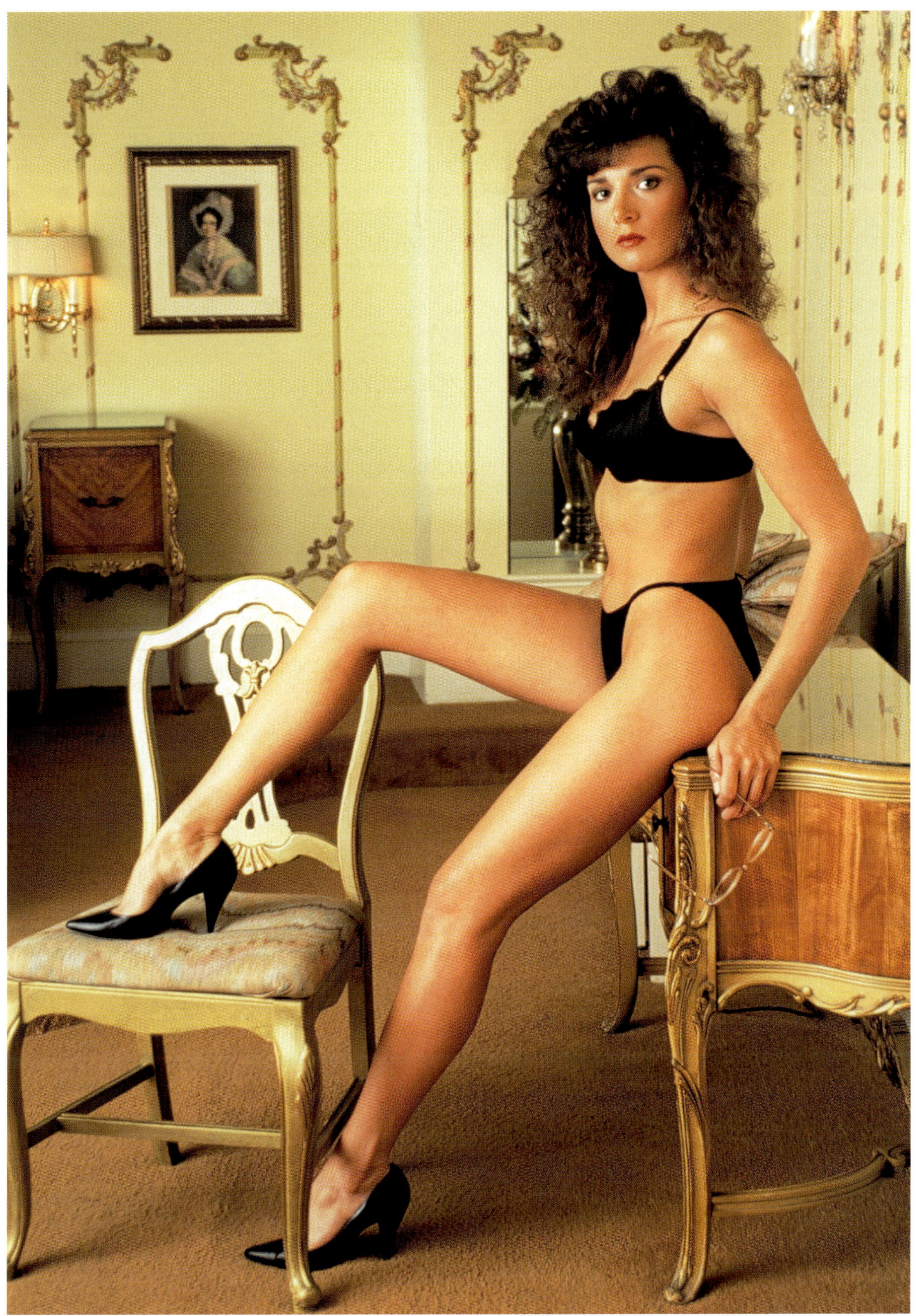

Some agencies, particularly smaller or relatively new ones, are more anxious to get new photographs into their files and might work more closely with their photographers. Occasionally, agencies will help finance stock photo shoots for selected photographers in an effort to fill gaps in their files. Ask them for the names of several of their represented photographers, then call these shooters to ask about their relationship with the agency. Find out how long they've been with the agency, approximately how many photographs they have in the files, and if they're happy with the results. While some photographers may be reluctant to discuss specific sales and income, they should be willing to share general information about their experience in working with the agency. You can use this information, along with what the agency tells you, to make your final decision.

Assuming all goes well and you find an agency that is a good match for your work, don't expect much to happen right away. Your first commission check is probably six months away, and you should not expect regular sales for almost a year. While this might be upsetting to a photographer anxious to see commission checks and tear sheets, keep in mind that your photographs need to be edited, categorized, captioned, labeled, and filed—all of which takes time. If your agency is large and busy, it might take months just to get your photographs into their files, and even then, your photographs will be competing with hundreds or even thousands of other photographs for potential sales. If you are doing a good job of supplying your agency with fresh images, and they are doing a good job of marketing them, it's just a matter of time until you see results. Stock photography is a long-term commitment, and if you're expecting quick sales, you may be disappointed.

SELL YOUR OWN IMAGES

While many photographers choose to have a stock photo agency do the selling for them, you might choose to market your photographs yourself. There are benefits and drawbacks to this method. The biggest advantage is, of course, that when you sell photographs yourself, you get to keep 100 percent of the income—you don't have to split the fee with an agency. The downside is that selling stock photographs takes time, effort, discipline, and marketing skills. Unless you plan to put sufficient energy into your marketing efforts, you may be more successful working through an agency.

The market for glamour photographs is international, and there is always a need for glamour and centerfold photographs, particularly for products such as posters, calendars, greeting cards, and magazines. Your first step in marketing your photographs is to locate potential buyers. One way to do this is by purchasing one of several marketing handbooks that can be found in any large bookstore. This will help you find listings of advertising and public relations agencies, publishers, and other companies that purchase photography. Potential buyers will most likely be found among the magazine publishers and poster, greeting card, and calendar companies. Scan the listings, which also include the type of images they are looking for as well as requirements for submission of images.

Some of these companies publish a "want list" detailing their projects for the next few years. For example, a calendar company usually plans their products three to four years ahead of time. They might be publishing a "Blondes on the Beach" calendar in a few years and will indicate on their list the photographs they need. Or their annual "Hot Cars" calendar might feature attractive young women next to the cars. To receive a "want list," you need only call and ask for the photo department, and they'll send you one. It's not a good idea to submit photographs before contacting someone at the company or without reviewing their submission policies. Professional photo editors have little time to review unsolicited submissions, particularly if they don't contain images relevant to future projects.

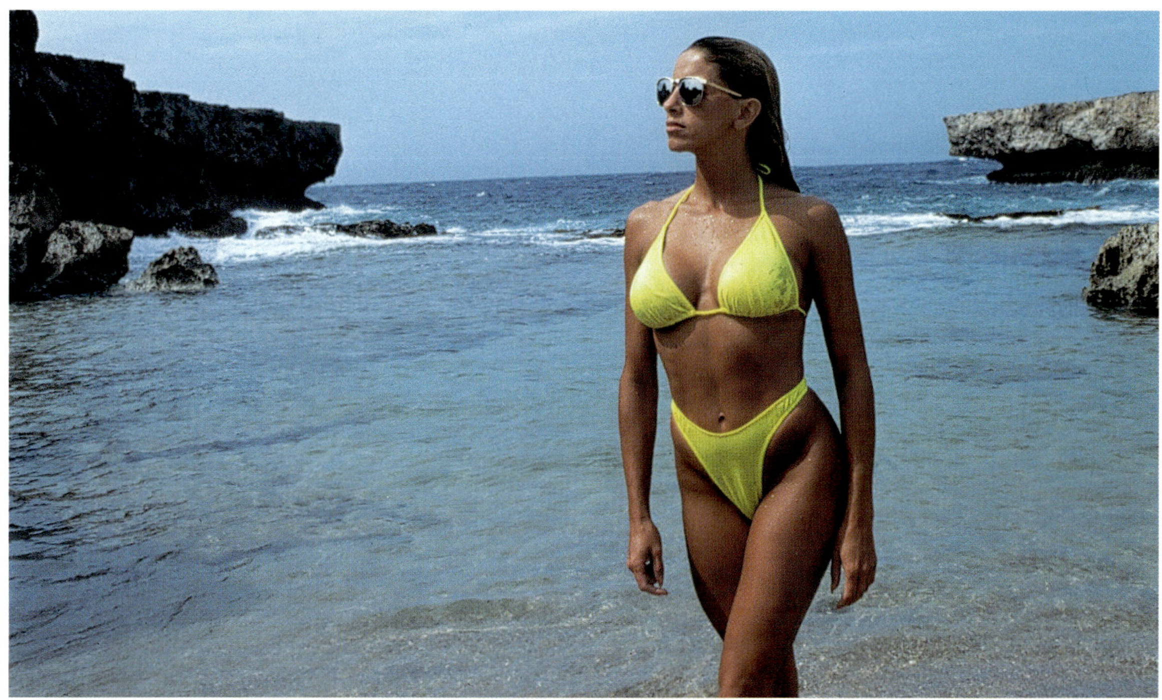

A simple outdoor glamour shot like this one has real sales potential. The model's yellow bikini contrasts nicely with the blue water in the background. Avoid using blue or green swimsuits—they don't show up as well. ©Glamour Portfolios

When submitting photographs for review, it is important to label and package your photographs carefully. Your copyright notice should be on each slide, and slides should be inserted into clean slide pages. Make sure you include a cover letter that has your name, address, and phone number. It's always a good idea to include a delivery memo, which can offer you some legal protection against the misuse or loss of your photographs; it also helps create a more professional image. You can use the sample ASMP delivery memo form found in their book *Professional Business Practices in Photography* or make your own using the sample that appears on page 134.

One of the key elements of a delivery memo is that it specifies how much each slide is worth (in case it is lost or damaged). The industry's standard amount per slide is widely quoted as $1500 per slide, representing future sales of that image, but I know that some photographers quote amounts as low as $200. They are your slides, and since you may have other, similar images on file, you can set the value at any level you want. It's a good idea to send any slide submissions securely packaged using registered mail or through an overnight delivery service, such as FedEx. This way you have proof that your package was delivered.

Although prices are sometimes open to negotiation, more often than not you will find that for such items as calendars, greeting cards, and magazines, the publishers have their own prices already budgeted. Rather than asking you how much you will charge them, they will tell you what they are paying for the particular usage. For example, a greeting card company might pay $250 per card, a calendar publisher might pay $400 per image, and a magazine might offer from $1500 to $3000 per layout. Don't expect much flexibility in their payments; it's often a take-it-or-leave-it situation.

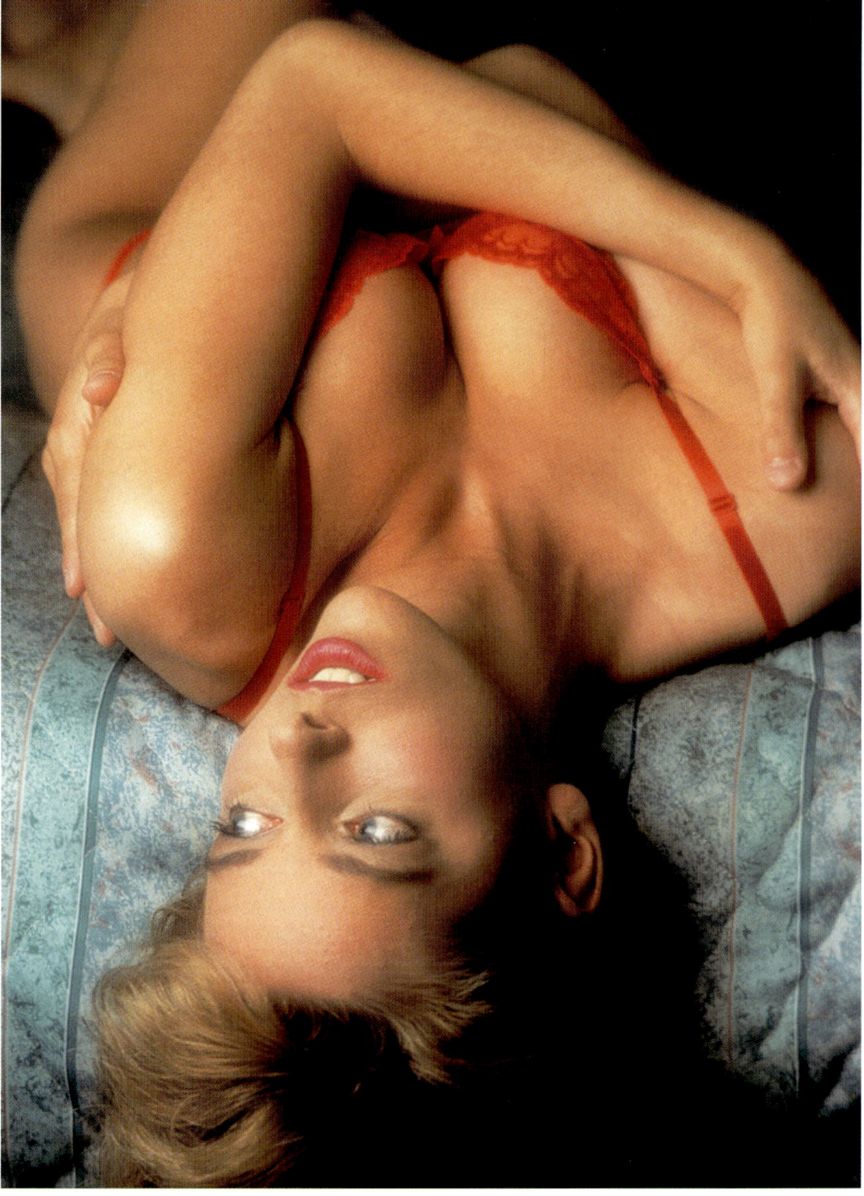

Here's an example of how a nontraditional pose can help produce an eye-catching photo. Rather than have the model sit on the bed, the photographer placed her at the edge. ©Glamour Portfolios

Digital Stock Photography

With a little ingenuity and creativity, you can become a direct marketer of your own glamour and centerfold images. In addition to selling your glamour photographs to companies that will use them in printed products, there are other markets you should consider. You can sell to the consumers who purchase calendars, posters, and magazines that feature glamour photography. They are often interested in buying photographs directly from photographers in the form of color prints, CD-ROM discs, or from your own Web site.

A relatively new and profitable method of directly marketing your glamour photographs is to place a collection of them on a CD-ROM disc. The average CD-ROM disc can store over 600 megabytes of information, which can include photographic images, sound, text, and video clips. If you have sufficient computer skills, you can design a master CD-ROM disc, which can then be duplicated in any quantity you want. If your computer skills are not at that level, or if you are too busy creating images, you can always utilize the services of a graphics design firm that will be more than glad to do it for you. Your CD-ROM collection can be as simple as a few hundred images stored on the disc as graphic files, or it may utilize a graphic interface that includes music, navigation buttons, icons, and other on-screen devices that are used to enhance the overall presentation of your photographs.

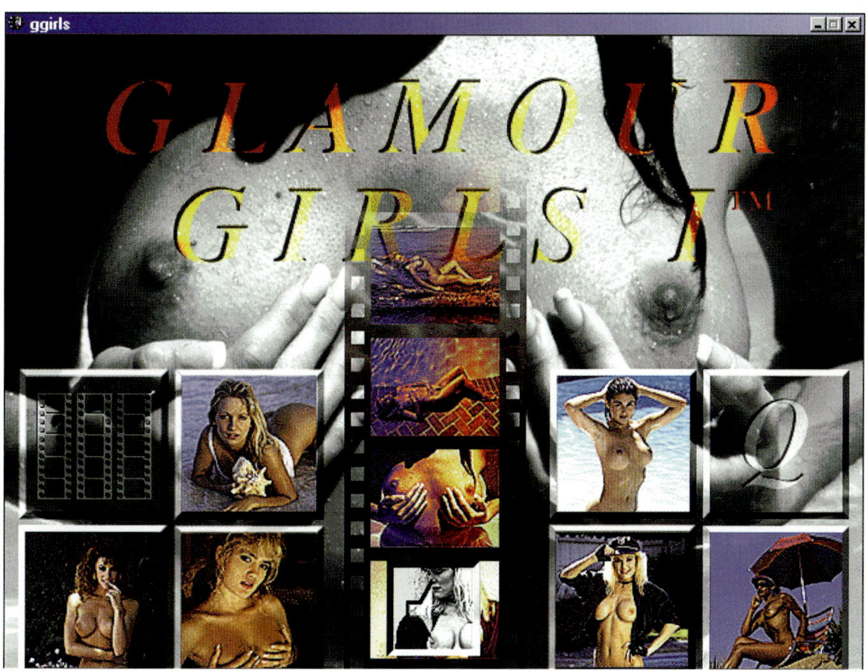

This is the interface for a CD-ROM collection called "Glamour Girls." Each CD-ROM in this collection contains several hundred photographs as well as QuickTime movies. ©Glamour Portfolios

Some of the major benefits of marketing your glamour photography in CD-ROM format is that there are relatively low start-up costs, little financial risk, high markups, and low storage and shipping costs. Once you've created the original glamour photographs, your only costs include the initial scanning, interface design, and pressing of the discs. Typical scanning costs, if sent to a photo lab or service bureau, range from $1 to $15 per scan. If you have the time and computer expertise, you might consider purchasing a scanner and doing this work yourself.

Depending on the complexity of the project, it will cost anywhere from $500 to $5000 to have a graphics artist design an attractive interface for your image collection and create a master disc. If you have the computing savvy, you can create your own CD-ROM interface using a program such as Macromedia's Director. The only part of the entire process that isn't practical to do yourself is the pressing of the discs. However, there are numerous companies that specialize in pressing CD-ROM discs, with typical costs ranging from $1.50 to $2 per disc.

Here is a typical budget to create 1000 copies of your disc, assuming a relatively simple interface that will display 500 of your photographs:

Scan 500 photos @ $1.50 each	$ 750
Simple interface design and master	600
Press 1000 CD-ROM discs @ $2 each	2000
Total	$ 3350
Your cost per CD-ROM disc	**$ 3.35**

To a part-time glamour photographer, spending over $3000 to create CD-ROM discs may sound like a lot of money, but there's one part of the equation that hasn't been considered—the selling price of the disc. Typical photo-collection CD-ROM discs sell for $19 to $29 each, with some selling for a lot more. If you price your CD at $25 with a production cost of $3.35, your gross profit per disc is over $20, which represents a 700 percent markup. Maybe that's why so many glamour and centerfold photographers are now marketing their images on CD-ROM discs.

There are other aspects of CD-ROM discs that make them particularly attractive. Unlike posters and calendars which can be large and bulky to store and ship, CD-ROM discs are small and lightweight. An inventory of 1000 CD-ROM discs can sit neatly on a shelf in your home office. Also, unlike posters (which can fade or be damaged) and calendars (which can be sold for only one year), CD-ROM discs are durable and last for many years.

Marketing on the Internet

Of all the methods available to photographers for marketing glamour and centerfold photographs, none is more exciting or profitable as the Internet. Over the past few years, the number of photographers using the World Wide Web to market their images has increased dramatically, and I expect this will continue. You can visit my Web site at www.hyperzine.com/writers/joef.html.

Web-based marketing is simple, inexpensive, and the perfect vehicle for selling glamour and centerfold photographs to the global market. If you have an interest in developing a Web site to market your images, the first step is to get on the Internet and see how other photographers are designing their Web sites and marketing strategies.

To surf the Net, you'll need a computer, a monitor, a fast modem, and Internet browser software. A Web browser's main function is to connect you to your Internet service provider (ISP) and take you to a home page that serves as a starting point for your Web explorations. Unlike a starting screen for CompuServe or America Online (on-line services that provide a cornucopia of information directing you to many different services), browser home pages are full of self-promotion—or nothing. So you need to know where you are going or at least what you are looking for. The two most popular Web browsers are Netscape Navigator and Microsoft Explorer, and most new computers sold today will have one or both of these programs already installed.

Once on-line, you'll quickly learn how to use search engines, such as Yahoo! and Excite, to find the kinds of sites you're interested in. Unfortunately, if you're looking to find examples of glamour and centerfold photography, you'll quickly realize that the Web is awash in pornographic images. However, if you take the time to search carefully, you'll discover a growing number of Web sites created by highly talented and legitimate glamour and centerfold photographers with beautiful, elegant, and professional images available for viewing and sale. Many of the photographers whose images appear in top magazines have their own Web sites, making additional images, CD-ROM discs, and other products available to photographic enthusiasts.

In general, professional photography sites fall into one of two categories. First, there is the free gallery or portfolio style of Web site where the photographer provides information about his or her studio, describes the types of assignments accepted, and displays anywhere from a handful to a few dozen examples of

Surfing the Net

The mechanics of producing a Web site go beyond the scope of this book. Technically inclined photographers can purchase appropriate site-construction software, such as Adobe PageMill or Microsoft FrontPage. There are also books specifically designed to teach you how to produce your own Web site, including my own, The Photographer's Internet Handbook. *This book is written for those photographers interested in taking advantage of opportunities on the World Wide Web but don't know where to start. It includes information on what you need to do before establishing your own Web site, examples of photographic Web sites, and a "behind-the-screens" look at how six photographers created their own sites.*

his or her work. The purpose of this kind of Web site is to give potential clients the opportunity to conveniently review the photographer's portfolio. Sometimes the design is simple, done by the photographer, while other times, the assistance of an experienced programmer or Web master may be required for a more sophisticated or interactive environment.

At the second type of Web site, the commercial or subscription site, images are sold directly. This has become an almost standard format for glamour and centerfold photographers who wish to showcase their images and make an income directly from customers on the Web. While visitors to portfolio sites include potential clients such as art directors and art buyers, visitors to subscription sites more typically include glamour and centerfold photography enthusiasts, usually the same market that magazines such as *Playboy* target.

When visitors arrive at the site, they are given the opportunity to review the entry terms. Because a glamour or centerfold site may contain nude images, it's important to restrict access. This is done by using "nanny" programs that when installed correctly on the user's computer can prevent minors from accessing any adult-oriented sites. While not foolproof, these software safeguards can be highly effective. Once visitors agree to the terms, which include age and copyright restrictions, they are shown a main index page with a menu of items that should allow them to navigate easily through the site.

Most commercial Web sites contain three basic components. The first is a free sample area, in which visitors can view a few dozen typical images. The next area is the main library, where visitors can view up to several thousand images. Some on-line libraries contain as many as 100,000 images, but Web sites operated by individual photographers usually contain a much smaller number. The third area might contain an on-line store where the photographer can sell signed prints, CD-ROM discs, books, and other products associated with his or her photography.

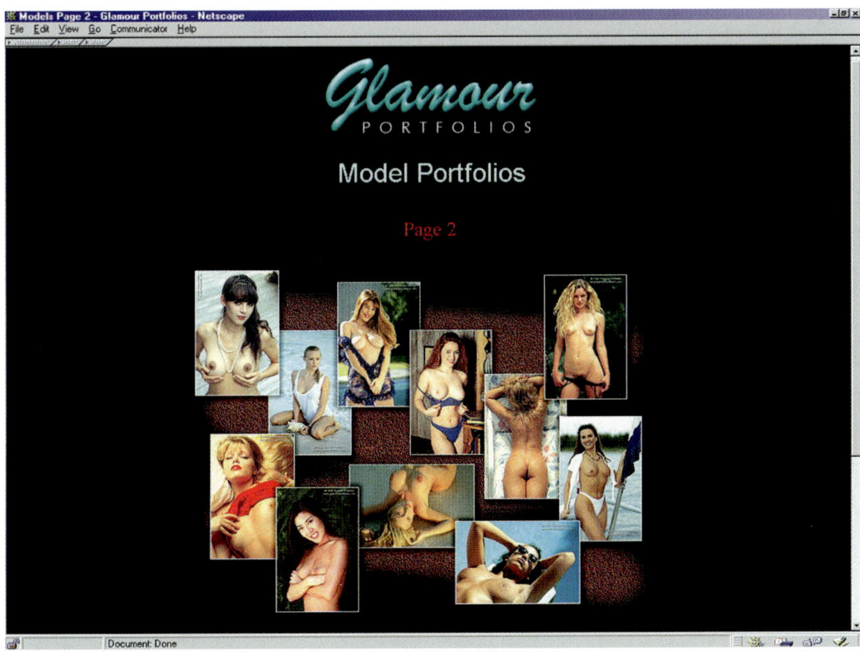

Glamour Portfolios' model portfolios page on the World Wide Web features a collage of images visitors can click on to see additional photographs of a particular model. ©Glamour Portfolios

Here's how a typical Web site can be constructed. Like the real world, there is a lot of competition on the Web. Since there are thousands and thousands of photo-oriented sites on-line, the big question is: How are you going to get people to come to your site? That's what building a successful Web site is really all about. Following are a few ways to increase traffic on your site and build sales.

Start with a quality product. Because on-line browsing is quick and easy, you must have high-quality photographs to attract paying customers. Otherwise, since there is no shortage of free on-line photography, potential customers might just prefer to cruise the Web looking for freebies.

Make sure your Web site has a clean design with navigational features that let visitors move easily from section to section. There's no quicker way to lose sales than having a potential subscriber get lost within your Web site.

Pornographic sites are everywhere on the Web, and you don't want to be associated with them in any form. Resist the temptation to display ads for adult sites. Even though placing such banners is one way to make a small additional income, doing so makes your site look cheap. The attractive, upscale sites are the ones that make money on the Web. Remember, you're known by the company you keep, and what's true in the real world is true for the Internet. Take my advice and keep your site respectable by staying away from porn-pushers.

Update your site regularly. If you're going to charge a subscription fee, it's important that new images be added regularly. While there's no magic number, you should add at least 100 images each month—the more, the better.

Hire a professional Web master to run your site while you concentrate on creating saleable images. Although this will increase your up-front costs, it will pay you back many times in the long run. The Internet is filled with sophisticated Web sites with slick graphics and programming; if you want to compete, your site must look good. Unless you're skilled at programming, you are better off letting someone else do it. You should consider finding a programmer who will act as your Web master, with compensation based on a percentage of sales made from the Web site. This arrangement will give your Web master incentive to keep the site updated regularly, find new links, and develop good marketing strategies.

You should price access to your site fairly and with an eye on the competition. Usually, subscription pricing is based on how long the user has access to the site. For example, the Glamour Portfolios Web site at www.glamourportfolios.com offers the following subscription rates to view its library of 2000 (as I write this) images:

one month:	$ 19.95
three months:	$ 45.00
one year:	$60.00

By using this price structure, Glamour Portfolios tries to entice subscribers into taking a three-month or one-year subscription—and it works. Unlike magazine subscriptions for which the direct costs are closely proportional to subscription length, with the Internet, incremental costs of providing service for one year are not that much more when compared to the cost of a single month, so you can offer much greater discounts for longer subscriptions. This is a win-win situation for you and your customer.

Make sure your billing page is located on a secure server, so your customers' credit card information will be encrypted and cannot be easily stolen. Many Internet customers will not enter any information on a non-secure page. Before signing on with your Internet service provider, make sure a secure server is offered, and make sure you inform your Web customers. The more secure a potential customer feels when reviewing your site, the greater the chances of that customer subscribing.

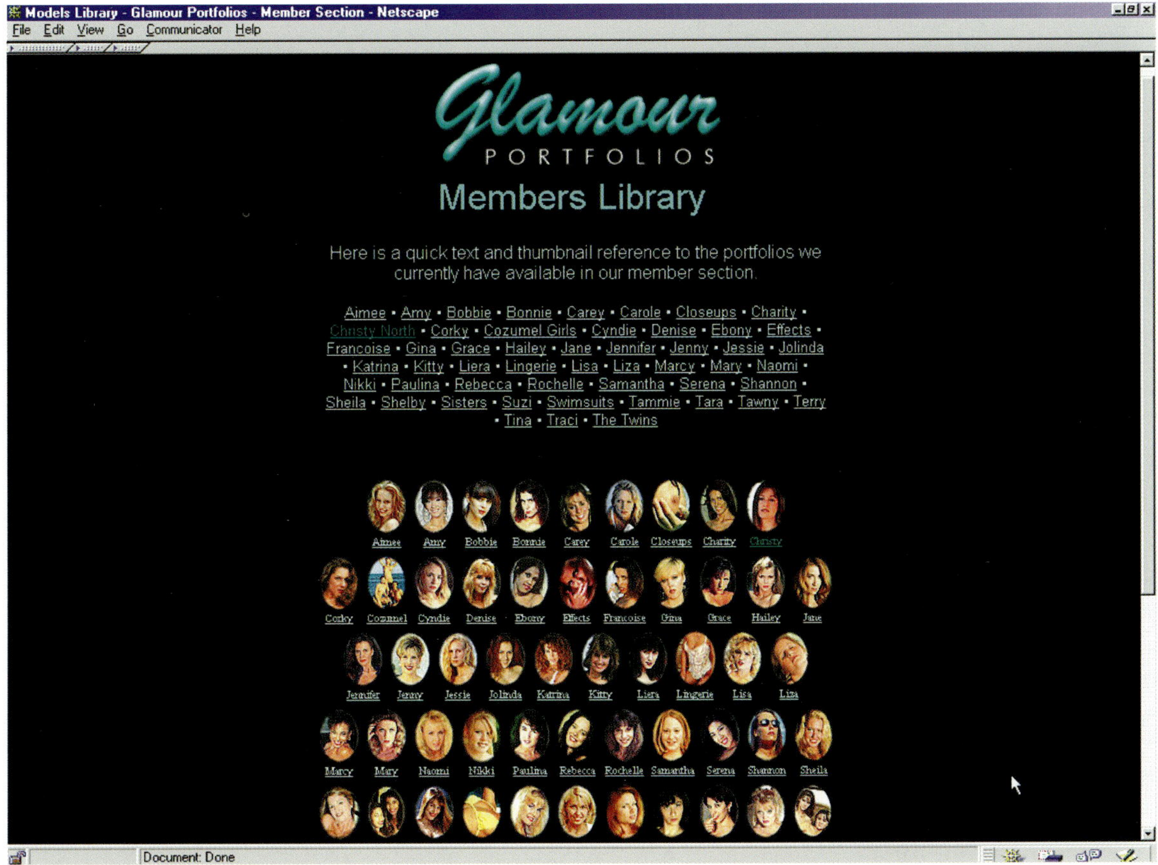

One of the pages of the subscriber's area of Glamour Portfolios' Web site shows thumbnail images of many of their models. Clicking on that thumbnail takes you to the model's portfolio pages. ©Glamour Portfolios

Make sure the site provides a way for customers to contact you via e-mail for service, to ask questions, to make comments, or to cancel their subscriptions.

Above all, be fair. Don't try to trick potential customers into subscribing using any sort of deceptive ads. Instead, offer free samples and some type of guarantee.

These are just a few basic concepts you should consider when offering your glamour photographs for sale on the World Wide Web. The best way to learn what works and what doesn't is by surfing the Web and reviewing other glamour photography sites. Although most photographers normally wouldn't check out a local competitor's studio, there's nothing wrong with subscribing to several photo sites to see what they are like and to learn what other photographers are doing. That's the way things work on the Web, where imitation is the sincerest form of flattery—and sometimes good business sense!

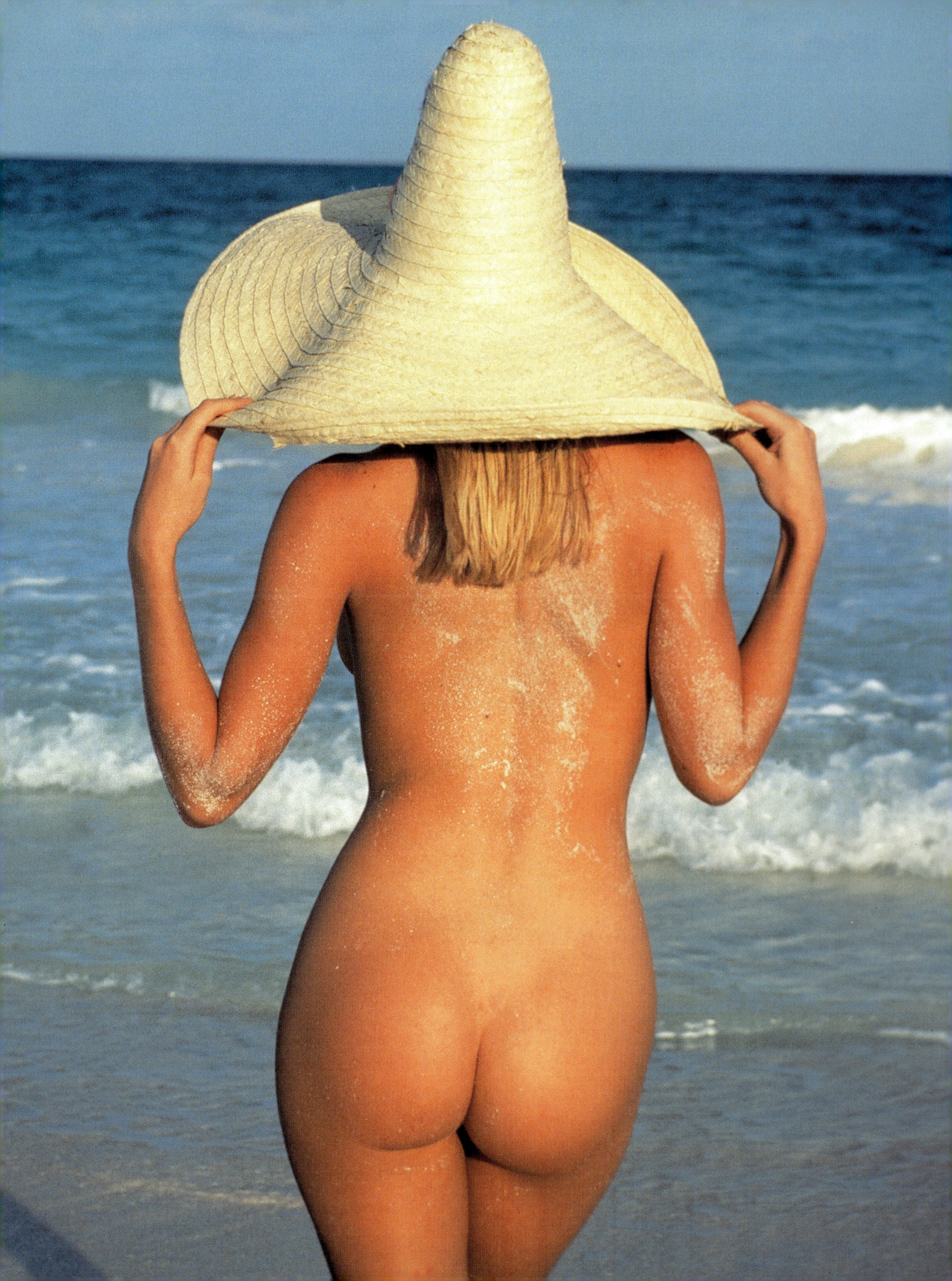

Forms & Appendix

Here a simple prop, nice lighting, a good location, and an attractive model combine to create a very marketable stock photo. ©Glamour Portfolios

CASTING INFORMATION

Date ______________________________

Name ______________________________

Address ______________________________

City ______________ State ______________ Zip ______________ Phone ______________

Height ______________ Weight ______________ Measurements ______________

Hair ______________ Eye color ______________ Size ______________

Date of birth ______________________________

Are you currently affiliated with any modeling agencies? Yes ❑ No ❑

If yes, which agencies? ______________________________

Have you ever appeared in any magazines? Yes ❑ No ❑

What modeling styles are you interested in? (Check all that apply)

Editorial ❑ Swimsuit ❑ Lingerie ❑ Topless ❑ Centerfold ❑

Are you available for travel within the United States? Yes ❑ No ❑

Outside the United States? Yes ❑ No ❑

Please list any special talents (dancing, sports, etc.):

____

____

____

____

____

____

____

____

MODEL RELEASE

In consideration of my engagement as a model upon the terms stated, I hereby give to Photographer ____________________, his/her heirs, legal representatives, licensees and assigns, those for whom he/she is acting, and those acting with his/her authority and permission (collectively, the "Authorized Parties"):

a) The irrevocable, exclusive, and unrestricted right and permission to create, copy, use, re-use, alter, publish, re-publish, license, assign, and distribute the photographic portraits or pictures in which I may be included in whole or in part as a result of my engagement by Photographer, whether accurate or distorted in character or form, without restriction as to changes or transformations (collectively, the "Released Images"), in conjunction with my own name, a fictitious name, or no name at all. Photographer is granted the foregoing exclusive rights regarding the Released Images in any and all media now or hereafter known, including but not limited to film, print, video, and digital reproduction for illustration, art, promotion, advertising, trade, or any other purpose whatsoever. I acknowledge that as between Photographer and me, Photographer is and shall be the author of all Released Images under the copyright laws and owns and shall own all Released Images.

b) I also permit and authorize the Photographer and any Authorized Parties to use any printed material or other materials or media they desire with the Released Images.

c) I hereby relinquish any right that I may have to examine or approve: (1) the completed product or products or any associated advertising copy or printed matter incorporating or associated with the Released Images, (2) any other materials or media that may be used in conjunction with the Released Images, or (3) the use to which the Released Images may be applied.

d) I hereby release, discharge, and agree to hold harmless the Photographer and all Authorized Parties, individually and jointly, from any liability to me or others associated with me by virtue of any blurring, distortion, or alteration of the Released Images, or use of the Released Images in composite form, whether intentional or otherwise, that may occur or be produced in the taking of said Released Images or in any subsequent processing, publication, or usage thereof, including without limitation any claims for defamation or violation of rights of privacy or publicity. I acknowledge and agree that this release and agreement to hold harmless shall continue indefinitely, regardless of whether any Released Image used within the scope of this Agreement causes me in the future to feel embarrassed, ashamed, degraded, or otherwise injured in any manner.

e) I hereby release, discharge, and agree to save harmless the Photographer and any and all Authorized Parties from any liability resulting from any injury or accident, regardless of cause, in which I am involved during a photo shooting.

I HEREBY AFFIRM THAT I AM AN ADULT OF LEGAL AGE AND HAVE THE RIGHT TO CONTRACT IN MY OWN NAME. I HAVE READ THE ABOVE AUTHORIZATION, RELEASE, AND AGREEMENT PRIOR TO ITS EXECUTION; I FULLY UNDERSTAND THE CONTENTS THEREOF. This agreement shall be binding upon me and my heirs, legal representatives, and assigns.

Description of photographs ____

____

All photographs taken at ______________ during the time from ______________ to ______________

As payment, I have received ______________ and expect no additional compensation.

Model's name (please print) ____

Model's signature ______________________________ Date ______________

Address ____

City ______________________________ State ______________ Zip ______________

SS# ______________ Date of Birth ______________

Telephone # ______________ Witness ______________________________

DELIVERY MEMO

Date ______________

SHIPPED TO:

Name ______________________________

Organization ______________________________

Address ______________________________

City ______________________________ State ______________ Zip ______________

Phone ( ) ______________________________

Photographs Delivered Via ______________ Airbill Package Tracking Number ______________

Enclosed please find the following original 35mm slides. This count shall be considered correct, unless this memo is immediately signed and returned with any discrepancies listed.
TOTAL NUMBER OF 35mm ORIGINAL SLIDES ENCLOSED ____________

Terms: By accepting these images, you agree to the following terms. If you do not agree to these terms, you must return the images immediately.

1. Images may be held for three weeks from the date of this memo. After such time, they are subject to a holding fee of $1 per week per slide.
2. Images are for review only. No usage rights are granted until an invoice is issued and paid.
3. Recipient accepts an insurer's liability herein for the safe and undamaged return of the images to the photographer. Such images are to be returned by FedEx or by registered mail prepaid and fully insured. Recipient is accountable for any loss or damage to the images, from time of receipt until they are returned to Photographer, and shall indemnify Photographer against any loss or damage to photographs in transit or in possession of Recipient. This agreement is not considered a bailment and is specifically conditioned upon the item delivered being returned to Photographer in the same condition as delivered.
4. The monetary damage for loss or damage of an original color transparency or photograph shall be determined by the value of each individual image. Recipient agrees, however, that the reasonable value of EACH lost or damaged photograph or transparency shall be FIFTEEN HUNDRED DOLLARS ($1500.00) each. Photographer agrees to the delivery of the goods herein only upon the express covenant and understanding by Recipient that the terms contained in Paragraph 4 are material to this agreement. Recipient assumes full liability for his/her employees, agents, assigns, represented models, or messengers for loss, damage, or misuse of the images.
5. This agreement, its validity, and effect shall be interpreted under and governed by the laws of the State of ______________________.
6. If Photographer is caused to present claim or suit as a result of breach of the terms set forth, it shall be made whole for such reasonable legal fees and costs by recipient or user herein.

SIGN AND RETURN ONE COPY

Date ______________

Signed ______________________________

Print name ______________________________

Companies and Organizations

Adobe Systems
345 Park Avenue, San Jose, California 95110-2704
(408) 536-6000, Fax: (408) 537-6000
www.adobe.com

American Society of Media Photographers (ASMP)
14 Washington Road, Suite 502
Princeton, NJ 08550-1033
(609) 799-8300, Fax: (609) 799-2233
www.asmp.org

Brother International Corporation
200 Cottontail Lane, Somerset, NJ 08875
(908) 356-8880, Fax: (908) 356-4085
www.brother.com

Canon U.S.A., Inc.
One Canon Plaza
Lake Success, NY 10042
(516) 328-5000, www.usa.canon.com

Cradoc Corporation
145 Tyee Drive, Suite 286, Point Roberts, WA 98281
(206) 842-4030 Fax: (206) 842-1381

DataViz
55 Corporate Drive, Trumbull, CT 06111
(800) 733-0030, Fax: (203) 268-4345
www.dataviz.com

Denny Manufacturing Company, Inc.
3007 Dial Street, P.O. Box 7200
Mobile, AL 36670-0200
(800) 844-5616, (205) 457-2388, Fax: (205) 452-4630
www.dennymfg.com

Eastman Kodak Company
343 State Street, Rochester, NY 14650
(800) 242-2424, www.kodak.com

Epson America, Inc.
20770 Madrona Avenue, P.O. Box 2842
Torrance, CA 90509-2842
(800) 289-3776, (310) 782-0770, Fax: (310) 782-5220
www.epson.com

Glamour Portfolios
www.glamourportfolios.com

Hewlett Packard
3000 Hanover Street, Palo Alto, CA 94304
(800) 752-0900, www.hp.com

Iomega Corporation
1821 W. Iomega Way, Roy, UT 84067
(800) 697-8833, (801) 778-1000, www.iomega.com

Light Impressions
P.O. Box 940, Rochester, NY 14603-0940
(800) 828-6216, (716) 271-8960, Fax: (800) 828-5539
www.lightimpressionsdirect.com

Lowel-Light Manufacturing, Inc.
140 58th Street, Brooklyn, NY 11220
(800) 334-3426, (718) 921-0600, Fax: (718) 921-0303
www.lowel.com

Macromedia, Inc.
600 Townsend Street, Suite 310 W
San Francisco, CA 94103-4945
(800) 326-2128, (415) 252-2000, Fax: (415) 626-0554
www.macromedia.com

Microsoft Corporation
One Microsoft Way, Redmond, WA 98052-6399
(800) MSPRESS, Fax: (206) 93MSFAX
www.microsoft.com

Minolta Corporation
101 Williams Drive, Ramsey, NJ 07446-1282
(201) 825-4000, Fax: (201) 423-0590
www.minoltausa.com

Nikon, Inc.
1300 Walt Whitman Road, Melville, NY 11747
(516) 547-4200, www.nikonusa.com

Pentax Corporation
35 Inverness Drive, E. Englewood, CO 80155
(800) 729-1419, www.pentax.com

Perfect Niche Software
6962 E. First Avenue, Suite 103
Scottsdale, AZ 85251
(602) 945-2001, Fax: (602) 949-1707

Photoflex
333 Encinal Street, Santa Cruz, CA 95060
(800) 486-2674, Fax: (408) 454-9600
www.photoflex.com

The Picture Agency Council of America
P.O. Box 308, Northfield, MN 55057-0308
(800) 457-PACA, (507) 645-6988, Fax: (507) 645-7066
www.indexstock.com/pages/paca.htm

Polaris
(see The Tiffen Company)

Silver Pixel Press
A Tiffen Company
21 Jet View Drive, Rochester, NY 14624
(716) 328-7800, Fax: (716) 328-5078
www.saundersphoto.com

Studio Press
4330 Harlan Street, Wheat Ridge, CO 80033
(303) 420-3505

The Tiffen Company
21 Jet View Drive, Rochester, NY 14624
(716) 328-7800, Fax: (716) 328-5078
www.saundersphoto.com or www.tiffen.com

F. J. Westcott Company
1447 Summit Street, Toledo, OH 43603
(800) 886-1689, (419) 243-7311, Fax: (419) 243-8401
www.fjwestcott.com

Photo Day and Glamour Workshop Sponsors

Bob Shell Workshops
P.O. Box 808, Radford, VA 24141
www.bobshell.com

"Get Published" Glamour Midwest Model Shoots/Workshops
P.O. Box 291, Bedford Park, IL 60499-0291
(708) 430-5425, E-mail: glamourmag@prodigy.com

Glamour Photographers International
P.O. Box 84374, San Diego, CA 92138
(619) 575-0100
www.glamourphotonet.com

Hudson Valley Model Shoots
RD 2 Box 60, Red Hook, NY 12571

Le Image Glamour Model Photo Workshop
259 Prospect Street, Nutley, NJ 07110-2267
(973) 661-3320, E-mail: leimage@earthlink.net

The New England Council of Camera Clubs
28 Silva Terrace, Oxford, CT 06478-1816
(while not specifically a sponsor of Photo Days, NECCC sponsors a three-day conference on the campus of the University of Massachusetts in Amherst that includes photo sessions with models)

Outdoor Nude Workshop
P.O. Box 2684, Chicago, IL 60690-2684
E-mail: f64clubmann@juno.com

Photo Shoots in New Mexico
Bobby Sargent, 818 Jester, Dallas, TX 75211
(214) 330-5362, Fax: (214) 330-6182

Books

Concept to Print: Advanced Techniques in Creative Portraiture
by Stu Williamson, Silver Pixel Press
ISBN 1-883403-28-6

Design Ideas for Small Spaces: Living Rooms and Home Offices
by Norman Smith, Rockport Publishers
ISBN 1-56496-304-7

Fantasy Nudes: Digital Techniques in Photography
by Jim Zuckerman, Silver Pixel Press
ISBN 1-883403-48-0

The Nude: Complete Photography Course
by Bruce Pinkard, Silver Pixel Press
ISBN 1-883403-60-X

The Photographer's Internet Handbook
by Joe Farace, Allworth Press
ISBN 1-880559-62-5

Photographers Market
edited by Megan Lane, Writer's Digest Books
ISBN 0-89879-851-5

Professional Business Practices In Photography
American Society of Media Photographers
ISBN 0-927629-14-3

Sell & Resell Your Photos
by Rohn Engh, Writer's Digest Books
ISBN 0-89879-774-8

Stock Photo Smart
by Joe Farace, Rockport Publishers
ISBN 1-56496-381-0

Periodicals

Model Look International Magazine
One Glamour Place, P.O. Box 1002
Charleston, IL 61920
(217) 345-9555, Fax: (217) 348-1211

Photo Stock Notes Newsletter
PhotoSource International
1910 35th Road, Osceola, WI 54020-5602
(715) 248-3800, Fax: (715) 248-7394
www.photosource.com